ADVANCE PRAISE

AF650398

"We believe in sustainability and inspiring change to help preserve a more natural world, alongside building Nature-positive cities of the future. Understanding the challenges of biodiversity and climate change is a minefield, and Sangeeta has done an excellent job of simplifying things, giving us the context of what is happening in our natural world. Her book shows us how to make positive choices for the planet, whereas her interviews inspire and offer a sense of purpose. This is a book of optimism and action."

Constructive Voices, a media platform and podcast series highlighting sustainable practices within the construction industry that benefit the sector and the environment

"Sangeeta has a unique ability to communicate vital information about some of the world's most pressing challenges in an easy style. Now in her very readable book, she shows how severe our problems are, but importantly, shines a spotlight of hope on global change-makers, giving us ideas about what we can all do to reduce the threats we face."

Mohua Chinappa, Podcast host, LinkedIn's Top Podcasting Host and founder of The Mohua Show – a popular podcast for entrepreneurs and change-makers with 1.5 million downloads; Mohua is also a poet, author and columnist

ADVANCE PRAISE

WHAT WILL YOUR LEGACY BE?

CONVERSATIONS WITH GLOBAL GAME CHANGERS ABOUT THE CLIMATE CRISIS

SANGEETA WALDRON

JAICO PUBLISHING HOUSE

Ahmedabad Bangalore Chennai
Delhi Hyderabad Kolkata Mumbai

Published by Jaico Publishing House
A-2 Jash Chambers, 7-A Sir Phirozshah Mehta Road
Fort, Mumbai - 400 001
jaicopub@jaicobooks.com
www.jaicobooks.com

© Sangeeta Waldron, 2024
© LID Business Media Limited, 2024

Published in arrangement with
LID Business Media Limited
LABS House, 15-19 Bloomsbury Way
London, WC1A 2TH, UK

To be sold only in India, Bangladesh, Bhutan,
Pakistan, Nepal, Sri Lanka and the Maldives.

WHAT WILL YOUR LEGACY BE?
ISBN 978-93-49358-53-9

First Jaico Impression: 2025

No part of this book may be reproduced or utilized in
any form or by any means, electronic or
mechanical including photocopying, recording or by any
information storage and retrieval system,
without permission in writing from the publishers.

Cover and page design: Caroline Li

Printed by
Parksons Graphics Pvt. Ltd., Mumbai

WHAT
WILL
YOUR
LEGACY
BE?

TO GODDESS PRITHVI – OUR EARTH MOTHER

CONTENTS

ACKNOWLEDGEMENTS

I would like to thank all the experts featured in this book:

Roberta Boscolo, Climate, Energy and Science Officer at the World Meteorological Organization

Dr Simon Nicholson, Associate Professor of International Relations at American University, Washington, DC

Stéphane Hallegatte, Senior Climate Change Adviser at the World Bank

Dr Kimberley R. Miner, Research Assistant Professor at the University of Maine and Climate Scientist at NASA

Jojo Mehta, Chief Executive of Stop Ecocide International

Jacob Dahl, Senior Partner Emeritus at McKinsey & Company

Nisreen Elsaim, Sudanese activist

Lieutenant Colonel (Retd) Langley Sharp MBE, Former head of the British Army's Centre for Army Leadership

James Cracknell, Editor at *Enfield Dispatch* and editor-in-chief at *Social Spider Community News*

Zed Anwar, Creative art director and creative specialist

Aaron Straight, Founder and senior creative director of Soulcraft

Karla Mendes, Award-winning Brazilian environmental investigative journalist

Sarah Bridle, Professor of Food, Climate and Society at the University of York

Kaddu Kiwe Sebunya, CEO of the African Wildlife Foundation

Michael Tingsager, Leading food industry expert

Shristi Adhikari, Agriculturalist

Sunita Narain, Environmentalist, activist and Director General of the Centre for Science and Environment

Sanjoy Roy, Managing Director of Teamwork Arts

Prachi Shevgaonkar, Founder of Cool The Globe

Shombi Sharp, UN Resident Coordinator in India

Ricky Kej, International Indian composer and environmentalist

Janina Rossiter, Artist, author and 'artivist'

Stevie Kalinich, American 'peace poet' and songwriter

Claire O'Neill, Cofounder and CEO of A Greener Future

Yamide Dagnet, Director for Climate Justice at the Open Society Foundations

Jim N. R. Dale, Founder and Senior Meteorological Consultant at British Weather Services

Nicholas Janni, Award-winning author and leadership practitioner

Malin Cunningham, Founder and Owner of Hattrick

Antoinette Vermilye, Cofounder of the Gallifrey Foundation and SHE Changes Climate

Pradeep Tripathi, Cofounder of Green Yatra

Rachel Cartwright, Naturalist and humpback whale researcher

Jim Cannon, CEO and Founder of Sustainable Fisheries Partnership

Nemonte Nenquimo, Indigenous Waorani leader

Julian Lennon, Founder of the White Feather Foundation

Marimuthu Yoganathan, South Indian environmental activist

Ingmar Rentzhog, Founder and CEO of We Don't Have Time

I would also like to thank my publisher, Martin Liu, and the incredible team at LID Publishing, for publishing my third book, which is a continuation of my previous book, *Corporate Social Responsibility Is Not Public Relations*, published in 2021.

And to my #TeamWaldron (Steve and Rory), who wrote this book with me, for dealing with my angst!

FOREWORD

Dear Divine Being,

Welcome to this book.

I am a visionary yogi, humanitarian and Siddha yoga master. My teachings come from the seldom-revealed source of yogic wisdom of the Siddha Sages, the liberated mystics of South India. My purpose is to awaken humanity, and Siddha means 'to awake the conscious being.' Consciousness offers the solution to the complex issues facing our planet. Increasing our consciousness will unite humanity through peace, coexistence, harmony and understanding. We can no longer be asleep. Rising sea levels, increasingly extreme weather patterns, alarming extinctions of species – these are the headlines that surround us daily around the world and are intensifying far more rapidly than we had thought. Global warming has reached new heights of severity, where our overconsumption has caused the extinction of many species. Put this alongside the powerful fossil-fuel lobby groups, the polarization of mainstream politics and the rise of fake news, and the climate crisis demands new action.

Amid these global threats, hope remains boundless, and it echoes throughout the pages of Sangeeta's new book, *What Will Your Legacy Be?* Sangeeta speaks with 36 leading change-makers and experts from around the world who are all committed to finding solutions to protect the planet and to benefit humanity. From the deep ocean to the remote Amazon forests to the peaks of Kathmandu, all the conversations – with Indigenous people, scientists, thought leaders, entrepreneurs and citizens – are committed to a common goal: protecting our home, Earth, and leaving a legacy.

Sangeeta has spent time researching this book, curating conversations with different voices from around the world, and has spoken with some of today's greatest influencers. They include Jojo Mehta, Chief Executive of Stop Ecocide International; Rachel Cartwright, naturalist and humpback whale researcher; Shombi Sharp, UN Resident Coordinator in India; Karla Mendes, award-winning Brazilian environmental investigative journalist; and Stevie Kalinich, American 'peace poet' and songwriter.

Each conversation within the book is insightful and different, unfolding to be a guide to action. Each noninterview chapter includes a takeaway to ensure you end every chapter with a thought about starting something new and being the change. Sangeeta has been ambitious and written a book for everyone, with the sole intention of empowering you to feel inspired – to know that each of us can make a difference in the midst of this destruction and uncertainty. From the moment you open the book, you can tell that Sangeeta has put you at the heart of her writing, wanting us to become beacons of hope and be informed, so that we can make better choices and keep these critical discussions at the forefront in these challenging times. She wants us to become conscious.

I have known Sangeeta for some time and regard her as an authentic example of a person who has always cared. There are people who have visions and there are people who act on visions, and Sangeeta does both. This book is a continuation of her previous successful book, *Corporate Social Responsibility Is Not Public Relations*, in which I was honoured to share my insights about sustainability.

Sangeeta is not afraid to give us independent and unconventional ideas to ignite worldwide action. Examples include music having power to connect us to Nature; the need for a new breed of bold, authentic political leaders; the idea that science cannot ignore the wisdoms of Indigenous people about finding solutions to climate change; the idea that communities are catalysts for change; and the potential for India to emerge as the new global voice for the planet. *What Will Your Legacy Be?* is a movement for the planet and for its people.

It is time for us to be conscious, to care and find solutions over despair. We know that the climate emergency is the most significant threat to civilization that we have ever faced, and *What Will Your Legacy Be?* educates and reconnects readers with their ecosystems so they can be part of the solution. This is a book for everyone. We should all be thinking about our legacy, irrespective of how old we are. We need to act now to create a better future.

Dear Divine Being, Mother Nature is asking you, "What will your legacy be?"

Nandhiji
Spiritual Leader and Yoga Master; visionary; humanitarian

INTRODUCTION

The song "How Do You Solve a Problem Like Maria?" from the film *The Sound of Music* (with Julie Andrews) strangely keeps popping into my head as I start to write this introduction. I think it's because we can't solve the climate crisis – we don't have time – but we can certainly manage it, make things better and improve things.

When I told people that I was writing my third book about climate change, some asked me, "Why climate?" or "What has that got to do with public relations?" or "What does that have to do with you?" I found the questions intriguing, as I had assumed the answers would be obvious to everyone. I realized that not everyone was aware of what was happening with this crisis, and this was exactly why I was writing the book! My answer to all these questions is this – I have cared about our planet and what has been happening to it my whole life. More specifically, my answers to the three questions are that I have always tried to give Mother Nature a voice; it has become clear that climate change is a communications issue, and we need more people to understand what is happening; and climate change has everything to do with me, just like it has everything to do with you.

I wrote this book to help connect us to what's happening and enable us to be part of the solutions. While it's now too late to reverse the temperature rises across the world and the way they are impacting ecosystems, there is time to learn how to care for our precious resources and make better decisions to help improve the future for those who will come after us. To help me get these points across, I wanted to bring in diverse expert voices from as many parts of the world as possible, particularly female voices, and including people from different ethnic groups and backgrounds. I was determined to be as representative as I could. This was important because too often these voices are missing from climate conversations, and they bring unique perspectives.

I partially grew up in India, spending my teenage years in the lower ranges of the Himalayas. I saw a rapid change in my surroundings, as forests were lost due to intense fires caused by the heat. The wildlife, mainly monkeys, were forced to live in the town, learning to forage for food from bins, gardens and vegetable stalls in the bazaar. It reminded me of the story, *Planet of the Apes*. But it wasn't just the environment being impacted. It was the elements too – water, the soil and the air. Severe water shortages in summer, late monsoons, and extreme rainfalls would occur out of season and oversaturate the dry earth, causing landslides. All this was happening 40-odd years ago in India, and now we are witnessing scenarios like this across the world.

What I have discovered is that all these outcomes are related and there is a domino effect. Climate change is not happening in isolation. The climate has changed because we have tampered with our planet's weather patterns by putting too much carbon into the atmosphere, used chemicals in our fertilizers (which has hampered our bees and other pollinators), depleted our fish stocks with overfishing, chopped down hectares of precious forest areas, destroyed natural habitats, and polluted our seas and rivers with water pollution. The list goes on and on, with the dominos falling into one another. But within all these gloomy scenarios there is still hope, and making change, no matter how small, has impact.

While living in India, I was introduced to the ancient Vedic Sanskrit scriptures. At the time, I had a limited understanding of this timeless Indian philosophy. It's only as I have become older that these words have begun to speak to me and I have gained a better understanding. In the chapter on India (*Chapter 9*), you will come across the phrase 'Vasudhaiva Kutumbakam,' which means 'The World Is One Family.' 'Vasudhaiva' refers to the Earth, where humans reside, and 'Kutumbakam' means a family, or the inhabitants of the Earth, where every particle of the Earth is equivalent to a member of the family.

The phrase remains relevant today as it emphasizes the global perspective – the world is a family. We need to be conscious – live consciously, eat consciously and shop consciously. But most of all, this profound concept has been a cornerstone of Indian thought for centuries, promoting interconnectedness, unity and global kinship. It means ensuring equality for all, irrespective of socioeconomic background. Inclusive development that leads to a more equitable ecosystem will help us manage the climate crisis.

WHY LEGACY?

I wanted to write a book that talked about the future, because there is still one ahead of us. Legacy is a perfect way to frame this conversation, because it can lead to action. We all want to be remembered for something – everyone wants to leave a footprint behind, both personally and professionally. While writing this book, I have learned a lot about this term, which can be a big, daunting word, even for the people who are doing the work. It also sounds like something for history books or, dare I say it, death. My conclusion is that it doesn't matter what age we are – what we do now matters and has a footprint.

I also discovered from speaking to the people who appear in this book that every one of them is unassuming and passionate, which you will see yourself. They are driven by their personal values, where their passion becomes a catalyst for hope not just for themselves but for us all. They are not giving up, even if at times theirs are the only voices or their voices are being drowned out.

Our personal values and relationships matter, as they form the building blocks of our legacy, which also need time for self-reflection. We need to step back to consider the bigger picture, especially what motivates us to give life a sense of intention that offers joy and purpose. We should all be wanting to leave something excellent and beneficial for those we leave behind and for future generations. Even if we are gone, if we leave something of worth to others, it's like we still exist in the world through their memories of us and our actions' effect on others.

This is where being connected to Nature is so vital. I encourage everyone to sit with Nature and think. Life can be fleeting, and your time may not be enough to do everything you want. It is noble to consider the welfare of others beyond what you need for yourself – even more so when those others will outlive you and may not have anything to do with you. And a good legacy can serve as an example for the next generation, so they can see the values you lived by and the positive impact left by your actions. People will know what not to do, so they can lead a better life, and they may be able to learn something from what you did.

Everyone creates and retells their own narrative; your life story connects you to your community and differentiates you from the lives that others lead. It is what makes you unique and fills you with a sense of unity and purpose. We are programmed by the need to belong and feel a sense of purpose. Belonging to a community and finding a purpose are interlinked. When you find your life's path, you'll most likely find others with similar values hoping to reach the same objectives. It is called creating your community. It's how you make a difference in the world.

Probably more rewarding is the fact that leaving a legacy can improve your own life by giving you better mental health, as consciously trying to leave something positive behind can make you feel happier and more satisfied. Living a purposeful life can make you resilient and less anxious. You gain a sense of satisfaction, happiness and personal fulfilment, which are positive emotions that reduce stress. You take control and become resilient to challenges. Ultimately, you gain a sense of hope and actually become inspired to live longer, because there is work to do. You don't have to be extremely popular or noteworthy to leave a legacy.

Take risks and follow your instincts. Don't be afraid to dream big, push yourself and be open to learning. Knowledge is infinite – it equips you with tools to share your wisdom and experiences with others. Share your wisdom, create conversations, and spread your legacy by sharing your values, know-how and experiences with the world. Find out how you can use your wisdom to help your community. Define how you'd like others to remember you and align your decisions and communications.

It is never too late to reevaluate and change course. Draw inspiration from others – people you admire. I believe our legacy is connected to our community, where it lives on in the relationships we build with family members, colleagues and friends. Recognize, celebrate and lift up your community's achievements. Doing so fosters a positive environment and inspires others to strive to be their best selves. Leading by example won't only contribute to your legacy – it will also create a shared legacy with a positive ripple effect on your entire community.

And at all costs, avoid leaving a bad legacy.

WHAT WILL YOU DISCOVER IN THIS BOOK?

Over the year that I have been writing this book, there was so much research and data being released that exposed the true plight of the world. In fact, as I continued writing, some of the latest data was replacing statistics that had been released less than a year ago. It was overwhelming. Significantly, this means that some of the science was becoming dated the moment it was being released. I did not want to date this book, so I have chosen to keep the statistics to a minimum. I am aware, too, that data can be a turn-off and it is not engaging – it doesn't really connect us. It can shock us and make us sit back, but then what?

What really speaks to us? What's the one thing that we all love? The answer is simple. It's a story, which is the crux of who we are as humans. It bring us together. I like to call the conversations in this book 'stories,' but they are real narratives. There's nothing fictious about them – they are all true accounts.

I found every dialogue rewarding – after I spoke to an expert, I was left feeling alive, hopeful and optimistic. I knew I was not alone. There were people with the same ideas, mission and determination. I was part of something bigger – a community of international beings who cared, who were doing something, who were intent on trying to make things better.

Each interaction spurred me on to continue writing this book, and I felt like a collector of precious conversations. No one account is better than any other; each is different and has its place in its chapter. You will read about the wonders of the humpback whale and its calf, and how mangroves are incredible ecosystems – what I would describe as magical forests. You will discover how some of these experts followed their instincts to do the work they are doing – their current path wasn't their original game plan. You will learn how scientists want to listen to the wisdom of Indigenous people, and you will hear from an Indigenous leader. You will also see how scientists deal with all the gloomy data that constantly reaches them. There are voices from the next generation and from community leaders, artists and musicians, not forgetting the change-makers who are drafting new laws, running innovative businesses or spending time on the front lines every day to support Mother Nature. The book explores theories and news relating to the cost of war and political leadership, and my own hunch about India's place in this fight against climate change.

I have endeavoured not to leave you with unanswered questions, and each noninterview chapter ends with a simple takeaway for you to act upon.

None of them are impossible to do, and I hope they will nudge you to take positive action – that is, if you are open to trying. Every takeaway goes toward building something better, to help foster your own connection with your planet. Remember, climate change is your problem, too. Your action makes a difference and is the start of your legacy.

CHAPTER 1

SCIENCE

Everything has a beginning – a 'once a upon a time' – and climate change is no different. Its story starts with science, which has been a constant and steadfast narrator clearly telling us that our systems are changing, and not for the better. Sadly, for a long time it fell on deaf ears, but now we are all starting to experience the weather patterns on our doorsteps, which are changing our lives and communities. International research and studies have documented these changes, creating an understanding of how our lives will continue to be impacted by climate change and what we can do to slow or reverse this change.

I grew up thinking that science was all about test tubes and learning the periodic table, and perhaps you did too – but we were mistaken. This is a discipline that has become key to knowing what is happening in our ecosystems and what we can expect. There have been many pivotal moments in the history of science and our climate – actually there have been so many – and I want to highlight some to show how far back we have been ignoring the warnings and also to give an insight into the science.

Let us start in 1896 with the Swedish physicist and physical chemist Svante Arrhenius, who won the Nobel Prize in Chemistry for what was, in effect, the first model of climate change. Arrhenius published a paper predicting that changes in atmospheric carbon dioxide levels could substantially alter the surface temperature of the planet.

Now let's hop to 1938, when steam engineer Guy Stewart Callendar decided to take a break from his day job and began to painstakingly collect records from 147 weather stations globally, doing all his calculations by hand. He discovered that global temperatures had risen by 0.3°C over the previous 50 years. He argued that carbon dioxide emissions from industry were responsible for global warming. Remarkably, his estimates of the extent of global warming were very accurate and in line with modern assessments.[1]

In 1958, a young geochemist, Charles David Keeling, decided to compare the amounts of carbon dioxide in the water and air. Nobody had ever really tried to measure the level of carbon dioxide in the atmosphere before, and there was no off-the-shelf equipment Keeling could use, so he designed his own. He set off to a weather observation station on the top of the Mauna Loa volcano in Hawaii and took measurements every day. Within five years, he had provided the first solid proof that carbon dioxide concentrations were rising, and he was able to attribute this rise to the use of fossil fuels.

In 1968, along came John Mercer, a glaciologist at The Ohio State University in Columbus, who predicted ice-sheet collapse, warning us that global warming could cause Antarctic ice sheets to fall, leading to a disastrous rise in sea levels. He found evidence that sea levels had risen six metres in the previous interglacial period, around 120,000 years ago.[2] He highlighted that atmospheric warming could once again cause the ice shelves to disintegrate, causing a sea-level rise of about five metres. This is happening today.

It was in the 1980s that things started to change. In 1985, Joseph Farman, Brian Gardiner and Jonathan Shanklin, three scientists from the British Antarctic Survey, discover a hole in the ozone layer above Antarctica. The ozone layer, part of the Earth's atmosphere, naturally protects us from harmful ultraviolet light. When these three scientists reported that they had detected abnormally low levels of ozone over the South Pole, the world was shocked. They suggested that compounds called chlorofluorocarbons (CFCs), used in aerosol cans and fridges, could be responsible. Their findings led to the 1987 Montreal Protocol, which called for the reduction of CFCs and ultimately their total ban. This protocol is one of the most successful global environmental policies of the 20th century and helped raise public awareness of climate change.

In 1988, the Intergovernmental Panel on Climate Change (IPCC) was established by the UN Environment Programme and the World Meteorological Organization. The IPCC became responsible for assessing the science related to climate change and providing regular scientific assessments on the current state of knowledge about climate change, heralding a new era of climate research. The first IPCC assessment report, in 1990, played a decisive role in the creation of the UN Framework Convention on Climate Change, a pivotal international treaty intended to reduce global warming and help humanity cope with the consequences of climate change.[3]

It was the IPCC's second report, in 1995, that led to the famous 1997 Kyoto Protocol, which committed industrialized countries to limiting and reducing their greenhouse gas emissions to individually agreed targets.[4] The fifth assessment report, in 2014, provided the foundation for the historic 2015 Paris Agreement, where 195 countries agreed to limit global warming to less than 2°C above preindustrial levels.[5]

In 1992, US scientists Stephen Smith and Robert Buddemeier discovered that coral reefs were at threat from growing levels of carbon dioxide in the ocean. When carbon dioxide dissolves in the ocean, it raises the water's acidity level and stops corals from sucking in a vital mineral called calcium carbonate, which they use to build their skeletons. It's not just corals that are at risk; all creatures that form shells are in danger, including oysters, mussels, clams and some planktonic species. Since 1992, this threat has continued to mount.[6]

Fast-forward to 2023, when research led by Geoffrey Supran with researchers from Harvard University and the Potsdam Institute for Climate Impact Research exposed that ExxonMobil had known of the dangers of global heating from at least the 1970s, with other oil industry bodies knowing of the risk even earlier, from around the 1950s. Guess you didn't see that one coming!

Anyway, for decades, some members of the fossil fuel industry tried to convince the public that a link between fossil fuel use and climate warming could not be made because the models used to project warming were uncertain. Together, they forcefully and successfully mobilized against the science to stop any action to reduce fossil fuel use. ExxonMobil's scientists were accurate in their projections from the 1970s onwards, predicting an upward curve of global temperatures and that global heating was human-influenced and would be detected around the year 2000.[7]

Supran and his team examined more than 100 internal documents and peer-reviewed scientific publications either produced in-house by ExxonMobil scientists and managers or coauthored by ExxonMobil scientists in independent publications between 1977 and 2014. Climate scientists from Duke, Brown and Cornell Universities have said the new study highlighted an important chapter in the struggle to address the climate crisis.

So there we have it: we have been short-sighted, and science is more far-reaching than we give it credit for. Today – at last – it is governing our understanding of what is happening to Nature, our local climates and our lives. While researching and writing this chapter, I discovered something called 'climate grief,' which some scientists are having to cope with. It struck me that we forget that they are people, dealing with the facts, the data and the research. This can be exhausting for them, knowing what they know. Science, data and research are crying out for us to start caring and making changes to combat what is happening globally with the climate. We are all experiencing how the Earth's climate is changing. Temperatures around the world are rising, traditional weather patterns are shifting, and extreme weather events – hurricanes and very high temperatures – are happening more frequently.

In fact, it was after scientists from the World Meteorological Organization and the EU's Copernicus Earth observation programme confirmed that July 2023 was on track to be the world's hottest month on record that we ended the era of global warming. "The era of global boiling has arrived," said UN Secretary-General António Guterres, adding, "Climate change is here. It is terrifying. And it is just the beginning." The steady rise in global average temperatures, driven by pollution that traps sunlight and acts like a greenhouse around the Earth, has made weather extremes worse. Guterres also said: "Humanity is in the hotseat. … For vast parts of North America, Asia, Africa and Europe – it is a cruel summer. For the entire planet, it is a disaster. And for scientists, it is unequivocal – humans are to blame."[8]

The science has been loud and clear – the planet is heating, and we are causing it. Scientists always focus on the evidence, not on opinions, and scientific evidence continues to show that human activities, mainly the burning of fossil fuels, have warmed our planet's surface and the ocean basins, impacting our climate. This is based on more than a century of scientific evidence. While the Earth has always had natural cycles of warming and cooling, these have not been like what we are seeing now. The ten hottest years ever recorded have all been since 2000.

According to the IPCC report on impacts, adaptation and vulnerability, at the current rate, the world could be 1.5°C hotter as soon as 2040 – that's only two decades away. And don't forget that the IPCC is made up of the world's leading climate scientists.[9]

Earth's climate is complex, where even a small increase in average global temperature means big changes, with lots of dangerous side effects with the potential for short-circuiting entire ecosystems. Scientific studies show that exceeding 1.5°C could trigger several tipping points for our climate systems. There are so many scientific reports and data that I could mention and throw at you, but it would become tedious. Respected scientists have been consistently showing us – proving to us – that the planet is getting hotter and that we need to do something.

CLIMATE CHANGE DENIERS

Following on from the ExxonMobil's story mentioned earlier in this chapter, the climate change deniers, many of whom have interests in the fossil fuels industry, continuously challenge the findings of scientists and downplay the significance of global warming. While I was writing this book, so many news stories broke about the underhanded way these oil and gas companies have played with our futures.

We live in a hyper-partisan media atmosphere, where people get their information from media outlets that reinforce their preconceptions and biases. This has aided and abetted the deniers. This brave new online world has also fuelled keyboard warriors and trolls, who cause a lot of hate, discord and unpleasantness. In 2023, a survey of 468 international climate scientists published by campaign group Global Witness found that prominent scientists were the most likely to face abuse, with half of those who had published at least ten papers reporting they had suffered online harassment as a result of their climate work. Most of this abuse took place on X (formerly known as Twitter) and Facebook.[10]

The survey highlighted that the level of exposure to harassment was linked to number of academic publications and frequency of media appearances.

Overall, 39% of the scientists polled (183 out of 468) had experienced online harassment or abuse as a result of their climate work. The rate was lower for those who had published fewer than six articles (24%) and increased to 49% of scientists who had published more than ten journal articles.

The results suggest abuse increases with both academic output and media exposure. Of those scientists who are in the media at least once a month (13% of respondents), 73% had experienced abuse and 29% reported having experienced 'a great deal' or 'a fair amount' of abuse. Even among those scientists who had never made any media appearances (19% of the respondents), 12% reported they had experienced online abuse.

Along with these keyboard warriors, many of us can get stuck in echo chambers where we are no longer in touch with the news, facts and reality. This is a dangerous place to be, as you are no longer keeping informed of what is happening in your neighbourhood, community, country or the rest of the world. You are asleep.

HOW DO PUBLIC RELATIONS AND ADVERTISING FIT INTO THIS?

I am ashamed to say that in 2022, for the first time, 450 scientists identified that public relations (PR – my industry) and advertising play a role in fuelling the climate crisis.[11] Fossil-fuel-linked groups spent around $4 million on Facebook and Instagram ads in 2022 spreading false climate-related claims during the UN Climate Change Conference (COP27). The 'big four' – BP, Chevron, ExxonMobil and Shell – funded over 3,700 ads that were identified as sharing false claims on the Meta-owned platforms. In 2024, another news story broke in the US, exposing how major oil companies have misled Americans for decades about the threat of human-caused climate change.[12]

Simply put, the advertising and media strategies of the fossil fuel industry are sophisticated and have sown doubt in the minds of the public and policymakers about the climate crisis. What they have done is created media campaigns to shift blame onto individuals and greenwash their way out of being required to take real action by governments. Agencies such as BBDO, Edelman, Ogilvy and nearly 90 others worldwide still represent these clients and put their leading creative minds behind the work to mislead us about the climate emergency. For instance, a report, *Three Shades of Green(washing)*, which is a

Harvard University investigation commissioned by Greenpeace Netherlands, reveals rampant use of greenwashing and tokenism by the largest car brands, airlines, and oil and gas companies in Europe to exploit people's concerns about the environment and spread disinformation online. Findings include that only one in five 'green' car social media posts sold a product; the rest were to present the brand as green. Companies used the imagery of Nature, women, nonbinary gender, nonwhite people, youth, experts, sportspeople and celebrities to strengthen their messages of misdirection.[13]

Interestingly, car brands were found to be more proactive on social media than airlines and oil companies, on average generating twice the amount of social media posts of airlines and quadruple that of oil and gas companies. Only a negligible handful of social posts made explicit reference to climate change, despite Europe's record-hot summer. The good news is that people working within these agencies are saying 'no' and no longer want to disguise the truth. There's been a turning point.

BEING OVERWHELMED

With so many reports coming out, it is hard not to feel exhausted by it all. Indeed, as mentioned above, some of us are now dealing with ecological grief or eco-anxiety. Until we get a handle on solutions, many more of us will start to experience the impacts of climate change on our lives – for example, if a natural disaster suddenly hits us or our loved ones. There is a growing awareness that things are changing, with feelings of grief, sadness and trauma because of the losses involved – lost landscapes, plants, animals and human life. We do not talk about grief enough. I believe that if it is not recognized or talked about, it can manifest as an anxiety where a deep feeling of uncertainty will creep in – and there is already a lot of uncertainty in the world.

Those who work in the climate space probably know of this kind of grief already. It doesn't just visit once but can come in waves, triggered again and again by the latest climate reports, extreme weather events or regressive environmental policies. A natural response is to push the feelings away. To help deal with this type of grief, look to Nature to inspire you; look for stories that tell about regeneration after damage; look to the science to help reconnect you to hope, because I have realized that science itself deals in hope and there is still time to rewrite this ending. We can't make change without hope. Hope is the catalyst for making the changes we need, and scientists are working to understand the role that hope plays. A review study funded by the US National Science Foundation found "partial yet inconclusive evidence" that increasing hope makes people engage more with the climate.[14]

CONCLUSION

We need facts to push back against disinformation and fake news, which are the main obstacles that prevent our progress in tackling this crisis. Deceptive or misleading content distorts the perception of climate science and solutions, which creates confusion and often leads to delays in action or even harmful action. We need all hands on deck to cut greenhouse gas emissions to net zero by 2050, and halving them by 2030 requires nothing less than a complete transformation of how we produce, consume and move.

One of the most important things about science is that it is committed to finding solutions that are based on action, but the scientists can't do this alone. They need us all.

TAKEAWAY

This might sound like an obvious and simple takeaway, but there is a lot of power in starting a conversation about climate change and talking to our colleagues, friends and family about the real facts of the climate crisis. This is one of the best ways to take climate action. Climate change can be complex, so keep reading regularly about what's happening and ensure your news sources are authentic and trusted. This will help you stay informed so you can make the right choices.

CHAPTER 2

IN CONVERSATION WITH SCIENTISTS

To explore the topic of science, I spoke to four leading scientists: Roberta Boscolo, from the World Meteorological Organization (WMO); Dr Simon Nicholson at American University, Washington, DC; Stéphane Hallegatte, Senior Climate Change Adviser at the World Bank; and Dr Kimberley R. Miner, who is looking at Earth systems and risks at the University of Maine and is also a NASA scientist. They all openly shared their thoughts, views and solutions. The one thing all four shared was hope, which is a natural resource because, like clean air and water, it keeps us all going for a better tomorrow.

ROBERTA BOSCOLO

CLIMATE, ENERGY AND SCIENCE OFFICER AT THE WORLD METEOROLOGICAL ORGANIZATION

I spoke to Roberta Boscolo, climate, energy and science officer at the WMO, in August 2023, a week after the devasting wildfires that took place in Maui, Hawaii. Roberta coordinates scientific efforts globally to address the knowledge gaps in understanding the Earth's climate system. She also leads a team of scientists at the WMO aiming to enable society to better manage the risks and opportunities arising from climate variability and change through the provision of science-based climate information and prediction. Roberta, with her team, advances the use of climate change research to develop climate adaptation and mitigation strategies, which have helped shape the vision of the UN-led initiative – Global Framework for Climate Services. Roberta leads the WMO effort in implementing climate services for the energy sector, particularly in developing countries.

In this interview, we see why solutions, adaptation and mitigation are critical – what I would describe as the next frontiers in climate science. We discuss many topics and discover that Roberta is one of the experts on the panel of the prestigious Earthshot Prize, which was founded by the UK's Prince William, who is the president. This is a prize designed to find and grow solutions that will repair our planet this decade.

The UN has said that the planet has entered a new era of global boiling. What hope, if any, can scientists give us?

Let me start by saying there is hope! Even with hurricanes and storms becoming stronger, with everything getting more intense and frequent, like we have seen in Hawaii, scientists still believe there is hope, because we know that what is happening is because of us, which also means we have the solutions to stop this trend.

The good news is that we can start a process of transition – a regeneration of our planet. We can stop what we are doing and go back to the state where we were before humanity started to pump huge amounts of carbon dioxide into the atmosphere. We have the tools and the ability to do it. But at the moment, what is missing is the will to make these changes. Even though scientists – such as the IPCC,[15] which is rigorous and carries out solid analysis – are providing the information, we are not listening. The IPCC is speaking loudly but is still not heard, and that's because there is no real will to stop climate change.

Al Gore gave a TED Talk in July 2023.[16] From watching it, people will understand that one barrier to making change happen is the lobby groups of big industries. Unfortunately, climate change is partly being caused by these big companies, which are the richest in the world.

Then, there's something else that I have noticed, which is that climate change has become a very politically polarized issue, which I don't understand as a scientist. I mean, do we have an opinion on gravity? No! Because everybody understands gravity is a physical fact. But somehow, because of misinformation that is put out by lobby groups, the climate facts have been distorted. Everyone should look at the data and listen to both the science and the scientists.

We also need to look at the tools, which are the solutions to climate change and very much part of our hope. For example, renewable energy has improved, becoming cheaper; it's cheaper than oil, which means it can be more attractive in the long term. Then we have regenerative agriculture, and we need to stop deforestation, since forests are a big sink of carbon dioxide. Companies can do a lot of things to decarbonize. We have the tools, we have the hope and we still have time to turn this round.

Collectively as a planet and a global community, we decided to limit the temperature and to not increase it more than 1.5°C. Though we might now overshoot this ambition, there is still hope. As scientists we don't say, "If we hit 1.5°C, then we all die." In fact, we are already 1.12°C degrees above the average and are experiencing dangerous weather. But what we need to do is to act fast. Otherwise, we will enter uncharted territory. Note that we say this in a 'scientific way,' as we don't actually know what will happen, because we cannot compare what is happening to anything that's happened in the past, and neither can we say definitely what is going to happen.

There are also issues of tipping points, where some of the scientists say if we reach a certain temperature, it may start some kind of mechanism where the Earth system will enter a new state that is completely different to what we are experiencing now. This may be positive for some nations but will certainly be negative for others.

The risk of climate change has three different aspects – the hazards, the vulnerability and the exposure. The results will be different from country to country, where the more exposed are the most vulnerable and will be hit the hardest.

Do you think governments are funding enough climate change research?

Certainly not. Scientists have a good understanding about the physical aspects, but now science needs to move toward understanding the impacts of climate change. This is a field that definitely needs more funding. I also believe science should be people-centred and this too is an area that is underfunded.

Science is for solutions, and solutions are for mitigation and adaptation. Scientists are producing a digital-twin Earth to help us make the best decisions in terms of adaptation. If we were to put big walls on coasts to prevent damage from storms and storm surges, would this be a good solution or not? We need more research to identify where the risk areas are, what can we do to help these regions, and what are the best decisions to reduce the risks. To reduce vulnerability, is relocation needed or should we rebuild? For example, there is new direct carbon-capture technology, but is this better than restoring our forests? What can we do to capture more carbon dioxide from the atmosphere? Also, what is happening in our seas? We don't have enough data and research, and the oceans are still a big unknown. Yet the oceans are critical, as they absorb 90% of excess heat, and as a result are becoming warmer annually. But what is happening to this heat – how is it being released? We have no idea.

It is all about how we make the best decisions to halt the damage we have created, and how we go back to the situation we had before we started our industrialization.

As you were talking, I was thinking that your job is fascinating. And yet, when I was at school, science seemed so boring. Science can actually give us solutions to the problems we've created.

Yes, I do feel that science is becoming more human and is solving real problems. When I started as a scientist, I was a theoretical physicist. I moved into climate change, but I was still among scientists. It was about ten years ago, while working on climate change, that I was attending conferences and meeting other scientists, where we were all talking, and on the same wavelength. But I felt that we were not going to have an impact if we continued to talk among ourselves, which is why I moved to applied science.

Now I work on the energy aspects of climate change and the energy nexus.[17] I started to work on projects in Africa, and in South America, focused on adaptation. It's much harder, and progress is very, very minimal. Yet, when you go and talk to people, and explain about the job you are doing and that you are there to help them, it is a hundred times more rewarding.

I don't want to go back and be in rooms with other scientists, looking at reducing errors in some little quantity, when we have a huge problem to solve, which is to help people thrive through this period, which definitely presents a big risk for many of us.

You're an action woman and a doer. Were there other women scientists at those conferences?

Very few, and it's still a very male-dominated discipline. Even at the IPCC, they have tried to get more women on board, but with little success. We also need young people, as I believe that they should be involved so they can be part of the solution.

Do you think climate activists are helping drive awareness of climate change? Or driving people away from the science?

This is a very good question, and my thought is that they are helping create awareness of climate change. When I say this, I am thinking of Greta Thunberg, for example, and the movement she started. She always references science and says we need to listen to the science – the science should be our compass. By doing this, she has raised awareness of the fact that we are actually far from really listening to the science.

I hope all these young people who started out as activists when they were 15 or 16 will now vote, because at the end of the day, what is really needed is a big change in the political arena. We need new and better policies, and for this we need informed politicians. At the moment it's not happening, and I wonder why it's not happening! And I think the reason goes back to the big lobby groups that put out misinformation that influences elections and drives political issues.

I do believe, in the end, we will arrive at the point where we will all recognize what needs to be done, and we will do it, because there is no business without our planet. But we need to act faster.

For the planet to thrive, as global temperatures rise, what types of energy production systems will need to be developed to adjust to the changes in climate that we will experience? What kinds of solutions?

Just let me start by saying that energy is a vital sector that needs to be decarbonized, because at the moment, it makes up almost 75% of the greenhouse gases in the atmosphere. Hence, this is a big sector that need to be looked at, changed and transformed.

When we talk about energy, we also need to think about cooling – about buildings, mobility and the transport industry, and of course how much electricity we use. We already have the solutions for energy, which are renewable energy and a low-carbon energy that can be used and deployed in a large scale.

Another solution is solar energy, and the progress we have made here is amazing. For example, in Africa, renewable energy has so much potential. Africa could be exporting energy to the rest of the world by covering the desert with solar panels that generate heat. Another example of an energy solution is wind power. Look at the UK, where the North Sea is full of wind turbines. This is clean energy that we can harness for our consumption. Then we have geothermal energy, which could be expanded, and I would also like to include nuclear – not because I think nuclear is a clean source of energy, as it is not, but because it is a low-carbon energy, and in this transition period, we might need it.

One other solution is the possibility of creating biofuels, which have very low emissions. There is also hydrogen, another technology that at the moment is just starting out. Green hydrogen, created with renewable energy, could be a new source of energy.

Another topic is energy efficiency, which is vital. It is how we can be more efficient with the use of energy in our buildings and our industries. My colleagues and I always say, "The cheapest energy is the one that you don't use!"

This means that we can be very, very clever and smart in how we use energy. We already have the ability to do this via digitalization of our appliances, which can be connected to see when the energy is cheapest or more available. I can put my washing machine on using digitalization, which is part of the system of being smart and efficient.

I also like the concept of energy communities being created in cities and villages, where people put solar panels on their roofs and are not just consumers but 'prosumers,' so they provide free energy – for example, to critical infrastructure such as local schools, hospitals and clinics. The energy that we capture and don't use can be given away for free to community projects. We have the potential to create a future where we will have an enormous amount of energy for free.

This is the world we need to live in – where energy is distributed everywhere in the world. You don't need to be sitting on a big source of oil and become a rich country and aim to rule the world because of this.

Instead, everyone will have access to cheap and clean energy. This is very transformative, not just from the viewpoint of energy but also for development. It would actually make energy democratic, where everybody can use it and can produce it.

Wow! That's indeed the world we need to live in.

Yes, so I am one of the experts on the panel of the Earthshot Prize. We review the ideas that have been submitted, and I was amazed to see these solutions. While I can't say too much just yet, what I can say is there have been pioneering ideas in cooling systems, solar panels and recycling of batteries.

There are solar panels that can be placed in a very remote area, such as a village in Africa, to produce their own energy, to allow the villagers to change the way they cook, to enable kids to be clean, to power schools and hospitals, and to improve agriculture.

One of the big issues in Africa is that when the farmers harvest, they don't know where to store their crops, and sometimes, because of the heat, their harvested crops can rot. What they need are large fridges. But of course, it's very difficult to create these big storage fridges, as they need to be connected to electricity. However, if you have solar panels to run these vast fridges, the farmers can store their harvest. This means that they can then sell their produce at a different time, which generates a big income. For small-scale farmers in Africa, it is life-changing and will ultimately benefit everyone. This could also be a chance to develop Africa.

I've got goosebumps – that would be fantastic for farmers, in Africa and in other vulnerable countries. We rely on them for our food, yet they are at the bottom of the chain. This would transform their lives. This leads to my next question. About 15 years ago, I met a futurist who said that one day climatologists and climate analysts would be a profession of extreme importance. They would equal doctors. Would you agree?

(Roberta laughs) Would I not?! Recently, I have been contacted to go on television to talk about the extreme heat. My team at the WMO were receiving calls daily from Al Jazeera, the BBC and other media outlets. I said to my father, who is not a scientist: "We are the new faces in demand, because during the global COVID pandemic, we saw lots of biologists who became familiar faces to us. Now, with the impact of climate change, it's our turn to be on the television."

We need to think about climate touching everything – all the socioeconomic aspects. We should have climate advisers everywhere, to ensure that the climate and the profession of climate scientist are applied to every socioeconomic area. This will enable good decision-making for adaptation and mitigation.

Currently, while we as scientists produce data to say, "This is what's happening," what is missing is why it matters to you! We need to go further, to show how it is impacting you. In order to do this, we need to know how people live, how people work, what problems they have to face and how we can help solve problems – practical problems, not just to say, "This is the data." Having climate advisers covering all aspects means we can go further and touch more on practical problems.

I've been reading a lot about this – that science now has to go further.

Yes, we need to work more with social scientists to understand how society works and how we can help. During the global pandemic, I started posting a lot about climate change and its science on LinkedIn, as I realized that just communicating within my own circle of colleagues had a limited reach, as we all already know and agree! But there was a large part of the world that didn't know or were unaware of the science.

I started because I wanted to be closer to people to say, "Look, this is what I know. And I think you should know too."

Which leads nicely to my final question: what do you want your legacy to be?

This is a tough question. In terms of how I see my legacy unfolding, to an extent this goes back to what we talked about before, which is how do we push the boundaries of science to be more people-centred? How do we become integrated into people's lives? I want to go further, and use the science to solve problems.

DR SIMON NICHOLSON

ASSOCIATE PROFESSOR OF INTERNATIONAL RELATIONS AT AMERICAN UNIVERSITY, WASHINGTON, DC

In August 2023, I spoke to Dr Simon Nicholson, Associate Professor of International Relations at American University, Washington, DC. His work focuses on global environmental governance, global food politics and the politics of emerging technologies, including climate engineering and carbon removal technologies. Simon is cofounder of the Forum for Climate Engineering Assessment and the Institute for Responsible Carbon Removal, two scholarly initiatives of the School of International Service at the university.

We've seen all these horrific global fires this summer, and currently we have the Canadian fires going on. Do these climate headlines alarm you as a scientist? Or did you expect them?

Yes to both questions, and you might have heard this from others as well. As a human being, it is clearly alarming. As a scientist – if, by scientist, we mean somebody who can be dispassionate and look from a distance at data and try to understand trends – then this is entirely expected.

We've known for decades that this is the trajectory that the planet is on because of climate pollution. And it's shocking! Just because one individual, me as a human being, knows that this kind of thing might happen, it doesn't mean that we're prepared for it.

I look at the news from this recent year, knowing that the news is probably going to get worse next year, and the year after, especially when we think about macro trends. To try to make sense of the human suffering, to try to make sense of all of the forces that are driving us in this direction is totally overwhelming.

> I think we underestimate the sense of being overwhelmed and we as a society have stopped recognizing scientists as people. We've forgotten that there are people behind the data who are doing the research.

There is an analogy to draw with the doctors who have been going through the COVID pandemic, where they have had to face up, every day, to the extent of the tragedy. To keep doing the work the next day, knowing that there's a whole bunch of people out in the world who are saying, "This isn't real, there's nothing that can be done, right?" and having to deal with all the big cultural countercurrents at the same time that the work needs to be done day to day. The analogy isn't quite perfect, of course, because of the direct and immediate horrors associated with the COVID crisis versus the largely abstract nature of climate change.

So, much of what we experience as scientists based in the Global North, when it comes to climate change, is read through data, not through lived experience. That's an important distinction that needs to be drawn. At the same time, it is about needing to recognize scientists as human beings, because people are experiencing this not just intellectually, but deeply and emotionally.

Are there more climate surprises ahead of us? If so, what should we be prepared for?

The basic story to tell about the climate system is that all of human civilization, all that we know as a modern human civilization, has grown up during a time of relative climate stability. When we think about the big, global, long-term record, these last tens of thousands of years have been relatively warm and relatively stable, according to global averages. But we, as human beings over the last couple of centuries, have taken that stability and beaten it up with a big stick. Now we're going to see some of the consequences, moving into a time of turbulence from a time of stability.

And quite what that means, with all of the details, is still opaque to us. We just can't know for certain because of the complexity of the system, but the big macro trends are clear and have been clear for decades. A warmer world is a wetter world. A warmer world is one where we're going to see more extreme weather events. A warmer world is one where we're going to see sea levels rise because of the thermal expansion of water and because of the melting of freshwater reservoirs. All of that is well established. We know that the world is going to become more turbulent in those ways.

As to your question, yes, we're also going to see surprises. One of the biggest surprises beyond the fires and so forth this year has been the crashing of Arctic and Antarctic sea ice.[18] It's been a terrible season. If you look at the trends, things have been worsening in terms of the summer ice pack and now we're seeing a collapse of those systems. To use scientific language, we're not dealing with a linear system – we're dealing with a system that's going to have jagged edges and surprises are going to emerge. This is what scientists mean by 'tipping points' when it comes to climate change.

People try to convey in certain media sources that this hotter summer that many of us have experienced is the coolest summer that you will see in your lifetime moving forward, because the trends are that things are going to get warmer and more turbulent. So, you can expect that things will get worse. Human beings are uniquely capable of just accepting change, which is one of the things that makes climate change such a difficult thing to deal with. We live in the moment, we live in the day-to-day, we look around and say, "Oh, it's quite a nice day." Climate change is not something that is at the top of people's minds, so then we go on with our lives. We will have the same conversation next summer, and the summer after. The climate scientists will be saying, "We've told you, we've told you." It's going to get worse, and it's quite hard to break through that.

So, how do we change the conversation to engage with the next generation, who may be not interested? Or those who actually believe it's too late?

I'll say a couple of things and they're loosely connected. The first is that we shouldn't let the current generations off the hook – that's people of our age and older. Bill McKibben, an influential environmentalist author, activist and former journalist here in the US, says we can't just push responsibility onto those who are coming after us – it's unfair, and it's also going to be overwhelming for those who are being asked to act as leaders and mentors and take action. The second thing that needs to be better understood is that we need to draw more attention to the fact that climate action has been failing, in part because of the actions of the mainstream environmental movement.

What's been happening for a long time in mainstream environmental circles is that there's been an individualization of responsibility when it comes to climate action. I've got colleagues who have written extensively about this topic. The idea is basically that if you plant the tree, ride a bike, recycle and do your part, then you, as an individual, are taking responsibility. But the actions we are asking people to take are inadequate, in ways that are disempowering. Instead, it is about equipping folks with the tools to act. That's the kind of education I want to be part of – we have got to move beyond this kind of individualized notion of what climate action looks like. People will get motivated and things will change when we work together in community, not on consumer-based stuff, and to actually make political change. That's what is empowering.

The next generation, it seems to me, is not turning a blind eye to the difficult nature of the situation – not turning away from Greece, or turning away from the challenges associated with a warming world.

Following on from the 'individualized' notion, do you think we have put too much onus on one individual, like Greta Thunberg?

Greta became an iconic figure and movement – we galvanize around charismatic individuals. In every social movement you can think of, the stories are told through charismatic leaders, even though the movement is doing the work. I think this is overwhelmingly positive because so many young people, in particular, have been energized and then brought into the conversation about what effective action looks like, thanks to the media presence and other things that Greta has cultivated. It's important to recognize this when we're talking about community.

Some years ago, a US sociologist named Robert Putnam wrote a book called *Bowling Alone*, which talked about civil society, its fragmentation and its dissipation in the US context.[19] He talked about how there used to be bowling leagues, church groups and protest movements that would meet in church basement, and all of these things would bring people together in the community.

Putnam identified that more and more we were seeing fragmentation, where people were bowling alone, going to the bowling alley by themselves. So, if you want to write a story about climate change, it isn't just about the products of burning fossil fuels going into the atmosphere. If you want to think about the social dynamics that are driving that, then the fragmentation of social life is part of the story. It's a key part. What we're seeing among young people is that they are pushing away from that individualizing approach to find community, and be part of the community that's acting against the climate crisis – that's energizing. People get into conversations with folks rather than feeling like they're all alone.

Being alone while trying to make a difference means you don't get invited to dinner parties anymore – because you will put people off by talking about doom and gloom that nobody wants to hear. But if I find my people and we work together to make change – that's an energizing thing, that's constructive and positive.

Has social media played a positive role in that connection? Because now it seems many churches in America have right-wing congregations, who tend to be climate deniers. Therefore, have online communities helped to bring people together?

That's an interesting question. I think social media on balance is an evil for the world. It's an unbalanced and dreadful thing, and it's dreadful for a number of reasons. One is that, of course, we disappear into confined rabbit holes where all we hear are points of view that we already agree with, and this reinforces the us-versus-them dynamic. This makes real change really difficult.

Social media also gives a false sense of collectivism, as some would call it, where you are online and you're raging against other trolls. It makes you feel like you're doing something positive when, in fact, what you're doing is arguing.

Real action, I think, means in some ways turning away from the online space and toward the human physical space and actually meeting physically in church and basements – coming together as a community to make change.

What are your thoughts, then, on people wanting to fly to other places to connect?

When it comes to the moralism in the climate change movement, there's an analogy that is used in the US context. It's a crude analogy, so do forgive me. The analogy is 'circling the wagons and shooting inwards.' It comes from the old American West, where the wagons would circle to try to fight off attackers. Here the environmental movement circles the wagons and shoot inwards, which tends to scare people and tear them apart. This happens when we say, "Oh, you're flying? That means you're not committed." There's also the climate denial movement, which is very well organized around a set of themes, such as "Al Gore is on a plane again." All of that is a sideshow – it's a distraction.

We live in a world of wonders – we can't just turn off electricity and go back into caves. That's not the world I want to live in. I want to have a world that is compatible with ecological and social realities, that's constructive and positive and can be maintained for the long term. And there are lots of different ways that such a world could look.

It's a world that needs to centre its conversations on justice for those who are most vulnerable and how to construct that world with those benefits. It's a world where we should acknowledge that lots of technologies are incredibly positive but that we need to get a better handle on them, to ensure that the technologies are not driving us, but rather, humankind is shaping the technological direction. We've got to find a place where we're coming together around solutions to problems rather than tearing each other apart for political gain. There's a whole bunch of stuff going on here that makes things really complicated, but also pretty exciting. Part of why I do this work is because it's enormously challenging, which makes it enormously fun.

You've mentioned solutions. Are any of these solutions making a difference? And if so, which ones?

So much of my work is about technology as a response to climate change and other environmental issues. I think there's a broad sense, particularly in the West, that technology is neutral. Again, from the US context, the language that's used is that "guns don't kill people, it's people that kill people." The subtext is that guns are off the hook in the gun conversation in the US. Similarly, there's a sense of technologies being neutral and that we can wield them in lots of different ways – and that's just not true!

Borrowing language from other folks who study technology, technologies are inherently political. This means we fight over the way the technologies emerge in the world, and then fight when we have technologies that shape the world. For example, there's a reason that oil companies have enormous amounts of power. The way the fossil fuel infrastructure is embedded in our everyday lives has enabled these companies to buy political influence, to make sure the entire system keeps running along to their benefit.

What it boils down to is this: we can't bank on having the technology we need for the kind of world that we're trying to create. It's not like some magic thing is going to come over the horizon, like some carbon-sucking machine or some reflective layer that will shoot solar radiation back into space and make climate change go away!

Climate change is now a perennial problem. It's always going to be with us, and we have to find ways to work on this more turbulent planet, to our collective benefit, which means wielding technologies rather than letting technologies drive us. Some of the most important climate technologies won't be things like solar panels or wind farms; instead they'll be things like AI and biotech. But AI is going to change everything about the way that the world operates over the next couple of decades, and that reshaping could be for the service of the environment. Or it could be environmentally detrimental. Exactly how it's going to play out depends on how people come together and wrap power around the technologies to drive them in particular directions.

At the moment, we've got some big corporations just deciding that AI is great for the bottom line, we're just going to use it, to make the existing capitalist machine bigger and more efficient – and that's going to be terrible for the environment over the long term. That's an unsustainable use of AI. We've got to get smarter in the way that we try to control and use technologies.

At COP26, I heard scientists from around the world say the same thing - we cannot wait for the technology to be invented, it might not be invented in time and we might run out of time. This message hasn't really filtered down. We all just seem to be waiting for a new messiah of technology to save us.

That's exactly what I mean. When I use the line "technology will not save us," I'm not anti-technology, it's that we can't just wait. We are not going to have some magical technology emerge and make all of these problems go away. We are not even sure that we can invent it. At the same time, technology is basic to how human beings respond, because we're technological creatures.

We've got everything available to us today to construct a world that's compatible with ecological realities. It's not like we need to wait for that new thing to emerge – it's that we need to construct our society and politics in ways that take best advantage of the technologies that are already available. We could have had the energy transition two decades ago, and it's not like we had to wait for solar panels to get as cheap as they are. It's the fact that there's a whole bunch of complex reasons, the main one being there was just no desire or will.

So, now we find ourselves in a more desperate situation, reaching for more desperate types of responses, without doing the basic work that needs to be done, which is to turn off the fossil fuel economy.

Do you think politics will change? Are we going to see a new kind of politics that we desperately need – a new kind of political leadership?

I don't know. I thought I understood the world before the Trump election in 2016. Now I just don't know, with the kind of right-wing swing that we've seen and the way the COVID pandemic has led us toward more authoritarian governments around the world.

The work has to be done regardless. I think politics is more than political parties and what happens between countries. Politics is about how power operates in society to produce certain outcomes. At some level, we're all wielders of power, and this goes back to that earlier question about how we motivate people to be more effective. I think it's to help people to see the power that they actually wield – as individuals in a community, not where people are individualized in ways that fragment them. How do we come together in ways that make a difference? I think that's the game.

Where do you draw your hope from?

I don't know if I'm optimistic by nature. I think I tend to see the dark side of the situation. What I've been told by others whom I respect, and who have kind of pulled me out of that slump, is that we don't have the luxury of despair. We're just not allowed to, and if do we find ourselves in situations like that, we need to do the work that makes a difference. We're not going to do that work effectively if we allow ourselves to dwell or lose hope.

I'm about to give my first class of the year. It's a graduate seminar that I teach on environmental politics, and for the last few years I've always given a talk on hope as part of the first lecture. It's the theme of the course. The talk that I give is drawn from David Orr, a US environmental author. David has this line that he uses: "If you consider the environmental situation and you're optimistic, then you don't know enough. But if you're pessimistic, then you're ineffective." We need to reach for the ground in the middle, which is hope. This is something we can't just draw on because it exists in the world – it is something that needs to be made. Hope is something that we manufacture. We get up in the morning and say, "Today, I'm going to be hopeful." And then we get on with the work, and we don't allow ourselves to give up.

Yes, we can't give up on hope, which leaves me to ask you, what legacy do you want to leave?

That's a lovely question and I've never thought in such grand terms about the kind of work that I can do. But if there's a legacy, then it's through the students and through programmes that I've been part of, building a few things that I'm proud of, which I hope will go some way to help motivate particular types of actions and conversations. The work I'm proudest of is with smart people who go out and do amazing things, which means I also get to take some credit – some small amount of credit for the great work that others get to do.

STÉPHANE HALLEGATTE

SENIOR CLIMATE CHANGE ADVISER AT THE WORLD BANK

In September 2023, I spoke to Stéphane Hallegatte, Senior Climate Change Adviser at the World Bank. His research interests include the economics of natural disasters and risk management, climate change adaptation, urban policy and economics, climate change mitigation, and green growth. Stéphane is the author of dozens of articles published in international journals in multiple disciplines and of several books. He is also lead author of the fifth assessment report of the Intergovernmental Panel on Climate Change (IPCC).[20] He was the team leader for the World Bank Group Climate Change Action Plan, a large internal coordination exercise to determine and explain how the group will support countries in their implementation of the 2015 Paris Agreement.[21]

You were the lead author of the fifth assessment report of the IPCC on climate change, which came out in 2014. At that time, the report announced that the atmosphere and ocean were warming, snow and ice were diminishing, sea levels had risen, and the concentration of greenhouse gases had increased.

Do you feel disheartened that we are seeing the same headlines in 2023 and that the world has been deaf?

You might be surprised to hear that I am more optimistic than you might think, and, of course, how you see change depends on your expectations. The change I've seen is much bigger than I expected. The fact that the physical changes that we see around us have become worse should really not be a surprise for anyone. It takes a long time to change our economic systems to reduce emissions. Plus, we need to understand that there is an accumulation of carbon in the atmosphere, and even if you reduce how much you add to it every year, it will still take time to make a difference to that accumulation.

It takes time for the system to respond to the climate, and the trends that we're seeing will continue for decades – whatever we're doing – and some will continue forever, because they have been triggered and there's not much we can do. For instance, the melting of sea ice will continue for centuries and is in the books already – we now need to deal with it. The positive side of the story is that people are aware of the challenge, which means we can be prepared with how we deal with things. If I met a Generation Z person ten years ago, I would have to do the full spiel to explain what it is all about, why it's important and so on. I don't have to do that anymore. Plus, now any person working in any ministry, agency or company knows the climate is changing. The fact that everybody making decisions within their own department is aware that this is happening – well, that's big progress.

The other thing is that we have nothing to compare what's happening now with the past, but I do think we're already avoiding some impacts because of people's awareness. Ten years ago, just before the 2014 report, the first time I was talking about getting to zero in net emissions, people were laughing at me, because it looked impossible. But now over time everyone has processed the fact that, whether we like it or not, it's everyone's job to find a way forward. These are the discussions we are having today, and nobody's laughing anymore. This is progress.

Also in 2014, all technologies that helped reduce emissions were more expensive than using fossil fuels. Today, it is very different: solar and wind power are cheaper than coal, cheaper than gas, cheaper than everything. And electric bicycles, cars and buses are everywhere. Technologies take time to adapt to systems – it's not always easy, it doesn't happen instantly, and you do need to invest more at the beginning, but then you have the savings in the long term.

I use an electric bike to come to the office. It's so much cheaper than anything else, and it's also good for wellness. People know what the goal is, and we have started to see technologies make a positive impact, where there's a win–win.

That was not there ten years ago, and I can feel the difference. People are really trying and you're much more likely to succeed if you try. Ten years ago, nobody was trying.

Have the policies implemented since the Paris Agreement had an impact?

Yes, they have had an impact, no doubt about it. However, the question is how much, and whether it's on the scale that we need. It's pretty clear that things are not where they need to be, but countries have made commitments that are getting closer to what we need. The EU and the US say net zero in 2050, China says 2060, India says 2070 and so on. The commitments are almost becoming aligned with the global objectives.

However, countries have not aligned their policies with their commitments. If you take all the countries I've mentioned, they are not on track to meet their own commitments. The policies are not there. But we have very empirical statistics showing that policies have an impact on emissions – and not only we do have empirical studies but we also have good stories.[22]

Germany puts a lot of money toward subsidizing solar panels. I remember in the past that Germany was under attack, with people saying, "Oh, they are wasting a lot of money, because the solar panels are so expensive." But that's what Germany did, and in doing so, it created a huge demand, which China responded to by creating a supply. As a result, the scale got so big that the cost of solar declined very quickly, and now it's cheaper than anything else. This did not happen simply because of progress – it was what we call *directed* technical change, where somebody decided to make something happen and invested in it.

Now that people see the value of green products, they too want to be part of these green value chains. This is a big improvement and shows how policies can create transformative change.

Do we have the ability to end extreme poverty, even in the face of climate change? If so, what needs to happen?

I have recently done a study on this.[23] It is possible to take people out of extreme poverty without compromising our climate objectives. Even if we use old technology like fossil fuels, it will increase emissions by around 5%, which is negligible – it will not radically affect the climate problem. So, that's the first thing I'd like to say, and that getting people out of extreme poverty should be a higher priority than anything else. I don't think a lot of people realize how hard acute poverty is and how it impacts quality of life. We should never say to somebody living in rural Mali, "That is not possible because of increased emissions," because the emissions from these populations are so small that they are insignificant.

But of course, today we should not introduce electricity with old technologies. Instead, we can use renewable energy, which is much cheaper. I think it is really important to point out that we've had fossil fuels for a long time and many people still don't have access to electricity. That's because fossil fuels are not an easy way to bring electricity to these populations. Africa has a low population density, and if you wanted to introduce electricity with coal, you would need a big coal power plant with a lot of long transmission lines, which would be super-expensive and difficult to maintain. It is much cheaper to have solar panels, bringing electricity production closer to where the demand is.

I think people are really playing politics when they say, "We cannot get electricity to these people because of climate policies," because 20 years ago, we had almost no climate policies, and those same people did not have electricity. But now, climate policies have helped us get cheap renewable energy that can provide electricity to a rural village for much less. When you have a lot of people saying, "We shouldn't ban countries and people living in poverty from using fossil fuels," I think that is correct: they have the right to use fossil fuels, but it doesn't change the fact that it's not what they need, because renewable energy is a better option.

My worry is not that poor countries don't have access to fossil fuels because of climate policies. My worry is poor countries don't have the financing to have access to the technologies that are better for them, which are renewables and electric mobility. If there is something for those countries to complain about, it's that the financial system doesn't make it easy for them to invest in the technologies of tomorrow – the technologies they need to get out of poverty and develop. It's the same story for agriculture, where farming in poor countries has productivity that's less than half the productivity in rich countries because of limited access to practices, equipment, technologies, the right seeds and so on. If we help these farmers use the best practices, it will do a lot to reduce poverty and will also improve soil. And it will help keep carbon in the soil, reducing emissions, so again it is positive.

If you look at what needs to be done to reduce extreme poverty, it doesn't have to increase emissions a lot. It will increase emissions a little bit because we don't have the full technological package to do zero emissions at the moment. So, I think this is a false narrative and it's political, where we have people who are responsible for a lot of the emissions saying we cannot reduce the emissions. And I think this will be bad for people living in poverty.

What do you think about India's commitment to renewable energies and about solar energy in India?

India is doing a great job on solar and has extremely ambitious objectives that will be tricky to achieve. Fossil fuels in India are very political, and of course, as renewable energy becomes better, it will displace fossil fuels. A success story is India's push for renewable energy: it has put in place the right systems to get people to invest in solar energy. There is a lot of room to make this bigger and continue the increased effort toward using renewables. Some things still need to happen, especially with how the grid is being managed, to enable it to accommodate all types of renewable energy.

India is interesting – or perhaps it is better to say difficult – because of the geography of the country. A lot of the renewable potential is in the west of the country and a lot of the coal is in the east. Because India is a federal state with a lot of decentralization, it is not straightforward to get the money flowing. There is a huge political economic challenge for the country, but things are moving incredibly fast.

How do we use engagement on climate change to create change overall, as part of the big picture?

Change, developments, progress and so on are all to do with institutions, and institutions are created when we get a consensus that we need something and that there is an opportunity. For instance, if a country creates an institution for better water management, it also benefits the climate.

When I was working in France, we had trouble with development and flood zones for a long time. It was because of the political economy, where you had people who owned land in flood zones and who wanted to build on the land to make money. It was a difficult and sensitive topic. Climate change was extremely useful in changing the narrative and allowing progress to be made. You put the blame on somebody else, saying, "You know, it's all of these bad people emitting carbon dioxide who are changing the climate and now we have a problem."

We have now all realized it's not only climate that's the issue, it's something else too, such as climate and access to energy, or climate and land use, or climate and urbanization, or climate and access to jobs, and so on. When we have momentum, we should really use the opportunity to fix other problems too. We need to be optimistic, to make things better.

What we see is that some countries have a narrative on climate. Let's look at Germany, where climate is an important part of policy in the political narrative. And India, which is developing solar energy – which is good for the climate

– but doesn't position this effort under the umbrella of the climate message. Instead, India's message is about energy security and the sovereignty of the country.

Each region has a focus and a narrative, depending on its politics. You might do exactly the same thing under the climate umbrella in some countries and under the energy security, energy access or industrial development umbrella in other countries. In the end, the same things happen – it just comes down to the narrative and positioning.

When the UK government talks about climate, is it a narrative about energy security? We've had so much debate here about whether the government really cares about the planet.

Initially, in the 1980s and 1990s, when people started to talk about the climate, it was all very much connected to questions around energy security and energy access. Margaret Thatcher was one of the first heads of state to talk about climate,[24] but of course, the idea in the background was that fossil fuels were running out and the UK would become more dependent on the rest of the world. No policy is ever driven by one single goal – it's always multiple goals.

I think, if you polled the UK population, most people would want to do something about the climate, and of course you would have a small part of the population who was against it. But overall, it is accepted that the UK wants to reduce its emissions, but this is not the case in all countries. There are countries where the dominant narrative is still "the high-income countries are not doing enough and we won't do anything until we see more action from them." I'm not judging. That's fine, because those countries saying that might be investing more than others in solar energy, because they want to be more independent.

But going back to your question about whether the UK's policies are making a difference: the answer is yes. And I'd include policies that don't have 'climate' in the title. It's about separating the narrative from the noise.

For example, countries that have reformed their energy subsidies because they cannot afford them, and that have then tried to sell the subsidy reform as the government's need to save money, have failed to win people over. The narrative that works is the one about energy subsidies helping people – where the government says, "We will change the way we help you and by doing this we'll be more efficient." When government narratives have come from the perspective of helping the population and being efficient, then those policies have worked, with much less pushback from the population. That's the power of the narrative: it is really important – it is crucial.

Do you think people will make the right decisions?

I'm pretty convinced that there are no right and wrong decisions. Knowing what is right and wrong depends a lot on how the decision has been made. Sometimes we make bad decisions and we realize it afterwards, even though they were decisions made by collecting the right information, consulting with the right people and following the right process – sometimes you're wrong and there is no blame. It happens. However, sometimes people make the wrong decision because they didn't get the information they needed, or they didn't consult with the right people, or there were hidden goals that were not communicated. That's when the wrong decision was made because of the process.

We need to take care to keep people accountable for the process. If they make a wrong choice in terms of the process, then something needs to change. But if they get the process right and the outcome is negative, then we need to understand that sometimes bad things just happen.

In France, I was working on a big storm that took place in 2010, where many died. Several mayors got into trouble because of the decisions they had made to allow new construction in flood zones. But what I found interesting was that if you looked at how those decisions were being made, the mayors had very little choice and were not given the tools to make the right decisions. I'm now obsessed about how when we ask people to make the right decisions, we need to make sure they have a fighting chance, and a fighting chance means resources, time to collect the information and do the process correctly, and clear instructions to mandate what they can and cannot do.

It is about strengthening systems to improve how we make decisions. Nobody likes to put money into this because it looks like paperwork and bureaucracy, and it's boring. No one is interested. But it's actually critical and comes back to the point I was making about institutions being the key to success. Institution-building is the most difficult thing on Earth but is probably also the most important thing on Earth. Getting the institutions right is key.

Did you ever think, when you were growing up, that you would be doing such fascinating work?

I thought that I would be teaching. It is valuable and you're really shaping things. I think what's nice is to see things change. I think what I am doing now is not that different from teaching in a way – it is still about communicating information that people need in a way that they can process. It's similar to the work people do in universities – when you're doing your research, doing your teaching, and the two feed into each other.

My last question is about legacy. What would you like your legacy to be in this climate change narrative?

One thing I've been trying to do is to make people realize that we're not talking about the trade-off between protecting the planet and our own wellbeing. In everyday discussions, you have people saying, "Oh, we can't do this, because of trade-off with developments, poverty reduction and so on." My impression is that people are being too abstract, because what we are actually talking about is protecting forests, improving a farmer's equipment, investing in solar panels and so on. When you look at concrete projects, this trade-off disappears. I've been trying to make things more evidence based, because I think that too often people discuss abstract concepts – green growth, degrowth and so on – and are not necessarily making the connection with concrete cases and situations.

I also believe it is important – especially for someone like me who is working in Washington, DC, within an international organization – to empower people who have a mandate to decide, are allowed to make that decision, without me making the decision for them. It's a fine line, as you're trying to provide advice.

DR KIMBERLEY R. MINER

RESEARCH ASSISTANT PROFESSOR AT THE UNIVERSITY OF MAINE AND CLIMATE SCIENTIST AT NASA

In October 2023, I spoke to climate scientist Dr Kimberley R. Miner, who is looking at Earth systems and risks at the University of Maine. Dr Miner has earned global recognition for her groundbreaking research that includes the Arctic and an expedition to the summit of Everest, where she and her team set a Guinness World Record. Dr Miner is also a Fellow at the Center for Climate and Security; cochair of the NASA Interagency Forum on Climate Risks, Impacts and Adaptation; and a scientist at NASA Jet Propulsion Laboratory.

Her research on climate risks has taken her to the most extreme environments in the world. She has sought out new scientific discoveries at the ends of the Earth, travelling to both the North and South Poles, as well as high mountain ranges in Asia, Europe and North America.

Is there one impact of climate change that particularly concerns you right now?

What I think is of great relevance is the cryosphere[25] – the poles, their stability and their coldness. This drives a lot of the atmosphere and ocean circulation that we rely on to keep our world and our climate steady.

There is a lot of overlap and it's hard to distinguish individual sources of climate change, because everything is connected. One of the things that really overlaps with the Arctic warming, and that I'm concerned about, is the ocean circulation and the potential for it to slow. This can be understood by thinking about the emerging tipping points and how close we are to crossing them. I personally think that we've probably already crossed the Arctic tipping point, across a variety of scales. However, there are other tipping points – including tropical forest stability and ocean circulation – I think, unfortunately, we won't know whether we've crossed them until it's already happened. Looking backwards is relevant for me, as it allows us to understand patterns and systems.

What are the Arctic tipping points and why should we care?

There's an example I like to use that explains this really well. The sea ice at the North Pole used to be older than a decade. It was pretty significant ice that was there all the time, but now what we're seeing is the ice getting younger and younger. Every year the ice freezes, then melts, then freezes again, and then melts again, and crucially we are no longer seeing an increase of legacy ice.

Until now we have never not seen an increase of legacy ice or had a decrease of legacy ice. Neither have we seen the ice refreeze repeatedly year after year after year. Instead of seeing a frozen North Pole ocean that has long-term ice stability, we are now seeing this ice freeze and melt annually. It is a completely different ocean pattern – and it is increasing.

We are also seeing changes in the thaw depths for the permafrost, where a deeper thaw occurs more frequently. We should care about this for the same reason: when we see a snow-and-ice event in Texas, it means instability.

The poles are the key to stability for the atmosphere and ocean circulation. Without their stability, the prevailing wind currents that keep our temperature stable, that give us regular seasons, will be out of sync and obviously mean things are unstable. These novel patterns mean everything is unclear, which will impact the uncertainty of the crosswinds.[26]

You have undertaken some insightful research that has included looking at Indigenous communities and the role they play in addressing climate change. What inspired you to look at these communities and what can we learn from them?

It's clear to me that we are missing generations of knowledge from communities that have been on the land since time immemorial. We only have just under 200 years of direct measurements, especially in the Arctic, where people were getting stuck and not doing a great job of exploring until very recently. This has really limited our ability to understand what happened in the past, and therefore understand or predict what might happen in the future.

It's always seemed short-sighted to me that some types of knowledge are considered not usable, not as reasonable, or not as academic or politically sound, and as a result have been discounted because of the group that the knowledge comes from. Some underlying social dynamics are at play here, such as colonialism and how we think about expansion.

It's important to me to value all types of knowledge and make sure that there is an ethical integration of different types of knowledge to protect everybody. The other reason is that these are people who are indigenous to the Arctic, or who are living in the Arctic. Part of my mission as a scientist, especially a government-backed scientist, is to bring the science to the people that have paid for it, and that includes people who live on the land and in Alaska.

What has science learned from these Indigenous communities? Have they thrown light on anything that was hidden?

I have ongoing collaborations where I am constantly in a learning mode with friends who have regional knowledge and traditional ecological knowledge. A friend of mine has built an AI model that looks at Inuit and Yupik knowledge about sea ice and that is able to make predictions using the knowledge it has collected. It gives a much better insight than what we're able to get with direct measurements. So yes, I think there's definitely a huge amount of information and knowledge that we can each share and that Western scientists can definitely gain from, although it needs to be conducted in an ethical way.

Your work is insightful. You also talk about climate grief, which is the emotional impact sparked by working as a climate scientist. How do you deal with it and still maintain hope?

Funnily enough, I was talking about this yesterday with colleagues and it is very overwhelming. I have a couple of other hats that I wear, including on the engineering side, which is nice because it gives me a little bit of work that's not directly looking at the terrible impacts of climate change and reporting them back. It gives me balance and a bit of a break.

What I like to say is that I don't work with hope – I work in action. Therefore, I don't necessarily see that there is a reason for me to have hope, because I know that I'm doing the work. Plus, there's a lot of people doing really interesting and different things, and it's all of these people working together and acting together that will make the difference.

This leads me to my last question. What would you like your legacy to be within the climate change space?

Wow, it's a big question. I guess off the top of my head, I'd like to think that I tell the truth. I also like to look for things that are being overlooked, that are still really important across physical and social dynamics. I like to think that I'm doing all I can do within my work.

CHAPTER 3

GLOBAL LEADERSHIP

Since the global COVID-19 pandemic, we have found ourselves living in a far more fractured world, with new wars, cost-of-living crises and more natural disasters occurring. In the past ten years things have dramatically changed. If we look back at political conversations, climate was never part of the same conversation, but thankfully that is changing. Climate is now playing a growing role, but often these communications are watered down, and we need better from our leaders. We need world leaders to commit, to promise, to take an oath to protect our natural spaces, resources and life forms. Protecting our ecosystems is one of the most effective ways to lessen climate change and build resilience, as well as addressing the extinction crisis that threatens over 1 million species, including our own.

THE NEED FOR TRANSFORMATIVE LEADERSHIP

Strong, fearless leadership matters in this fight against climate change. Up to now there have been very few credible leaders, but what makes a credible leader? Well, it's things like decency, integrity and authenticity. It's a bold vision, and ideas to improve the world, because until now ideas have been an underestimated ingredient in politics. We need the big ideas to inspire innovation beyond what people currently think is possible.

We need leadership that shakes people out of their collective slumber, because we are sleepwalking into an abyss. The whole world needs transformative leadership and direction from national governments and people in all areas of society. But most of all, we need leaders who are not afraid to lead – we need courageous leaders who stick to their plans.

From talking to people in my networks and listening to groups, I think it's fair to say that wherever we are in the world, we are all tired of leaders who go back on their promises and manifestos. The world lacks truth and we are living in the age of fake news, where everything can be doctored to appear as truth and fact.

But most of all, we need global transformative leadership on climate adaptation to create safer, stronger and more thriving communities around the world. These leaders will recognize that the majority of measures to reduce greenhouse gas emissions have multiple economic benefits, such as job creation to improving public health by reducing local air pollution, which impacts millions of people around the world each year. The transition to the low-carbon economy will mean better economic growth, higher living standards and a reduction in poverty. There are some businesses and governments that do understand that the transition to low-carbon economic development and growth presents vast opportunities and will spur a new generation of jobs and innovation.

We desperately need the political will for governments to offer ambitious, equitable and credible national targets, and reach an agreement that commits all countries to increase the strength of their action to avoid dangerous climate change. This will require two important goals to be reached: zero deforestation by 2030, and zero emissions from fossil fuels by 2050. This is everyone's problem and all countries have an important stake in addressing this emergency.

There are already regions on the cusp of disappearing, such as the low-lying atoll nations, with many islands mere metres above sea level and subject to more frequent and intense extreme events. Mitigation is critical for the survival of atoll nations. At the same time, ambitious adaptation actions are required to prevent them from becoming uninhabitable. Several atoll nations, such as Kiribati, the Maldives and the Marshall Islands, are protecting their coastal areas by planting mangroves, restoring wetlands and improving water systems. But they also need the rest of us to change and to do our bit, otherwise their efforts will be futile.

If the world does not act together, we risk a 'climate apartheid' scenario where the wealthy pay to escape overheating, hunger and conflict while the rest of the world is left to suffer. Environmental degradation increases everyone's vulnerability to climate change, but it most acutely affects Indigenous peoples, rural communities and others who depend directly on healthy ecosystems for their livelihoods. There is still time to work with Nature to build resilience and reduce climate risks at all scales, such as by restoring forests to regulate water flows and sequester carbon, and by creating green spaces in cities to help control temperatures. However, the window of opportunity is closing quickly.

Reinforcing this thought, a Politico Morning Consult Global Sustainability Poll conducted in 2022 revealed frustration from citizens who felt that they were being left on their own to take climate action, when they believed governments and the companies with the most resources, which tend to have the most responsibility for carbon emissions, should shoulder the burden. The poll showed that adults globally have damning opinions about the performance of their political leaders when it comes to climate change.[27]

Even when the risks are understood, knowledge is often lacking on appropriate solutions, including what works, what doesn't, and the costs and benefits of specific options to reduce vulnerability. Governments lack incentives and funding for agencies to grapple with knowledge gaps, collaborate across silos and implement innovative solutions. In most governments, few incentives exist to foster collaboration across sectors – between ministries, between official bodies and affected communities, between the public and private sectors, and even between nations. This is where big businesses come in. As I said in my previous book, *Corporate Social Responsibility Is Not Public Relations*, some businesses have more money than governments, and more resources that can be used to help fix things.[28]

We need political leaders who have the audacity to think long term and not just focus on short-term policies. We need leaders who will put the future of the planet before their own political gain.

WHAT ABOUT THE CONFERENCE OF THE PARTIES (COP)?

You've probably heard of COP, which is the main decision-making body of the UN Framework Convention on Climate Change (UNFCCC). COP includes representatives from all 197 countries that are signatories to the UNFCCC. The objective of the UNFCCC is "stabilization of greenhouse gas concentrations in the atmosphere at a level that would prevent dangerous anthropogenic [human-induced] interference with the climate system."[29] COP assesses what each country has been doing to limit climate change against the overall goal of the UNFCCC.

So, is COP still relevant? This question is especially important given that many think COP has become an ineffective bureaucracy, with people flying in from around the world to discuss the same things as last year. Every nation has its own domestic agenda, making global progress slow. Things need to speed up or time will run out – the science is clear.

However, in spite of the lack of speed, COP is the best process that we have. Beyond the negotiations, there are real opportunities to increase external pressure on governments to create real opportunities for today's youth and future generations. I have been following the COP process since 2000 and I have participated in several COP meetings, and I think it's true to say that COPs are more than just summits; they present a determined global hope to make progress. We just need to ensure that they have the right sponsors and keep our governments on track, so they don't become glorified talking shops. Talk is cheap.

CLIMATE ACTIVISM

So, how do we keep governments alert? Many will say through action and that activists have a role. Climate activism is not new – it can be traced back to the early 1970s, when activists called for more effective political action regarding global warming and other environmental anomalies. Earth Day 1970 saw the first large-scale environmental movement that called for the protection of all life on Earth. Since then, the idea has grown, with more young people joining the movement for positive change. However, a report from the nonprofit Global Witness shows that at least 177 people were killed in 2022 for defending the environment, with a fifth of killings taking place in the Amazon Rainforest. That's a rate of one environmental defender being murdered by organized crime groups and land invaders every other day. Colombia was the deadliest country, recording 60 murders. Indigenous communities were disproportionately represented in the figures, making up 34% of all murders despite representing about 5% of the world's population.[30]

In 2023, a Norwegian study found that anger is by far the most powerful emotional predictor of whether somebody plans to take part in a climate protest. The research asked 2,000 Norwegian adults how they felt about the climate crisis and found the link to activism was seven times stronger for anger than it was for hope. The effects were smaller for other actions, but fear and guilt were the best predictors of policy support, while sadness, fear and hope were the best predictors of behavioural change.[31]

I guess the question is – is it time for more of us to start to rally together in order to peacefully protest for climate action? History has shown us that it does work. Gandhi organized peaceful protests against British rule, inspiring people all over the world, including civil rights leaders in the US such as Martin Luther King Jr. The civil rights movement went on to secure African Americans equal access to restaurants, transportation and other public facilities. It enabled Black people, women and other minorities to break down barriers in the workplace.

When political systems start to fail or when regimes become oppressive, activism starts to fill the void. People should feel angry because they have been deliberately deceived by fossil fuel companies and governments have let it happen. People are losing trust. We're still pumping oil; we're still digging for coal. There are thousands of people dying around the world due to the impacts of climate change. The world is still burning and flooding.

But if the global pandemic has taught us anything, it's how connected we all are – and that the world has changed not because a president, a prime minister, a CEO or a celebrity decided it had to. It changed because we changed – people decided that the working world could and should be different.

GLOBAL HOPE AND ACTION

Sir David Attenborough said, "Surely it is our responsibility to do everything within our power to create a planet that provides a home not just for us, but for all life on Earth."[32] Hope can be found in action, and when it comes to action there has been some there has been some good news.

In 2022, the US made a huge leap forward when it passed sweeping new laws to confront climate change, with the Inflation Reduction Act aiming to reduce US greenhouse gas emissions by 40% by 2030.[33] The measures resulting from this act have been the biggest investment in climate solutions in US history, which is a sign of progress. The act aims to make green energy the default in major sectors like electricity, transport and industry. It is important to mention that the US is home to the largest ideological divide on climate action. Among Americans, a survey found that 97% of left-leaning voters expressed concern about climate change, compared to 51% of right-leaning voters.[34]

In the UK, a 2023 focus group for the newspaper *The Guardian* showed UK residents backed net-zero policies. Those in the focus group were happy to change their habits to be more environmentally friendly but felt held back by high rail fares or a lack of charging points for electric cars. They also had wider concerns that politicians might only tackle the climate crisis if there was a financial incentive for them. One suggestion made was that politicians were too exposed to vested interests because they took second jobs. Across the focus group, the main worry was that politicians either wouldn't be bold and forwardthinking enough to take the long-term steps necessary to reach net zero or would see net zero as a money-making opportunity.[35]

China plays a complicated role in global climate action. Unlike the countries in the developed world, it is not responsible for the historical greenhouse gas emissions that scientists say have caused climate change so far. But it is a huge polluter because of its very rapid economic growth. However, China is by far the biggest investor in renewable energy – a quarter of newly registered cars in China are electric.[36] The country is making efforts and setting demanding targets, including peaking its carbon emissions by 2030, and it has big ambitions to address carbon emissions by planting trees. At the World Economic Forum Annual meeting in 2022, President Xi Jinping pledged to plant 70 billion trees by 2030.[37]

THE POLITICAL LEADERS MAKING CHANGE

There are many bright spots, where political leaders around the world have stepped up and are doing good work to combat the climate crisis. Here are a few who will go down in history with a legacy of bringing about change.

I have to start with Al Gore, the American politician, businessman and environmentalist who served as the 45th vice president of the US from 1993 to 2001 under President Bill Clinton. He is founder and chairman of the Climate Reality Project, a nonprofit devoted to solving the climate crisis, and is founder, chairman or trustee of a whole host of other organizations. He was the subject of the documentary *An Inconvenient Truth*, which won two Oscars in 2006, and a second documentary in 2017, *An Inconvenient Sequel: Truth to Power*. In 2007, he was awarded the Nobel Peace Prize for "informing the world of the dangers posed by climate change."[38]

Who can forget the explosive COP26 speech of Mia Mottley, prime minister of Barbados, who called a world that warmed by 2°C a "death sentence" for many in the Global South.[39] Since then, Mottley has been building climate partnerships between developing nations, combining their efforts to push for greater action on climate change and the delivery of climate reparations. She is known for creating The Bridgetown Initiative, which is growing a global coalition of nations committed to overhauling the financial system and funding climate investment to the tune of trillions of dollars. She has a particular focus on supporting vulnerable countries facing a combination of financial stress and climate threats.

Next is Luiz Inácio Lula da Silva, president of Brazil, who managed to turn things around regarding Amazon deforestation, which fell by at least 60% in July 2023 compared to the same month in 2022.[40] This rapid progress highlights the importance of political change. In 2021, under the far-right President Jair Bolsonaro, the Amazon was suffering one of the worst cutting and burning seasons in recent history. However, since Lula da Silva took power, his administration has penalized land-grabbers, mounted paramilitary operations to drive out illegal miners, demarcated more Indigenous land and created more conservation areas. There is now hope that these improvements can be a springboard for a new cycle of prosperity in the Amazon. Lula da Silva has committed his political future to zero deforestation and will push for continued reductions in the run-up to COP30, which will be held in the Amazon city of Belém in 2025.

Then there's Carlos Manuel Rodríguez, the Environment and Energy Minister and former Vice President of Conservation International's Mexican and Central American programme in Costa Rica. He has pioneered the development of payments for ecosystem services to incentivize farmers and landowners to use their land for environmental good. This policy helped preserve ecosystems and contributed significantly to Costa Rica's economy.

Robert Habeck, who has been billed as the "world's most powerful green politician,"[41] wants to transform green politics and for Germany to be a global leader in renewable energy.

In India, Harsh Vardan, the Union Minister for the Environment, has focused on motivating scientists to develop new technologies that address social and environmental problems. However, he is likely to be best remembered for making India a leader in environmental preservation. In 2008, he launched an anti-plastic-bag campaign in Delhi and the Green Shopper Campaign, which promotes business partnerships with manufacturers of environmentally friendly products.

In Indonesia, Tri Rismaharini is the country's Minister of Social Affairs and a former mayor of Surabaya. She has transformed the city, previously known for its pollution and congestion. It has emerged with an emphasis on sustainability and rich green spaces. There are now 11 landscaped parks. In recognition of Rismaharini's impact, she has been declared one of the World's 50 greatest leaders by *Fortune* magazine.[42]

Virginijus Sinkevičius, a Lithuanian politician who is European Commissioner for the Environment, Oceans and Fisheries, deserves a mention. In his previous role as Minister of the Economy and Innovation, he helped make Vilnius one of the greenest cities in Europe. In his current role, Sinkevičius has pioneered legislation to reduce chemical fertilizer overuse, which is a major driver of both climate change and ecological decline.

Someone who is perhaps a little less known is Anne Hidalgo, who has served as the mayor of Paris since 2014. Using the disruption from COVID-19, she turned many of the city's most traffic-filled areas into cycle-friendly neighbourhoods.

In Spain, Teresa Ribera, Spanish Minister for the Ecological Transition of Spain, is aiming for Spain to be carbon neutral by 2050 at the latest.

Finally, I'll end with the much-admired Caroline Lucas, former leader of the Green Party in the UK, who made history when she was elected as the Green Party's first MP in 2010. She was the first Green Party candidate to be elected to the House of Commons and has showed that a different kind of politics is possible.

We need this list to continue to grow. We need to see more political leaders who are committed to fighting for the planet and who will stay on track with their policies and manifestos.

CONCLUSION

We have trouble trusting governments to lead us in much-needed collective action. We have trouble defining the links between power and accountability. While change is happening, it is far too slow, marred by private interests and a powerful conservative majority that continues to deny the truth: that we are on the edge of disaster. Is this the fault of governments? Yes. They are failing to care for our needs and have instead succumbed to the pressure of profit-driven corporations and fringe stakeholders.

Governments need to realize that old patterns cannot be broken with old ways. All they have achieved is to buy time for an unsustainable system to briefly flourish until a complete breakdown is reached. In a system dominated by short-term policy, there is little appetite to adequately address climate change. Governments are failing to safeguard the integrity of democratic life. If this does not change, our political ideals will be undermined. We need to restore, through government and other means, our trust in collective action.

Globalization also ensures that responsibility for climate change remains difficult to pin down. It is easy for leaders in rich, advanced countries such as the UK and US to blame industrial nations such as China and India for the production of greenhouse gases. However, the actual role wealthier nations play in this pollution, through consumerism and a demand for lower prices, is rarely ever addressed. What we need is a new generation of fearless leaders who want to move the dial on climate and who are here to fight for the maximum possible ambition and action. We need governments that see the opportunities, that think outside the box, that believe in innovation, that want to inspire and above all that genuinely care about achieving a better world for all.

TAKEAWAY

We can all take political action by voting, and other ways include sharing petitions, joining campaigns and organizing events for the causes we care about most. Writing to your local MP or government official also helps create change to help stop the loss of wildlife and prioritize climate issues. Encourage the people you know who are eligible to vote to do so. It does matter – look at Brazil, which voted for change in 2022. Look for ways to meaningfully participate in democracy. There are so many organizations you can get involved with to have an impact in an upcoming election.

As an aside, in some countries, refugees and migrants are unable to participate in the voting process because they are not considered citizens of the country, but that doesn't necessarily mean they can't take part in the political process. In Germany, for instance, even as a non-German citizen, you are allowed to join a political party. This will become important as we see more climate migrants and refugees.

Another tip relates to your money, as money is power. Many institutions, such as banks, are funding the coal, gas and oil industries, often using our money. Removing your personal finances from any institution that invests in fossil fuels is one of the most impactful things you can do for the planet as an individual.

CHAPTER 4

IN CONVERSATION WITH GLOBAL THOUGHT LEADERS

I have gathered the voices of four thought leaders for this chapter, to show us what is possible, how policies can make a difference about what we should be thinking, and that we deserve better from our governments, political systems and leaders. The four are Jojo Mehta, Chief Executive of Stop Ecocide International; Jacob Dahl, author and a Senior Partner Emeritus at McKinsey & Company; Nisreen Elsaim, a Sudanese activist; and Lieutenant Colonel (Retd) Langley Sharp MBE, former head of the British Army's Centre for Army Leadership.

JOJO MEHTA

CHIEF EXECUTIVE OF STOP ECOCIDE INTERNATIONAL

In September 2023, I spoke to Jojo Mehta, Chief Executive of Stop Ecocide International. Jojo cofounded the organization in 2017 with the late Polly Higgins. Stop Ecocide International is behind the growing movement to make ecocide an international crime.

What is ecocide legislation and why is it important to recognize ecocide as a crime?

Ecocide law relates to a new international crime that fits precisely into existing legal systems and is compatible with them – it is a lever that can create real change. By introducing ecocide as a new crime against peace, we underline how seriously we take severe damage to the environment and so strengthen existing environmental laws as we create a new one. This is not without precedent. For example, murder has been a crime since time immemorial but the concept of life as a fundamental human right is a relatively new discourse.

There were obviously working definitions of ecocide and people ask, "What exactly do you mean by ecocide?" Polly Higgins, our late cofounder, had a definition that she submitted to the International Law Commission in 2010 as a proposal, but in a sense, it was just one lawyer saying, "I think it should look like this."

In 2020, some parliamentarians from Sweden approached us and said, "This is your area of expertise. Can you commission a draft that has a level of credibility and consensus, that we could then propose to our government to put forward to the International Criminal Court?" However, since then Sweden hasn't done that, and the country has had a change of government.

But this request prompted us to bring together a remarkable panel of experts that included Philippe Sands KC, a renowned international lawyer who is also an authority on the origins of international crimes.

He cochaired the panel with an eminent Senegalese jurist who had been a judge on the people's tribunal of Monsanto, which had discussed ecocide. Together they were a dynamite pairing, and we also brought together 12 lawyers from around the world. This ensured that the panel had a diversity of legal backgrounds, ranging from climate law to public law, humanitarian law, environmental law and criminal law. This meant that there was the necessity for a considerable degree of intellectual and professional generosity in terms of drafting, because they all had to make concessions to arrive at this definition:

> Ecocide means unlawful or wanton acts committed with knowledge that there is a substantial likelihood of severe and either widespread or long-term damage to the environment being caused by those acts.

This definition of ecocide is brilliant – it is so succinct. If you're talking to a politician, who rarely has time to read through your 20-page report, you can just hand it to them on a business card, or to anyone, and say "this is what ecocide is – it's very simple."

This definition emerged in June 2021 after a six-month drafting process. The press was fascinated by it, and it opened up political discussion all over the world. There were a few reasons this happened. One is that it focuses on consequences, and of course, one of the dangers that you always have when you legislate in the environmental arena is that in a sense, you permit by omission, which is why environmental regulation is often so detailed. If something isn't listed, then somehow it feels okay to do it, or rather companies think so. It was fascinating hearing a panel of lawyers drafting this definition of ecocide law, discussing whether we should list certain acts in the definition, or whether the definition should be based on the consequences.

I think it's absolutely key that it ended up with a vote for the consequences, because what this means is that no matter what ecocide or nonsense somebody dreams up in the next decade, it will still be covered by the fact that if you create a certain level of harm, it will be a crime. And that's dynamic!

Why hasn't it been done before if it's that simple?

It is crazy, isn't it! When the Rome Statute, which is the governing document of the ICC,[43] was being drafted in the 1990s, there were a number of clauses that were in play that could have ended up in the statute. For example, the severe, widespread and long-term harm to Nature was one, but it didn't make it into the final treaty in 1998. Significantly, it was dropped without a vote. When we look back at the relevant papers, we find that there were certain countries that spoke against it, and there are no big surprises about which they were – the US, the UK, France and the Netherlands.

What's very interesting is that all of those countries are oil states. Moreover, these four nations were either engaged in or considering engaging in nuclear testing, so you can imagine the implications – you can't do a test without committing ecocide. I think that is probably the most likely explanation for why ecocide didn't reach the statute at that time. What I often like to point out to people is that if ecocide had been accepted into the statute at that time, the world might be in a different place.

'Ecocide' is a term coined 50 years ago to refer to the damage created by Agent Orange in Vietnam.[44] It was first mentioned on the diplomatic stage by the Swedish premier Olof Palme in 1972, but it was put on the back burner, legally and politically, after that. There were people who did draft papers around ecocide, such as Professor Richard Falk, who drafted a convention on ecocide in the 1970s.[45] There were ideas of ecocide that have popped up in various aspects of international law, most significantly in the ENMOD Treaty, which deals with modification of the environment as a weapon of war.[46]

Then in the 1990s there was a decision from the International Court of Justice acknowledging that the environment was a legitimate subject for the protection of international law. This was significant, although specifics were not set out. I think what Polly did was to put ecocide back on the map, in terms of what we needed to do to bring its seriousness home. Finding the word 'ecocide' to describe what we were trying to do was a eureka moment for Polly – it is the word we need, and it belongs at the international level.

Many environmental laws have been put in place over the last few decades, including multilateral environmental agreements such as the 2015 Paris Agreement and the Montreal 2022 agreement.[47] However, one of the biggest issues we have with environmental protection is that many of these international regulations are nonbinding. Hence, they are not taken seriously. This is a fundamental point. We have a natural taboo around destroying people – it's deeply ingrained that killing people is wrong – but we don't have that same reaction to the destruction of Nature. Putting ecocide with the worst crimes that we currently do acknowledge will be momentous, as we will be saying it's just as bad, just as wrong and just as dangerous.

Do we now have more political will and determination to make this law?

I think there are certain key factors. First are the effects of climate change and the effects of environmental destruction. For example, currently in the UK, there's the pollution of the rivers and the granting of new oil licences. Globally, we are all far more aware about what's happening in the Amazon, of the rising sea levels and all of these different things. There's a visibility that hasn't been there before. There's also scientific acknowledgement that has now reached governmental level, such as the Intergovernmental Panel on Climate Change's reports.

But I think what has also been absolutely critical is grassroots mobilization, such as the school strikes, the Sunrise Movement[48] and Extinction Rebellion, also called XR.[49] If we look back in history, we see in the movements that have had an impact – whether that's the abolition of slavery, the suffragette movement or civil rights – there's always been civil disruption. This pushes things to a point and then comes legal change. That's what happened here in the UK. Efforts toward recognizing ecocide coincided with the XR launch – or, rather, the first rebellion that took place in April 2019. The founders of XR told us that they were going to open the rebellion with an ecocide focus action at Shell. It was a very significant time for us because that's when Polly passed away.

In 2019, we had a different organization name, and I remember sitting in the garden with Polly, who was quite weak by that point, and we knew that we needed to rebrand. We ended up launching our 'Stop Ecocide' rebrand during the rebellion, where there were all these placards. For Polly, who was on her deathbed, watching everything unfold on the internet and seeing it for the first time on the streets was very poignant. Polly had been working on this for years. She said, "It's going to happen now." It was an extraordinary moment.

I know we will talk about legacy, but in a strange way, Polly really was a martyr to the cause. When she passed away, suddenly people who had been sitting in their armchairs thinking about what Polly was doing, they got in touch, asking, "What can we do to help?" There were politicians, lawyers and campaigners in different countries. We started to realize that there was a real impetus for this and the dots started to join. It has become clear to me in the last couple of months that our organization is shifting from the start-up phase to a globally influential organization.

There are other key milestones that have made a real difference. Since 2015, we had been in discussion with the Pacific Ocean state of Vanuatu, which stepped things up in 2019, at the ICC's annual assembly, which is where all the member states meet. Vanuatu announced publicly, from the government's perspective, that all member states should consider the addition of ecocide to the Rome Statute. This was a big milestone that really triggered conversations at the political level, to the degree that we're now seeing the definition being used.

A couple of things sprung to mind while you were talking.
I remembered the Bhopal tragedy.[50] Would that have come under ecocide, if it had existed then?

Very probably yes, though I don't know the full details of the case. But if, at that time, it had been ascertained that the action needed hadn't been taken, then yes. However, if something is genuinely an unforeseeable accident, then it's very difficult to touch it. But my guess would be there were probably safety protocols that weren't followed.

That was certainly the case with Deepwater Horizon.[51] In the case of Fukushima, that could have been ecocide, from what I've read, as there were design recommendations that would have prevented the incident, but they were not followed, possibly for financial reasons.[52] But you can imagine that if ecocide law had been in place, those decisions would have been very carefully considered, and the incidents may have been avoided. The pollution in the Chevron case in Ecuador, for example, would almost certainly have been avoided.[53]

What kind of penalties can be expected? Would it be people, government officials or corporate personnel who would go to prison? What would happen?

I think the criminal law aspect is so vital and it's why it's important for there to be individual responsibility. The ICC can't prosecute companies, only actual people. I think this is very important, because ultimately, it is people who make decisions.

While it may be a board of people, it's still people. A board of directors will have a very different approach to its environmental obligations if they know that they could be in breach of law and may be at risk of committing ecocide. Such a law could give them a tap on the shoulder to let them know their freedom and reputation are at stake.

Most of this activity is located in the corporate world. I'm not suggesting there are no state-sponsored corporations, but on the whole, it's the corporate world that's in question, because if a C-suite executive is accused of a crime, it's not just the executive that's affected – the stock value of the company plummets, as we've seen with Enron.[54] There's a double level of deterrence, as it's personal and it's also about the corporation.

It's actually very important that the individual is being held responsible because that is where true deterrence happens. When it comes down to it, these big CEOs can still walk away with their bonuses, and they either go get another job or simply carry on with business as usual. This needs to be avoided.

When it comes down to it, we tend to see these potential perpetrators not as villains, as such, but as the logical product of a culture that has evolved over quite a long time.

But in terms of the actual level of policy and regulation at that top level, we should never approach this as a fight. We don't want to create opponents, because if you have a personal conversation with any of those C-suite executives, they will be completely on side with you – they will want the world to be protected. They want their kids to be okay. But the system they operate in prioritizes the bottom line and they are often constrained to do that, whether they like it or not.

Do you think this type of legislation will inspire a new type of political leader in mainstream parties?

Really interesting question. I hope so and I think it may have to. For example, the narrative coming from Indigenous cultures, and their worldview, is that if you damage Mother Earth, there are consequences – it's a matter of cause and effect. It is a fact, and we can see it happening.

It's not rocket science to realize that there are limits to nature's resources and we cannot keep drawing on them. This law creates a connection with reality that politics would have to deal with, and it would also equip the future with the safety rail that is going to be needed – especially if we're ever going to establish a harmonious relationship with our surroundings and actually make it through as a civilization.

In a sense, however ecocide manifests in the law, what is ultimately going to happen is a deep sense of taboo around the mass destruction of Nature, which is absolutely primary to survival and at the basis of a thriving civilization. I firmly believe introducing this law is possible, but I certainly don't believe the next few decades are going to be easy.

What do you think of ExxonMobil, which has privately sought to discredit climate change?

What I would say is had ecocide law been in place, I see no reason whatsoever why those executives would not have been prosecuted. However, the law doesn't work in retrospect. This is actually often the first question we get asked by the corporate sector – as you can imagine, they want to know if they will be prosecuted for something the company did years ago. When you think it through, for reasons to do with the rule of law, that's not possible.

While obviously Stop Ecocide International recognizes the desire for justice, it's also very important to understand that the ultimate goal of this law is not throwing people in jail – it's actually about protecting the planet. What we really want is changes in behaviour, and how you get changes in behaviour is by people having a compliance period, which is why what we're doing as an advocacy organization is fundamentally important.

It's going to take some time for the laws to come into place, with proposals being discussed that then go through the parliamentary procedures, and they may emerge in slightly different forms from what we anticipate. The important thing is that the general direction has already been established and there's a logical endpoint, which will ultimately be making it an international crime to severely destroy the environment.

Now, what that will do, and it's already happening, is to create a steer at the decision-making level among policymakers, but also at the decision-making level in industry. This has already been acknowledged by various UN bodies. For example, the UN Climate Change High Level Champions, which have spent some years encouraging voluntary action from businesses toward net zero, in 2022 finally acknowledged that voluntary action wasn't going to cut it, and that policy and regulation were required. They included a whole section on ecocide law in their report *The Pivot Point*, saying this initiative is a driver and an influencer of change, which is very important.[55]

I think it's interesting, for example, where we all know how that advocacy piece within the corporate world is hugely effective and is called lobbying; and is effective in terms of having the right conversations with the right people. Five years ago, no one was talking about ecocide law. Now I'm not saying that we've been the only people doing that, but we've been driving the conversation and that is what brings politicians on board. No politician wants to be the first person at a party – they haven't got the courage. They want to know the space they're entering into is safe, and that is about creating a conversation.

We have come to my last question. You've already touched on Polly's legacy. Is there anything you would like to add? And what kind of legacy would you like to leave?

Thinking about Polly's legacy, I would say that she was our figurehead, the catalyst of this movement, but more than anything, she was hugely inspiring. Polly had a great energy, which galvanized a whole new wave of action, where she created a huge legacy.

Somebody once said to me that organizations, particularly this transformative type of organization, have three stages. First there's the initiator, who's the torchbearer and figurehead; next comes a person who is like a mechanic, the doer; and then the third stage is the person that keeps it stable and growing. I am the second stage, a communicator and operator – communicating what we're doing to different audiences across the board with lots of different networks. For me, it is about nurturing and expanding the conversation.

My legacy is about the communication because this law is something that will affect everybody, in a very positive way. If I was going to be remembered in any particular way, it would be as the person who helped the world understand what this is about and why it's worth doing.

When it comes to that third stage of the organization, I fully anticipate not being present once everything is in place. I am not the sort of person that sits in an organization and makes it stable for 20 years – that's not me or my territory. Neither am I the sort of person that's going to retire overnight, by any means. My ideal is to work myself out of a job, and actually, to be honest, that's what the entire environmental world should be doing.

But right now, I honestly cannot imagine anywhere more exciting to be – it's just extraordinary watching what's happening. Ecocide law is so important because it's something that everyone can get behind and say, "We need this," and ask for it at local, national or international level. It speaks to that top level. It is about taking the responsibility up the chain to where it really needs to be because no matter what consumer decisions we make, if the government doesn't stop subsidizing the wrong things, if the industries don't take their production or supply chain responsibilities seriously, then no progress can be made.

JACOB DAHL

SENIOR PARTNER EMERITUS AT MCKINSEY & COMPANY

In October 2023, I spoke with Jacob Dahl. As well as being a Senior Partner Emeritus at McKinsey & Company, Jacob is a board member and investor who has worked as a management consultant for 26 years and lived in Denmark, elsewhere in Europe, Africa and Asia. He is the author of *In Search of Time: Understanding the Nature and Experience of Time for a Better Life*, an excellent book that looks at time through different perspectives.[56] In October 2023, I heard Jacob speak in London, which was fascinating – he delved into some of the ideas from his book. I knew then that I wanted to talk to him to further explore the concept of time in relation to the climate crisis, governance and political decision-making.

Climate scientists and research tells us that we're running out of time to address the climate challenges. Is there a way to beat the clock by changing our relationship with time? And are there opportunities to improve our societies if we accept a more relaxed attitude to time?

There are two very different answers to these questions. Answering the first question, I don't think we can beat the clock on the climate crisis, as we need to act as fast and as forcefully as we can. We don't have the time to waste to address this crisis – it is as simple as that. We cannot fool ourselves and think we can stop time to fix the problem. This is a serious issue that humanity is facing, and we need to address it urgently and with all our energy.

In answer to the second the question, I think that to improve society, and the world's future, we need to have a different view of time itself. In my book I talk about a few things, and one is how corporates view time. The world of business associates the idea of time with the labour market, which is based on the concept of selling time and is old-fashioned and an unhealthy idea. Essentially, it means that a lot of people are going to work to spend and sell their time on something. Even when employees have completed a task, they will keep inventing new stuff in order to fulfil the 40 hours that they are employed to work per week. I came across this so many times when I was a consultant, where people were inventing new things to be done, in part to not lose their jobs. People invent things to do because they are paid by the hour instead of being paid by impact. Therefore, one of my big ideas for a better society is that we need to turn our labour markets into impact-based markets instead of time-based markets.

Staying with large corporations for a moment, as they have a huge impact on the world we're living in, I also believe that the idea of running a corporation according to the 12-month calendar cycle is not productive. We have the majority of corporations, including the public sector, operating on a calendar wheel based on a year. This means they will have a strategy at the beginning of a year, with all kinds of other streams falling out of that yearly strategy – HR plans, communications, finance etc. – and it's all repeated the year after. The actual value of this is close to zero – it's always last year plus or minus 5%. There are thousands of big corporations that are using this method, and regulators are measuring corporations this way too. It is a whole system that is built on an unnecessary time wheel.

In contrast with this, let's look at when real change was needed. The global COVID-19 pandemic is a good example: we saw a tenfold increase in productivity because real change was needed. It was not driven by an artificial time frame; it was time that actually drove the change that was needed.

So, I would argue that we can actually have a much better society and better corporate wealth if we leave this corporate calendar of time and instead govern ourselves in large corporations. If we really look at the individual – because a big part of this is how we as individuals are dealing with time – in my view, we have been quite unhealthy in dealing with time. We become unnecessarily stressed for time, or we have huge anticipation for the future, but we are typically disappointed because our expectations are not met. Having high hopes for what the future will give you is almost certain to disappoint you at some stage.

I believe we can learn a lot from Asian and Indigenous cultures on this. We need to readjust our anticipation of the future and learn to live in the present. This will create better health and mental wellbeing for our youth and most adults. Just acquiring more time itself is not valuable. We see this when people retire, where suddenly they have all the time in the world yet become miserable. That's because even though they now have the time they hoped for, thinking the free time would create a whole new inspiring life for them, it doesn't happen. Time itself doesn't have value. It is your interest, your impact, your social connections that give time value.

Time has no meaning as a value and neither is it a happiness generator – it is what you do with your time that matters.

How do we bring the voice of future generations to the negotiating table regarding the climate crisis decision-making, and are there any examples of this happening?

This is a super-interesting topic and there are two key examples happening. One is in Wales, in the UK, and the other in Japan, where they have specific roles that sit below the ministerial level, called commissioners. In Japan, these commissioners have the responsibility of taking care of the Japanese generation of 2060, which means those born in 2060. When the commissioner sits in policy meetings, they will put the voice of that generation into the decision being made, whether it is about infrastructure, renewables, schooling, healthcare – any kind of decision. The commissioner is the voice of the future generation, which is so important. There is something similar happening in Wales, and we are also discussing it here in Denmark with politicians, so we will hopefully gain a minister, or at least some politician, who will have responsibility to bring the voice of the future into the room.

In fact, we have adopted from some Indigenous cultures. For example, in Native American cultures, there are several tribes that have this idea, known as the 'Seventh Generation Principle,' where they are looking even further ahead. So, when they make a decision, they need to hold it up to the question, "Will this make sense in seven generations?" If it won't, it is not considered.

However, I am not advocating that we should be naive and say it's all about the future, because of course we need to take care of people today, but just to have perhaps one or two voices advocating for the future would be helpful. For example, if we look at the climate crisis today, could we have avoided it? Well, let's imagine that in 1960 or 1970, when making decisions about oil and gas, we raised a finger to say, "Let's think about 2023 – how would the world look from a carbon dioxide perspective?" Let's think about that and where we would be now if we had embraced that debate back in that period. I'm not saying we would have changed the direction of the world, but it's an interesting thought. I believe we have lost our connection to our future, and we have lost our responsibility to future generations.

Could generational thinking create a shift in political thinking? A lot of it is based on short-term strategies.

I don't think there's an easy solution or answer. One of the elements would be what we just talked about, where the voices of the future are included in the policy decisions made today. But then you could argue that there could be other experiments. For example, there could be an experiment around longer election cycles, as most election cycles last four years. Of course, there are downsides because you could be stuck with ineffective politicians for longer periods. But why is it four years? Why not ten years? Or maybe there's an opt-out after four years.

We could experiment to see what works and start having a real dialogue about what would happen if we got more timeless. However, while the premise here is that we should be more timeless, we shouldn't discount the future, as the future is as important as the present.

I think we need discussions to update our democratic systems, where we create improved machines. If we look at Native Americans, whose governance pre-dates parliamentary systems, it's interesting because they allocate power locally or to smaller decision makers who are familiar with the needs of the community and at the same time connected to the future, because they know their grandchildren, their future grandchildren and the grandchildren of other people will be affected. This devolved structure gives more commitment than when you scale the whole thing up to a national level. So perhaps a part of the answer is we should allocate more decision-making locally, because it tends to be more future-oriented, as local people care for their community and take care of each other. This can be coupled with Seventh Generation Principle.

Or we could have more women in power?

Exactly right! Since 2007, McKinsey has been extensively analysing women in the workplace and has shown that having women in power, or at least a balanced leadership team, both politically and in cooperation, just gets better results.[57]

What would you like your legacy to be with respect to this climate change conversation?

Unfortunately, in the context of the climate crisis, I think we're so far down the track – this conversation would have been relevant 50 years ago. We should have had this discussion in 1973, and it would have made a difference. I don't believe that thinking about time differently will help the climate crisis. Instead, I hope that we will start to take this crisis seriously and that I can contribute to us avoiding a future crisis, because I'm sure there will be one.

I would like to help individuals think in a more nuanced way about how they spend their time. Today we are all extremely stressed about time, including our youth, and I don't think that social media is helping. If we are able to manage our time, it will improve our mental world. I also want to unlock productivity in the corporate world by avoiding some of those time traps that the corporate worlds falls into. I believe this will make a better, more fulfilled world.

NISREEN ELSAIM

SUDANESE ACTIVIST

Nisreen Elsaim is an activist from Sudan, a country plagued by the adverse effects of climate change and now a civil war. We spoke in mid-June 2023. Nisreen is based in Sudan, where she has been at the forefront of raising awareness about climate issues since 2012. In 2019, she was named as one of 30 UN youth special envoys, and in 2020 she was appointed chair of the UN Secretary-General's Youth Advisory Group on Climate Change until 2022. She is regarded as one of the leading figures on climate and security issues in the world, and in 2020, the Africa Youth Awards named her one of the top 100 most influential young people globally.

A member of Youth Environment Sudan, Nisreen was appointed cochair of Sudanese Youth for Climate Change and leads the African Youth Conference. If that wasn't enough, she is an active member of the Pan African Climate

Justice Alliance, a consortium of more than 1,000 organizations from 48 African countries that work together to address climate issues and environmental challenges facing humanity and the planet.

Sudan is ranked as one of the most vulnerable countries to climate change and is experiencing several harms, including increased frequency of droughts; high variability of rainfall, which jeopardizes agriculture and grazing livelihoods; health problems related to pollution; disease outbreaks; overexploitation of land and water; and food insecurity.

Nisreen, how frustrated are you with how slow global governments have been to tackle climate change?

This is a complex question to answer, but my first response is that while I am very disappointed, I am not surprised. Some people are disappointed and surprised. But for me, it's no surprise at all. Changing our current economic systems to become more sustainable and aligned with climate change takes a lot of nerve. It also takes huge political will, not only from the governments but specifically from the private sector, the oil and gas companies. This 'will' doesn't exist right now. There is no unity around the need for urgent action to move from fossil fuels to a more sustainable way of producing energy.

I am also frustrated that there's little effort to mitigate the climate problems, particularly regarding emissions. But what makes me really frustrated is that there's not even the drive for adapting, which is really sad. Let me explain: if you're burning someone's house down as a result of your emissions, the very least you can do is help them rebuild their house from better, more sustainable materials. Not having the 'will' to do the very least in making change really frustrates me, more than the actual challenge of climate change.

Would you call it climate change? Or a climate emergency?

I call it climate change because climate emergency is a situation and not the problem itself. The problem is definitely about the climate changing, while climate emergency is the situation created because of climate change.

I guess being a young Sudanese woman must have challenges, especially as a young activist?

Well, I'm from Sudan, and as you know, Sudan is a country that has a long history of different problems. These are nowhere near ending soon, especially now with the current situation of the war.

Growing up in Sudan, I was regarded as someone who did not have the right priorities, especially as a lot of people thought and still think that climate change doesn't matter, particularly in a country with a lot of other problems. I spent a decade trying to explain that most of the problems we are facing in our country are because of climate change.

My other challenge was that when you are a teenager, you are not taken seriously, nor are you old enough, but then you are also not young enough. You are not treated as a kid or as an adult. While I'm not a teenager anymore, it is still tough to be heard and seen as an adult.

Professionally I am at a stage where when I apply for senior-level management jobs, I am treated as not having enough experience, and then when I apply for junior roles, I am told I am too old or experienced. This is a huge challenge and is one that I and others of my age are facing right now.

Another challenge is about the lack of support. From my experience, the people who have support are already privileged. They have access to the media, campaigns and a lot of resources. Those of us who don't have this support or privileges or access don't have the opportunities to participate as speakers, or be on panel discussions, except when it's for diversity. We are invited to speak or be part of a photo line-up, because we are a tick-box exercise. Yet, we will never get the resources that we need to keep us going forward in our climate activism work. We need to acknowledge that this is a big challenge.

I also want to mention another challenge, which is a new one for me, and that's being a mum. My baby is 11 months old, and being a mother in our field is not easy. When I am invited to participate in events, it is costly, as I need to get a babysitter, and if it involves international travel, I need to take my baby with me, but then I face problems in terms of visas. While I can get a visa support letter for myself, I might not get one for my son.

There's a lot of motherhood-related problems. What I have discovered over the last few months is that while many organizations and multilateral bodies claim that they want to support women and that they are with women workers, it's actually not the case. They have created a system that doesn't allow mothers and women to interact effectively.

There are so many things that I want to follow up on from what you have just said. The first is, do you think the climate change movement is a white, middle-class movement? I ask because you said a lot of the engagement seems like tokenism, where they line up diversity and women of colour.

In a word, yes! But there is a deeper answer to this question. Let me explain: for a long time, climate change, plastic pollution, conserving oceans and water, and any other kind of environmental problem was always a white, middle-class problem. That's because the rest of the world did not have the time, the energy or the education – and it is a matter of education to actually think about these problems.

Things are changing, and they are changing because of the impact of climate change, where people in the developing world are experiencing things on a greater scale. Yet still people from the Global South are not able to control the conversation.

All of the multilateral processes, all of the UN processes, are always trying to create this balance by having cochairs, one from the Global South and one from the Global North, but the reality is the Global South chairperson has no real power. Plus, when you explore what the Global North cochair gained, you will see that they gained more from the process than their Global South cochair.

It's always easy to do partnerships with the Global North, as it's an easy transition, where they can go from a job to a better job, with a better offer. It's definitely not the same in terms of the Global South. Many of the Global North activists do recognize this and try to bridge the gap, but at times their efforts can feel patronizing.

Have you found any solutions to these problems?

There is a solution, of course, and it is about speaking out louder and louder! Making your points boldly and clearly. And, while you might be hated for saying things out loud and boldly, there could be someone who benefits from you standing up.

I am also trying to address the balance of power within organizations. These environmental issues have always existed, since well before the climate change movement started, but the Global South is poor and, crucially, the Global South doesn't control the media. We know that every big news and media company – Fox News, the BBC, CNN, France 24 – is in the US, Europe or the UK. And it's not helping our case.

Has Al Jazeera helped at all?

Well, it is in the Global South. But really how much influence do they have? Compare them to the other media organizations.

What motivated you to get involved with the fight against climate change?

The first time I ever heard about climate change, I was a freshman at university in Khartoum and we had a major incident. The government's loyalist students had a violent interaction with the other students on the campus – they threw two students from a balcony on the fourth floor. One survived with severe injuries and one passed away. I was studying physics as an undergraduate and the university had to close for three months.

I was so science-oriented at that time and had the belief that I could solve every global problem that way, but when this incident occurred at the university, it made me realize that we could have thousands of scientists around the world, but they're not the ones that make the decisions. And if we were actually listening to scientists, we would not be living in this world in its current state.

I began to seek to understand how science can influence politics, policies and decisions, and I discovered science diplomacy and climate change. Climate change was closer to science, and that got my attention. I started reading more and more about climate change, and because the university was closed, and I was only a freshman, I volunteered in one of the local organizations focused on climate change and the environment. I learned a lot there.

You're a remarkable young woman, and you are still young. You have had the drive from your university years to make a difference. So, who inspires you?

Survivors inspire me. I've been through many situations in my life, being Sudanese, and the last situation was only a month ago, in Sudan, when the conflict started. I didn't know if I would make it to the next day or not. I didn't know whether I would lose my child, or whether we all might be gone. Sadly, there have been entire families who have been wiped out because of the military clashes. But I have been lucky, and my situation is actually better than others. This made me realize that if others can survive the worst things and get through them, then so can I.

This is why survivors inspire me a lot, not only the survivors of climate change, but also the women who take the lead in their communities, along with the people who recover after a huge injury or serious mental health problem or other challenge.

How would you encourage others to get involved with this fight against climate change?

First, I don't believe that we should encourage everyone to get involved. That's because climate change is not easy advocacy work to do. There's a lot of frustration, many sleepless nights and a lot of responsibility.

My message is more to the people who are already encouraged but don't know where to start. My advice to them is that whatever you do is important. If you decide to switch off the lights to reduce energy use or if you are planting trees, or if you decide to use public transportation instead of your car. Or if you decide to get involved in a local organization or movement to combat climate change or push your government to do more – everything you do counts.

And for those who don't have the desire to do work on climate change, I say, it's unfortunate, as the fight against climate change is just like the global COVID pandemic – no one is safe until everyone is saved. So, even if you don't want to take action, it will get you, unfortunately, and this is the reality that everyone needs to be focused on.

You've mentioned the conflict going on in your country right now. Would you like to say anything further about how it's affecting climate change?

Sudan has a big geopolitical role to play. It was the only safe, stable spot in this very disturbed region. Central Africa is in a mess, South Sudan is in a mess, Ethiopia was in a mess, Eritrea is so isolated, Chad and Libya were in a mess. So, Sudan has an important role to play. It was the market and path to the Red Sea, the Gulf and the rest of the world. It was the basket where most of the countries accessed their products, including agricultural products.

Unfortunately, no one looks at this whole situation. Sudan was fine when they needed their raw materials and minerals such as iron ore, marble and mica, etc. But they don't care how Sudanese people are living, and Sudan is very vulnerable to climate change.

Currently, all the international and national government efforts to combat climate change in Sudan are no longer in force because of the conflict. People can't plant anything, so the harvest season will be disastrous. We also experience floods on average every two years, and there was no flood last year, so it might happen this year, but there are no precautions for this situation.

I'm really sorry for everything. The world is so upside-down now.

Yes, very much.

> My last question is about legacy, which is the focus of this book. You are still young, but what legacy do you want to create? And what is next for you?

The biggest legacy I really wish to create is to bridge the gap between the youth movement and heads of state and high-ranking governments officials at the UN. Because currently young people are pushing for things that are needed but they don't have the tools to implement them.

Governments think that the young people don't have ideas or are a bunch of hippies or that as young people they just want to scream, which is not true. Young people have a lot of ideas that can help governments to do positive things.

And what's next for me? I really don't know. I get asked this question a lot when I am travelling, from "Where are you based?" or "Are you going back to Khartoum?" I am like, "Guys, don't ask too many questions, because I don't know." So, I really don't know what's next for me. All I know is that I will do my best to at least make the world a better place for my son and the next generations.

> Just as you're talking, it occurs to me - and this really is my final question - do you think Greta Thunberg has raised awareness? Has the Greta effect been a positive?

My problem with the Greta effect is this: why did it have to be a young Swedish woman who is, again, white and is very much from a privileged upbringing, compared to a lot of people I know? I want to stress that I don't want to undermine the effort that Greta has made, as she has done some amazing work, and a lot of people have got engaged from her work. But I feel the problem has been the publicity created by the people around her. It looks like a show, and right now, I don't believe Greta is a climate activist. She is more of a Hollywood star, and this kind of stardom is erasing the soul of the climate action movement.

Greta's publicity and image have blurred the vision of other young people, as many now think they need to be famous, or need to have hundreds of followers on social media, which is not true. There is now this inaccurate perception that it is about quantity over quality, where the more followers you have, the stronger your climate work will be. You're a climate change activist, not an artist – there's no money coming from people watching your actions. Yet, we do need everyone to know that there is a climate change challenge, and it is very hard to engage people.

LIEUTENANT COLONEL (RETD) LANGLEY SHARP MBE

FORMER HEAD OF THE BRITISH ARMY'S CENTRE FOR ARMY LEADERSHIP

Lieutenant Colonel (Retd) Langley Sharp is a former head of the British Army's Centre for Army Leadership and served in the British Army for 23 years. We spoke in August 2023. He began as an officer in the Parachute Regiment, having graduated from the Royal Military Academy Sandhurst, and was deployed to Afghanistan, Iraq, Macedonia and Northern Ireland. During his military career, Langley led a counterinsurgency task force operation, commanded a Parachute Regiment battalion and delivered the London 2012 Olympics venue security training programme for the Ministry of Defence – for which he was awarded an MBE. As head of the Centre for Army Leadership, he was responsible for championing leadership excellence across the British Army.

Langley is the author of the bestselling book *The Habit of Excellence*, a unique insight into the British Army's leadership that explains what makes it unique, what makes it so effective and what civilians can take from it to become better leaders themselves.[58]

He is founder and director of the consultancy firm Frontier Leadership and is dedicated to sharing his experiences to help individuals, teams and organizations perform at their best. Langley is a passionate believer in the power of leadership as a force multiplier for social good.

Do you think we need stronger political leadership when it comes to fighting the war on climate? If so, what kind of political leaders do we need?

The issue we have is that our current political system, in terms of trying to deal with the existential crisis that is climate change, is culturally flawed. It is consistently framed through a narrative of 'them and us,' or the 'in-group and the out-group.' It is, as Francis Fukuyama would say, 'identity politics,' where people identify themselves as either Conservatives, Labour or Liberal Democrats in the UK, for example, or Republicans or Democrats in the US.[59] The debate, therefore, is often one of offensive and defensive in regard to the narrative and language, and subsequently the thinking and behaviours, and this in turn becomes culturally ingrained. It makes it very difficult to make tangible gains in the long term if the narrative is all about doggedly protecting one's own position.

Climate change is an issue that requires true collaboration. Strong political leadership requires humble leaders who are able to effectively collaborate, as no one party, nor indeed nation, can solve this problem. The fact is, however, that every party will maintain their own views and perspectives on the issue, and competitiveness will always be a reality of political life, so the challenge is, how do we break this down? How do we move beyond? How do we have strong political leadership that drives true collaboration, that understands that this is one of the fundamental issues of our time? I believe that we need a different approach – we need to get over our political differences, to get beyond the narrative and the short-term thinking, in order to really drive the solutions.

This means we need to focus on the collective purpose – the 'why' – identifying and acknowledging the challenge of alignment on the 'how.' Even within a political party there is unlikely to be true alignment, let alone between parties. A collaborative approach is absolutely critical – across all public and private stakeholders, noting that this is not just the responsibility of the political elite – together with the courage and the conviction needed to drive that collaboration.

It requires leaders with the ability to understand and listen, and then be able to communicate with clear intent about what we need to do. Communication is critical, accepting that narratives will change over time, because people's perceptions of climate change will shift as new evidence and research emerge. Narrative fatigue is a reality. The ability to communicate effectively to multiple audiences is vital. This is, of course, easy to say but difficult to do.

Strong political leaders also need to be strategically focused, and by that I mean engaged in long-term thinking and planning, which invokes the classic dilemma of the urgent versus the important. Too often, because of the nature of our political system, the debate and subsequent policies are framed in terms of the urgent rather than the important. The important is what we know is necessary for the long term, but, politically, thinking is too often focused on short-term objectives. Political leaders need to have the courage to say, "No, this is necessary for our future – it is absolutely critical."

In reality, of course, it requires a balance of judgment. Long-term strategic thinkers need to be able to balance both the urgent and the important, because the reality is that climate change doesn't sit in isolation from what people perceive to be today's priorities. We need to recognize that not everything can be driven solely by the most important long-term issues, because inevitably what often matters most to people is that which impacts their lives in the here and now – the cost of living, health, education and so on. Take, for example, the ULEZ[60] issue that the current mayor of London is implementing, and that recently seized the news headlines and influenced local elections in London. The ULEZ is a good example of an issue that has been brought in for the health of our people and the good of our planet, to help drive positive behaviours, putting climate change at the heart of policy, and yet it has become an issue politicized, by both politicians and voters, to support understandable short-term interests.

There will have to be compromises on all sides of the climate debate. But the ability to think and have the courage to stay around for the long term is going to be really important, and that's too often missing at the moment. I often refer to Jim Collins, who talks about the 'level five leader' in his book *Good to Great*,[61] where he advocates that the most successful leaders across industry lead with humility matched with an indomitable will to win – "a paradoxical mixture of personal humility and professional will."[62] That's so important. People that absolutely have the determination to succeed need humility to do everything that we've been talking about in terms of collaboration, listening, empathetic understanding and so on. Blending a conviction to persevere, while not letting ego get in the way. That 'level five leadership' that Collins refers to is a good framework for the sort of character of leader we need to drive this forward.

I want to delve a little deeper into what you've just said about the importance of clear communications and communicating with intent and purpose. How important, then, is truth within communications? Does it play a part or are leaders just delivering a message, whether it's right or wrong?

It's critical and is yet another significant issue of our time – people's perception of truth and trust. Trust is linked to truth, and we can get into a philosophical debate about what is truth, as one person's truth might not be someone else's. There's so much out there at the moment, it is hard to distinguish what to trust and that's one of the problems, especially because of social media and now the emergence of AI. This is one of the key issues that politicians are going to have to grapple with – how do you convince people that what is being communicated is the truth?

How does the armed forces do it? Is it true because it's an order, or do they trust the order because they trust the leader?

It boils down to the trust in one another within the organization, which is institutional trust. At its core, it is an organization with a set of clear values, and if culturally we're driven to live by those values, then that instils a foundation of trust, acknowledging that we are also human and might not always adhere to those values every day. Reinforcing this, we've got a common doctrine, common training, common language, traditions, heritage, everything that builds in a sense of collective and shared identity. This all inevitably creates trust in one another.

Clearly, trust is hard won and easily lost; it's very easy to lose that trust when the decisions made turn out not to be deemed the right ones. We've got to be very careful of that and I guess there's an element where there's trust in our politicians that they are making the decisions that are right at the time, that represent the best interests of our nation. Ultimately in the armed forces, we serve our politicians, and our politicians serve our society. We've got to have faith in that political system, that the decisions being made are the right ones at the right time with the information that is available. The problem might come in hindsight when it is realized that some decisions have been flawed. That erodes trust. You can see trust lost in America and the West because of some of the grand-strategic[63] and military-strategic decisions that have been made over the past 20 years. But at the time, we had to have faith in our political masters and in the decisions that were made.

That's why values and character are so fundamentally important to any organization. If people are seen to undermine them, and are not held to account, then trust is eroded. It goes back to one of the fundamental issues we face as a society – the ability for people to trust not just our political systems, but business, government departments and public bodies. If people don't have trust in such institutions, then we really are screwed when it comes to matters such as climate change.

If we don't have trust, then who do we believe? Who do we follow? There's a great article that a friend of mine in the US, Stephen Scott, wrote, in which he said the reason that humans have not just survived but been able to advance so significantly, beyond other species, and particularly in recent times, is because of a 'trust infrastructure,'[64] meaning we developed trust beyond the family, tribe or clan, and institutionalized trust to enable collaboration at scale.

Scott also echoes concerns about the erosion of this institutionalized trust, where we lose faith in our politicians, multinational corporations or state institutions. If that happens for all the reasons we've been talking about, particularly with advancing technologies etc. – and God forbid it should get worse with the negative aspects of emerging technology – then our ability to fight existential issues like climate change will be significantly undermined. We follow people because we trust them – it's as simple as that. If trust isn't there, then how we can effect the change we need?

Yes, we don't even trust the science right now. Forget about political leaders!

I think it's because climate change doesn't affect most people's lives every single day. When the cost of living means you can't afford *X* that you're used to, for example, that becomes a priority. If you can't get admission to a hospital when you've got an ill grandmother or sick child, then that becomes your most pressing need. But if there's a wildfire in a faraway country and the reality is that it just doesn't impact you directly, irrespective of how scary the statistics or science might be, it is not a tangible problem, so doesn't register as a priority. Until people can see the immediacy of the issue and feel it personally, it will be challenging to drive the behavioural change we need in the timeframe we need it.

Take the global pandemic as an example. We came together through COVID because people felt it every day; it was an immediate impact on their lives. While there were and still are doubters and critics around that whole crisis, it is still a good example of how, when things became urgent and impacted everyone, it drove collaboration. People conformed within days and changed their behaviour because there was a war on COVID. We need that for climate change, but we're not going to get that because it doesn't impact people in the same way, as tragic as that is. So, you can understand why people doubt or are not willing to take immediate action, even though the science is irrefutable.

As you were talking, I was thinking that all our political leaders should go through military training, where they'll be trained about values.

I think we give our politicians a hard time. The reality is that we often see the worst of our politics because that's what makes the news. I believe the media plays a role in shaping this often unhelpful dialogue. Sometimes, when I listen to the radio in the morning, I get infuriated with the media narrative when they are interviewing a politician, because all they want is a sound bite, which inevitably puts the politician on the defensive.

I know that there are some political leaders who don't necessarily have the values we would all proclaim to aspire to, but I do think there are many values-based politicians who are genuinely trying to make a difference. There are lots of cultural flaws within our political system, which doesn't necessarily generate good behaviours.

I was chatting with a friend of mine who is a Labour MP and whom I trust implicitly, and he said, "You know, the reality is that what we see on the news is often the worst of it, because it's newsworthy. Behind the scenes there are actually a lot of good things happening, but they don't meet the news agenda. There's a lot of collaboration, laws and policies that are getting pushed through every single day, built on cross-party consensus." Hence, I've got a bit more faith in our politicians than others may have, but I don't disagree that there is a lot more that needs to be done.

What happens when, for example, you have the king, who is very pro-planet and driven about his sustainability initiatives, and then you have the leader of the day, who is saying we are not going to honour all the green initiatives. How does a military person balance that?

In simple terms, I think we've got to have faith in the system that we live in, a democratic society. I believe in the principle that the public has voted for a political leader, regardless of whether it is the current prime minister who was voted in, or whether the political leader is following the mandate that they said they would commit to. It's not just one person driving their own agenda, necessarily, as there are checks and balances, and increasingly so. I have faith that those individuals collectively are making the best decisions they can with the information they have at hand at the time, given what they believe is the right thing to do, amid all the competing demands they face.

The system is not perfect and when decisions are made at the very senior levels, that then filter down to the military to deliver, we ultimately behave within the context in which we find ourselves. We try to behave in a moral and ethical way, do our part and deliver as best we can. I think that's the most we can do.

I wanted to ask you about intelligent disobedience. What does it mean? Do you think it has a role in this fight against climate change?

The idea is that people, for the right reasons, intelligently disobey an order, directive or law. It is referenced in the Army's Followership Doctrine and is also mentioned in my book, *The Habit of Excellence*. Ira Chaleff is one of the world's leading authorities on followership and also wrote the book *Intelligent Disobedience*.[65] His opening story is about a guide dog refusing to follow their blind owner's direction to lead them across the road because the dog is intent on protecting them. My understanding is that intelligent disobedience has its origins in the work of service animals.

It is the ability, often the need, and the courage to disobey a directive, if you deem it to be unlawful or unethical. Every soldier has this right. If an order is deemed immoral or illegal, then they have not just a right but a duty to disobey it. But 'intelligent' is the key word here and again, from a military perspective, this is not disobedience. There is far more empowerment than people think there is in the army – a lot more devolved decision-making. We don't command through blind obedience to orders. It doesn't work like that, with people shouting at each other. That's too often the misperception.

We have in the army what we call 'mission command,' which is intent-based execution. This is where the commander, the person in the position of authority, who is ultimately held to account, is responsible for giving their intent. They state the 'what' – what needs to be achieved – and the 'why' – the purpose. This empowers their people to deliver the 'how.'

This approach empowers your people, on the battlefield or at the point of delivery, such that in the moment, amid the chaos and complexity of the situation, they are able to make the most appropriate decision within the intent. It may be that the senior person is too far removed to decide themselves or that the individual at the forward edge has more information than the leader does because the situation has changed. As such, they may choose to intelligently disobey a direct order but do so with an understanding of the intent and wider mission.

Do you think the Just Stop Oil protesters are implementing the principles of intelligent disobedience?

I can see how they might argue they are intelligently disobeying but I suspect the majority might not agree with the intelligent aspect of their actions. Personally, I think they're in the realm of just disobedience and disruption. Though they may have the right intent, raising awareness and demanding action, I am not convinced this is the right way to go about it. There is a risk that they will alienate the majority rather than building a meaningful movement that takes the majority with them. I think many people perceive their protests as generating a negative impact, which outweighs the positive impact they're trying to have. I'm not convinced by this type of activist approach.

How do we get more leaders to think about the planet? Is it about instilling more courage and conviction as values?

It's very easy to focus on political leaders, who obviously have a pivotal role to play. However, the reality is that there's a finite amount they can actually do. What our politicians are able to do is to implement policies and adapt the law, in time influencing changes in behaviours and, in turn, habits and cultures.

If you're trying to drive cultural change, one approach is to implement what Richard Scott, Professor Emeritus in the Department of Sociology at Stanford University, describes as the regulative, normative and cultural cognitive.[66] The regulative involves influencing the rules, which drives behaviour, which in turn evolves the norms – the accepted way of doing things. The cultural cognitive is the deepest sense of this, an almost intuitive acceptance of behaviour, embedded in our values.

While a politician can drive change through policies, it is in business where a lot of the required changes can and must happen. And it is education that sits at the core of this change. It is through education and awareness that climate change is now so high on the agenda, and many aspects of society are moving in the right direction to tackle its effects. We are better educated, better informed. But of course, more is required.

There's a lot of evidence to suggest that climate change matters to the younger generations, who have been educated about it as part of their everyday school narrative. But we need to see this increased awareness infused across society, where everyone is exposed to the implications of climate change. Education is the fundamental driver for change.

Plus, we need the courage to do what we know is right. As Winston Churchill said, "Courage is rightly esteemed the first of human qualities." It is the primary value, or you can argue virtue, because if you've got courage in your convictions, which encourages you to do what you know is right, then that's moral courage. That's what we're talking about here – the moral courage to do the right thing, regardless of the opposition.

This reality goes back to the urgent versus the important. Change invokes resistance because people don't like it. Change requires greater collective courage, founded on an enhanced understanding of what is the right thing to do. It requires looking beyond the short term, whether it be short-term politics or short-term financial gains in business. We've got to have the courage to look at this from a long-term perspective but do so knowing we have to act *now*. You might say that climate change is one of those issues that fuses the urgent with the long-term important.

Education does play a critical role in countering incorrect assumptions.

It's critical. The more aware people are, the more they can empathize, because you can understand another person's perspective. It gets us out of the 'them and us' mindset – a tribal mindset. If you're educated, and of course I don't just mean in the formal sense but more broadly, you can see other people's points of view. Only then can you start to genuinely collaborate and move forward. Education opens eyes and opportunities.

Our conversation is very timely. On 18 August, *The Guardian* newspaper published an article with the subtitle "Defence committee report says British military needs urgently to adapt over coming decades to be effective."[67] Do you think the climate crisis will have an impact on how the armed forces train and prepare for war? If so, how?

That's a big question and there are certainly people more informed than me to answer it, but yes, I think the climate crisis will significantly change the way we train and prepare – there's no doubt about it – from where we train to how we train to the tactics we employ and the equipment we use.

Defence, and how it does its business, is driven by threats, because its whole *raison d'etre* is to defend our nation and national interests. Those threats are changing and morphing now as climate change has its impact.

The spectrum of roles and responsibilities is likely to increase, as we have seen in recent times, from traditional warfighting to humanitarian assistance, disaster relief, migration control, security assistance, partner training and support in combating wildlife trafficking. By way of example, there appears to be an increased reliance on the military to aid in the event of natural disasters, whether in the UK or abroad. And our military allies are experiencing the same pressures. You can see this now with the Canadian military fighting wildfires, the same in Europe, or indeed UK service personnel responding to flooding in the UK. More recently, of course, the navy has been supporting the response to the so-called 'small boats crisis,' which is a result, in part, of climate change driving migration.

The spectrum of responsibilities of the military is not going to reduce, and if anything, I believe it will only increase. The article from *The Guardian* talked about where we train, which will be driven by the threats our nation faces. There will almost certainly be a need for a greater spectrum of capabilities to operate in different environments, whether it's increasingly very hot environments or extreme cold.

There's going to be an impact on the way we prepare in terms of our industrial base, and the kit and equipment we use. By way of example, the Ministry of Defence is currently responsible for 50% of all government emissions. Approximately two thirds of that are from aviation fuel. Therefore, there's going to have to be a very different approach to how we plan, fund and procure our equipment, particularly our big equipment such as tanks, aircraft and warships. Crucially, not only will these major platforms need to be sustainable from an environmental perspective, but also affordable and relevant for the long term.

There are a lot of political incentives behind supporting the UK industrial base. Increasingly, equipment will need to be able to be retrofitted for emerging technologies, as it might have used fossil fuels five years ago, now electric and hydrocarbon, and in 30 years' time something we've not even considered yet. Sometimes that's the problem: the pace of emerging technological solutions outstrips our ability to procure – not least because, ultimately, the Ministry of Defence, like every other government department, has a finite budget that needs to be balanced. It goes back to what we were saying right at the start of this conversation, that in all of this, there's a balance of judgments to be made.

The other thing that will need to evolve, as it does in every aspect of life, is the mindset and culture of our people, in terms of being climate aware in decision-making at all levels. Not just a senior decision maker authorizing what warship we are going to invest in, but the way we conduct our military business every single day, at the operational and tactical level.

It goes back to education, where everyone is part of the solution, where there's an onus to change, at every level, underpinned by a sense of responsibility to do the right thing – from the simple things, like how to reduce waste or use less energy. If we're going to make a difference, it's the cumulative gains, not just the big-ticket items, that will matter. It will also require persistent communication – two-way communication – with our people to drive that mindset of change, to ensure the necessary behaviours become culturally intuitive.

Actually, we are seeing this within the military now, and not just in a top-down direction. People are talking about it, driven both from the younger generations, who are demanding these conversations, as well as from the top. Real change needs this top-down and bottom-up momentum. There are conversations continually happening, including a Defence Green Network that has thousands of volunteers sharing ideas and collaborating, both informally and formally.

The military owns about 1.4% of UK land and is the biggest owner of Sites of Special Scientific Interest. A lot can be done with that in terms of sequestration and driving good examples of stewardship for our country.

Does the climate crisis pose a danger to the existence of the armed forces?

Definitely not to their existence. There will always be threats, and our armed forces will always adapt and morph to meet the requirement. There is plenty of evidence to show how climate change is creating and exacerbating conflict. A good example is in Africa, where climate change has made large areas of previously habitable land unsustainable, forcing migration to urban concentrations, which in turn fuels all sorts of problems from organized crime to extremist groups and migration flow, many of which are interrelated and generate broader instability elsewhere. We only have to look across the Sahel and the recent coup in Niger. There is very troubled territory across that whole continental belt, which is exposed to, again, extremist organizations and destabilization effects.

Another example is the Arctic. I was fortunate to spend a year in Canada, whose defence forces have been concerned about this issue for some time. Evidently the melting ice is impacting large parts of Canada's land mass and exposing hitherto inaccessible trading routes. Russia has long identified this and significantly enhanced their Arctic capability. China too is very interested, and given their geography, it obviously makes economic sense for them to invest in their ability to operate through such environments. New trading routes in the High North will undoubtedly create new types of competition for global trade. Where there is significant competition, conflict, or certainly preparation for it, often follows.

Well, this leads me to the last question: what would you like your legacy to be?

I came across two quotes recently that really resonated with me, and they both went something like this, with the first from Will.i.am, a remarkable man and a true leader. He urged us to "contribute in some way that brings progress to yourself and others." I thought that was a really simple and humble way of approaching life. In whatever way is right for you, have a positive impact.

The second is from Dr Andrew Szydlo, a brilliant British chemist who finished an enthralling lecture to a captivated audience by saying, "And remember, all that really matters in life is that you be kind to people and try your best."

If I can live by either of those mantras, ideally both, I'll have left a legacy.

CHAPTER 5

MEDIA

Headlines make the world go round, and how they have changed in the past 20 years! I remember in the mid-1990s, while working for small UK non-profit as a media officer, that trying to interest the British media, specifically the environmental journalists, in sustainability and climate news stories was near to impossible. It wasn't that they didn't care, because they did – they knew a crisis was looming – but as they used to tell me, their editors did not see it as news. It wasn't news affecting their readers. So, stories about water shortages, famines and intense heat were buried in the inside pages of the newspapers – and online news didn't exist then. Fast-forward to now, and a day doesn't go by when either a domestic or an international climate story doesn't hit our headlines, where the science and meteorologists have become the news.

There are discussions of climate fatigue, and that people are switching off from these news stories, that the big dark headlines are making us apathetic – what's the point of trying to make change if things are now predestined to combust?! But I trust, now that you have read this far, you know that hope exists. While we can't travel back in time, we can certainly forge ahead to make things better.

Research shows that climate change news ranks lower in markets where interest and attention are polarized, such as Australia and the US. A comparison of Australia and the US flags the role that polarized politics and media coverage play in driving down interest in and attention to climate change as an issue. Attention to sources across the board is low in both Australia and the US despite the visible effects of climate change witnessed in both countries in recent years.[68] While a 2024 study by the University of Michigan made for shocking headlines, revealing that nearly 15% of Americans don't believe climate change is even real. It sheds light on the highly divided attitude toward global warming. In contrast, countries like Chile and Greece do not appear to suffer from the same levels of audience polarization and see higher rates of attention, and this is perhaps because both these countries have been hit by severe climate extremes.[69]

SOURCES OF CLIMATE CHANGE NEWS

Environmental journalists play a key role, as they inform and raise awareness of topics such as sustainability, biodiversity and renewable energies, which are becoming essential. Today, with the changing face of news, I believe we can describe environmental journalism as current affairs reporting related to Nature and the environment.

The media allows debate on issues related to the environment, involving all agents in these issues, including organizations, politicians, corporates, community groups and others, giving a voice to marginalized communities and individuals. This type of reporting highlights stories of environmental injustice, Indigenous knowledge, grassroots initiatives and the importance of wildlife conservation. By amplifying these voices, journalists raise awareness of the disproportionate impacts of environmental degradation and inspire action for social and environmental justice.

Today the role of environmental journalists has changed, and they have become similar to war correspondents, often reporting from dangerous places – areas that are flooding or experiencing intense heat, where they are reporting from the front line. They investigate corporate activities, government policies, and industry practices related to sustainable development, renewable resources, fossil fuels and ecotourism to expose wrongdoing and support transparency.

By uncovering environmental violations and advocating for responsible behaviour, journalists contribute to creating a more sustainable and accountable society. Through their storytelling, journalists inspire individuals and communities to act. They showcase successful environmental initiatives, innovative solutions and inspiring stories of conservation efforts. By highlighting positive examples and sharing success stories, journalists encourage readers to make environmentally conscious choices and contribute to a more sustainable future.

LOCAL JOURNALISTS AND LOCAL NEWSPAPERS

We must not forget local journalists, who play a unique role in changing the narrative around the world's environmental breakdown, becoming an essential part of the solution. They help put the pieces of the jigsaw together and, very often, local environmental stories become national news stories, which in turn go on to become international news stories. These stories start in local newspapers, which play a vital role in communities across the globe.

Crucially, local newsrooms are making more connections between global climate change and climate-related problems in their own areas. They have the opportunity to localize problems, making them relevant to people in their everyday lives, which could inspire people across regions to find solutions together. We need local news to educate and inspire policy action. However, sadly, we have seen local journalism in decline over the past two decades, as technology has fundamentally altered the market for journalism. Print circulations have declined as people increasingly consume their news online, from smartphones and via social media feeds. We must not forget the role local journalism plays. It can increase turnout at elections, create economic value by encouraging people to buy locally, and foster a sense of cohesion and pride in where we live.

DO WE NEED A NEW MEDIUM TO TACKLE CLIMATE CHANGE?

We have seen documentary makers and feature film directors become important storytellers, using the impact of visuals to tell compelling stories about the environment. Through their work, they have the ability to reach a wide audience and create lasting impact. Along with film makers, environmental photographers capture powerful images that show what's happening and evoke emotions. They are able to document environmental issues and their work may be featured in publications, galleries and online platforms, raising awareness and inspiring change. However, something I keep wondering as I write this book is whether we need a new approach to tackle the climate crisis to reach a wider audience and engage people – an approach that includes a new way to tell the story, a new language that will inspire hope and change.

Who can forget the success of the Netflix film *Don't Look Up*, which came out in 2021 and gave us a different approach, using comedy and satire? After the film premiered, climate scientists took to social media and said they felt seen at last. Big, gloomy headlines don't motivate us and can make us feel helpless. However, on the whole, Hollywood films have a lopsided record of depicting the climate crisis, where some movies have made their villains eco-terrorists or have featured ecological collapse plots – think *The Day After Tomorrow* (2004), *Wall-E* (2008), *Interstellar* (2014) and *Tomorrowland* (2015). Environmentalists seem to make useful villains, and rare is the film that imagines a world where humans successfully work together to allay the worst of the crisis, save Nature and find alternatives to fossil fuels. We need a better way to engage and include the next generation.

I am not alone in my thinking, and I have started to see more parody being used in raising awareness about the climate crisis. Oscar-winning director Adam McKay's climate-focused production company Yellow Dot Studios, launched in 2022, is a nonprofit studio producing short-form videos aiming to push back on climate disinformation. McKay was also the director of *Don't Look Up*. Satire is a great way to combat the fossil fuel companies and lobby groups – it will help to disempower them and become their Achilles heel!

CONCLUSION

Without climate and environmental journalists, we would be ignorant of the truth and what's happening in the world. They play a pivotal role in raising awareness, informing us, holding entities accountable and inspiring action toward environmental conservation. They are becoming a trusted source. These journalists contribute to shaping a more informed and engaged society. We should appreciate and support their vital work in driving positive change for our environment. Through various mediums – such as reporting, writing, filmmaking, blogging and photography – environmental journalists bring attention to critical environmental issues and hold those responsible accountable.

This type of reporting will become increasingly relevant as climate-change-related issues begin to affect more and more people. It will be at the forefront, as we need independent, unbiased reporting on the effects of environmental change on society.

If you choose to become an environmental reporter, science writer, investigative journalist or any other professional in this field, your work will contribute to a better understanding of our environment and drive us toward a more sustainable future.

TAKEAWAY

We all need to keep reading and learning. We cannot afford to ignore the news; ignorance is no longer bliss and we all need to become beacons of light. Make sure you read one trusted source of climate news a day and share what you have learned with friends and family. Here are some trusted daily sources that you should be able to rely on: your local newspaper, *The Guardian*, NASA, Reuters, and the news reports published by any environmental organization of your choice, such as Greenpeace, Save the Children or the World Wildlife Fund.

Another important action you can take is to fact-check things you see posted online, as these can spread very quickly. Find out who created the post, what sources it is based on, who paid for it and who might be profiting from it.

CHAPTER 6

IN CONVERSATION WITH THE MEDIA

In this chapter, I have gathered different voices to give their views about climate news, reporting and the nature of climate storytelling. The four voices are James Cracknell, editor of my local newspaper, *Enfield Dispatch*; the award-winning creative art director and creative specialist Zed Anwar; Aaron Straight, founder and senior creative director at the award-winning agency Soulcraft; and the award-winning Brazilian environmental investigative journalist Karla Mendes.

JAMES CRACKNELL

EDITOR AT *ENFIELD DISPATCH* AND EDITOR-IN-CHIEF AT *SOCIAL SPIDER COMMUNITY NEWS*

In March 2024 I spoke to James Cracknell, editor of my local newspaper, *Enfield Dispatch*,[70] and also editor-in-chief at *Social Spider Community News*.[71] James is an experienced journalist who understands the power of regional news and the importance of communities.

How important are local newspapers for communities?

Local independent newspapers are hugely important and have a democratic role. We provide information for voters about what's happening in their area, telling them what councillors and local politicians are saying and doing, which is useful when people go to the ballot box. Without local newspapers, I believe local democracy wouldn't really exist in the same way.

They also play a key role in keeping the community together, because good local papers should be promoting the positive things that are happening in the community, from charity fundraising campaigns to community projects. This helps residents find out what's happening and then decide if they want to get involved to volunteer or even donate money. The community is represented, and I see the role of local newspapers as stitching everything together and providing a platform for people. Local newspapers are championing the community, ensuring that people have a voice.

You used an interesting phrase – you referred to 'good local papers.' Are there bad local papers?

Yes, there is such a thing as a bad local paper. While they don't actually cause harm, they are fairly pointless because they don't do all the things that I have just described. Invariably they don't have any locally based reporters and instead employ people who are part of a nationwide organization, which is probably owned by a US corporation, where decisions are made in a New York boardroom, and therefore there is no connection with the local community and the paper becomes irrelevant.

Sadly, this type of local newspaper group is typical in London, where local newspapers have been hollowed out, where they don't actually have locally based reporters, with local knowledge or connections. If you don't have local people, or local reporters with local connections, and knowledge of the area, then what is a local newspaper?! It's just a distant office somewhere, trying to put news together for the sake of it, without having any insight into or context for why those stories are important to local people.

What role do you think local media or newspapers play in the understanding of climate change?

It is about giving the news piece context and a relevant angle. For instance, when I worked at a newspaper in West London, we were near Brunel University, which had a climate change professor whom I would interview to give a local story context. It's not easy to make data on weather patterns relevant to an area, but I do find a way, such as working with a weather station in the vicinity to provide relevant data on how summers are getting hotter, or whatever is going on.

I interviewed an activist about a year ago who was a youth delegate at the UN climate talks in Dubai in 2023. She was a local person who knew the issue well and understood the talks that were happening on a global level, and as someone from the community, she brought a unique insight to the paper. She gave us a comparison between those global talks and what was happening on the ground in Enfield. Local papers give a voice to community groups focused on climate action or specific projects such as ones for woodland restoration. But it is not always easy to take a global issue and drill it down to a regional level.

Do you think local reporting on climate change has altered in the last five years? Or does it depend on where you live?

There are parts of this country that are very affected by climate change right now, and then there are parts that are less obviously so. For instance, flooding risks, coastal flooding and coastal erosion are happening in places such as Norfolk in the East of England. Or the Welsh towns that have river flooding, along the River Severn.[72] All these residents are very aware of climate change because they are being impacted. In contrast, here in Enfield, North London, we have no pressing issues right now, though we have had flooding in the past and there's certainly a possibility that we could have it again.

But overall, I've been trying to do different things and I think, as time goes on, things will change and awareness will get better, not just for people but for journalists too. Things are improving all the time. When I think back to 2007, as I was starting out in my career as a journalist and trying to report on climate change, it was viewed as an incredibly niche subject. I had difficulty as a reporter trying to pitch a story idea to my editor, who would say, "This isn't really our problem, is it?" It was a much harder argument to have in those days. Today, there's a general acceptance and understanding of it as a problem.

What do you think about building on greenbelt areas? Is it part of the local climate change news conversation, because it will change the local ecosystem, and are people connecting the dots?

I think the argument around the greenbelt doesn't usually get connected to climate change. I think people just tend to look at it in terms of "is this a good place to build or not?" and it gets tied up to housing targets. But you know, it's possible to build homes with solar panels on their roofs, and if you're doing tree planting at the same time, then it can be good for the environment. So, house building itself isn't necessarily a negative thing.

I do think people are very protective of green spaces because we know how valuable they are. We know that they're going to help and they're going to be increasingly valuable. In big cities, there's the heat island effect – for example, when you're in the centre of London, the average temperature is a degree warmer than if you're on the outskirts, which makes green spaces incredibly important. But I don't know how many people understand that.

Do I think local people are interested in local news about climate change? Yes, I do. Again, ten years ago, that wasn't the case, as it was regarded as an obscure topic, but these days it's accepted.

Do you think climate change is a middle-class issue or is it something that's understood across the board?

Well, of course it does affect everyone, but I think that the environmental movement has always struggled to know how to engage with poorer parts of society and how to bring in activists from more marginalized communities. The simple reason is that it's a secondary issue. If you're poor, you're worrying about paying the bills and you're worrying about where you're going to live. You have more pressing concerns than the temperature rising. However, we know it's always the poorest in society that are affected by these things more than others, so that understanding will naturally improve as time goes on.

My last question: what legacy do you want to leave regarding both climate change and news?

Well, you know, everyone just wants to leave something better than how they found it, but that is hard with climate change, because we know it's going to get worse. I want people to be better informed about everything. Climate change is an existential threat to all of us and will be the biggest threat we face this century, and so, if I can play a small part by improving people's understanding of what it means, then that's great.

Also right now, as a journalist, I am focused on highlighting the issue of housing here in the local area, which is dire. It interplays with climate change, and we need people in good housing. We can tackle the housing problems and climate change simultaneously, because if you give people better-quality homes with better insulation, their energy bills go down. There are so many other benefits, such as creating jobs by putting solar panels on roofs, which provides opportunities for people and helps the economy. Housing should be at the top of the agenda along with climate change, and hopefully people are going to understand that eventually.

ZED ANWAR

CREATIVE ART DIRECTOR AND CREATIVE SPECIALIST

In March 2024, I spoke to the award-winning creative art director and creative specialist Zed Anwar. Zed has worked on campaigns for well-known brands such as Guinness, Greenpeace, KFC, King of Shaves, Nivea, Ocean Saver, the Dian Fossey Gorilla Fund and WWF (the World Wide Fund for Nature, previously the World Wildlife Fund). Zed has many accolades, but perhaps his standout achievement is his award-winning C-Word Isabella Campaign for childhood neuroblastoma (a rare cancer), which gained over 50 million views across all social media channels.

You have created some very successful and provocative content for WWF's campaign #WorldWithoutNature, which has won awards. Why do you think this campaign was so successful? And why did it capture people's imagination?

Good question! As individuals, we like to uphold the brands that we have an affinity with, giving them respect and becoming loyal fans. What I wanted to do was to reach a new audience who wouldn't necessarily pay heed to climate issues. To do this, I started to look at famous brands and their logos, particularly brands using animals in their logos, such as the car company Jaguar, or Penguin Books or the sports brand Puma. The animal gives each brand an energy and power. I imagined what would happen if that animal disappeared from their logo, and the answer was that it would weaken their brand energy.

I wanted to connect people in a visual way, drawing their attention to climate change and how it affects biodiversity. I wanted to raise awareness about those companies that use animals in their brands, and also in a subtle way shame them too, because we know that corporates don't do enough for the planet and that a lot of greenwashing happens.

But overall, I think campaigns like this hold a brand to account about climate change and it's a good way of storytelling, showing us how life could be without these animals. This campaign was a way to start these important conversations.

Do we need a more visual way to communicate climate change to engage people, especially the next generation?

Visual storytelling has great impact and engages people. It's like a beacon and I am of the view that as humans we are affected by images, where if we see a picture of a burning forest, it will spark interest. Personally, I think we could all be doing more as humans to solve these issues. For instance, there is a lot of negative impact on the natural world from our electrical goods that we don't see because we live in our bubbles. But this story needs to be told because it affects countries and cultures. Here in the West, we have a great way of brushing everything under the carpet, but it doesn't magically go away.

What happens in the developing world matters. There are people in Africa who are breaking down TVs, computers and mobile phones to take out wires and other components. They are doing hard and horrible work. They then repackage these elements and send them back to make some trainers! We can't allow the developing world to become our dumping ground.

The best way to communicate this is to visually seize people's attention. That's what I try to do in my work – grab people in the first few seconds to keep them engrossed in the message I want to get across. That's my job. I consider my posters to be similar to movies, as they too are designed to capture people, horrify them and make them happy. It's all about emotion.

Talking about the next generation, we need to create meaningful conversations with them, which is about more than using a hashtag. A lot of these types of campaigns need to have longevity. They need to be more than just a day of 'celebrating' tigers, elephants, etc., where the next day you're celebrating pancakes! We need real engagement for these campaigns to really make an impact and each one needs to be a collective issue. How else will we make brands responsible? We also need to get children talking.

Along with this, we need more environmental charities and nonprofits to hold corporates to account. While it is all fun removing part of a logo, I do think that we need to then follow through with real action, such as making sure that Jaguar the brand is actually helping with the conservation of jaguars in the wild. That's the value of longevity in campaigns.

If we look at what's been happening in Gaza, for instance, are we talking about the impact of the pollution from this war? No one is talking about this and it's a fact of conflict. The funny thing is, while I've made a comparison with what's going on with Gaza, what is working is the boycott. If we had that same kind of attitude about conservation, where we forced brands to make environmental changes, then we would start to see things happening. A boycott is a sad way to look at a situation, but it works.

Do we need to be more provocative and use more satire in our campaigns?

Satire and irony do work, but they depend on the mood, the timing and how you set things up. A lot of agencies do a campaign today and next week, they're working on something else and they've forgotten about last's week project. It makes me wonder, what are we really in this for?! Is it to just create pictures? If so, we are mocking the seriousness of the situation.

At the end of the day, the corporates and the advertising world are the ones who have billions and billions of pounds, with the power to change the world. We need to give back to whatever we owe. I also think we need to pay for the image rights from the last 100 years or so, where we have photographed lions, elephants, tigers etc., and put that back into conservation.

Where do you draw your inspiration from?

From my personal experience. I've been ostracized by my industry due to my ethnicity, which has made me the creative that I am and been a catalyst for how I use my skills. I also draw inspiration from my children and other people's children. I then look at what's going on in the world and I know that I want to make the world a better place.

I resonate with what Spider Man says – "With great power comes great responsibility" – and I possess the power of communication and visual storytelling. So, instead of promoting sugary brands that feed kids with diabetes, I want to make a positive difference using a language that people understand, where I feel and learn how to talk to people, encouraging them to do things.

I've always been an animal and Nature lover, and when I see things destroyed or gentrified or anything like that, it raises the artist in me. I am driven to make change through my work, so if I'm making people sit up to take note then I am doing my job.

What legacy do you want to leave?

My legacy is to help leave a planet that's fit for our children. We know where we're heading, and the future is going to be a hard place in the next few years. I want to know that I did something and that includes stopping the exploitation of children in the developing world who are dying for minerals for our electrical goods. No one is talking about it.

I want to stand back to take stock of what's going on to find better ways of doing things. I am of the view that we are forced into a lot of these routes. I want people to question everything, don't take everything as gospel, hold everything to account. We should become accountable for our time on Earth and for the future of children. I just want everyone to find a balance and harmony in life. We need to fix things.

AARON STRAIGHT

FOUNDER AND SENIOR CREATIVE DIRECTOR OF SOULCRAFT

In April 2024, I spoke to Aaron Straight, founder and senior creative director at the award-winning agency Soulcraft. Soulcraft's mission is to amplify the positive impact of businesses that strive to make a difference. Prior to setting up Soulcraft, Aaron worked in the music industry, managing tours for artists such as King Sunny Adé and Youssou N'Dour. This was where he first encountered the transformative power of corporate social responsibility storytelling, where some musicians and bands were focused on creating positive impact for the planet. Aaron was inspired to use film to help bring awareness to campaigns. This led to the successful launch of the Fair Trade Certified brand, which set the stage for what Soulcraft stands for today.

How important is storytelling to make the world a better place?

As a filmmaker, I believe storytelling is the most important thing – it is central to my craft. It is also part of human communications, separating us from other animals, and is one of the oldest human activities, going right back to when we sat around campfires. Stories have the power to connect us to something deep within ourselves.

If we look at the problems that we are facing as a global community, we urgently need great storytelling to unite us to see beyond our fears, so we are able to work together to find solutions to allow all species to survive and thrive. This is a big test for us – are we going to destroy everything because we couldn't cooperate with the ecosystem that we're in? Or are we going to be wise enough to look around and find how we can live in harmony with our surroundings and tell a better story, where we innovate and create something that's good for people and the planet?

So, what is climate storytelling? How can we use it to find a way out of the climate crisis?

Great questions! Climate storytelling is the most important thing that we have to address this crisis, and in order for human beings to work together, we have to believe in uniting a story. Climate storytelling is an ecosystem of different types of stories – scientific, social, environmental, spiritual and economic. All these aspects are part of the human experience. We are the audience – a vast audience made up of different perspectives, where we have a lot to learn from Indigenous people. What is working against us right now is time, but I'm optimistic and believe in our ability to tell great stories, to unite us to find solutions.

For seven years, I worked in Haiti on a conservation initiative that was linked to human survival. There's no way to tell a story in Haiti about conservation that is not a humanitarian story. In Haiti there are limited resources, and the conflict between human and animal needs is as plain as day. The project I was working on was about a bird on the brink of extinction that lived in the mountains, where the last 2% of Haiti's forest remained. This forest was slowly being cut down by farmers who needed land to grow food. For this conservation project to work, we needed to find out why those farmers were cutting down the trees – and the answer came down to survival. The farmers were trying to take care of their own children and grow food for their families. It was a choice between their children or this bird.

At this time, one very wise Haitian said to me, "Aaron, conservation is for rich people." This was a powerful and true statement. Working there, we realized that we had to invest in the community, from helping them install cisterns to catch water to investing in their gardens to ensure they had seeds and plants; all these things improved their quality of life and wellbeing. When this community eventually took over and ran these programmes themselves, that's when the forest and the birds were protected. You can't ask people who have nothing to give up something – they have to feel connected to their own livelihood and outcomes. It makes sense, and this would be true for you if the roles were reversed. In climate storytelling, we have to go to people where they are located. We have to speak a language that relates to them, their own survival and their own struggle.

I was just on the phone with this guy who was talking about his community in Texas. He was frustrated and believed people were not taking care of the natural resources or the local ecosystem. I had to remind him that many of the people in his community might be struggling. In America right now, people don't understand the difficulties that many are facing. It is complicated here – there's a spiritual crisis and an economic crisis, there's disparity of wealth, and there's a lack of community spirit. All these things make a rich country feel poor. I had to remind him that those folks probably didn't have the time to be good stewards of their land, because they were focused on their own survival.

Climate storytelling is multifaceted, and it is important to connect to individuals to show them their association with the Earth. It is also about partnering with powerful entities that can make significant changes – from how we use resources to how we dispose of them and how we treat communities. We need to use storytelling to help big organizations make those changes, and then share their stories. Companies that are brave enough to do the real work, and not greenwashing, inspire us to support them.

I had this amazing experience during the pandemic of working on a project that ran from the top to the bottom of the Mississippi River. There was this connection between the farmers, ranchers and fisherpeople, who were all linked by this river. These people are all in traditionally hard-working agricultural communities, from multigenerational families and from family farms, in a very politically conservative part of the US. They were connected to the land and the river and wanted to leave something better behind for their children and grandchildren.

When we first spent time together, they admitted that they were nervous about me coming because they saw me as a liberal outsider. But we had this connection and realized we agreed on 95% of the things about life. We had a wonderful time working on solutions and exchanging stories. While our political differences might have ended up being a big deal online, in person they didn't matter at all! This Mississippi story is a great reminder of how there's a lot we need to do to get past these political differences.

This is a big question! If Mother Nature came to you and said, "I want you to create a film to make people climate aware and you have an unlimited budget," how would you approach it?

Oh, this is a really tough one! In fact, I've thought about this a lot over the years and I do have a couple of story ideas that I've written that I would love to explore. Essentially, I think it is important to not feel overwhelmed about the climate crisis and believe that we can make a difference; a lot of us think this problem is so big, and we're so small.

I would like to tell a very human story that links us to a life experience – perhaps adventure or falling in love – and that contains a message of transformation. No one likes direct sales or to be told what to think. So, this would be a story that allowed us to start to see the world in a different way, not from fear or desperation, but from unity, showing that we have been connected to this planet for a long time, spanning different civilizations. I would use the power of great music, wonderful acting and cinematography to take us back to the moment when our ancestors felt in awe of being a part of this planet.

The film would talk to everyone, including those who watched it and had no idea that it was about climate change, and those who understood the issue and wanted to be inspired to do the work that they are supposed to do. The greatest thing you can do as a storyteller is to be a catalyst for others. The unification of art and science is what often really makes changes for humanity.

Science without art doesn't reach or inspire people. I would like to read this quote from John Steinbeck, which is the essence of what we're talking about:

> It is a strange thing, that most of the feeling we call religious, most of the mystical outcrying, which is one of the most prized and used and desired reactions of our species, is really the understanding and the attempt to say that man is related to the whole thing, related inextricably to all reality, known and unknowable. This is a simple thing to say, but the profound feeling of it made a Jesus, a Saint Augustine, a Saint Francis, or a Roger Bacon, a Charles Darwin, and an Einstein. Each of them in his own tempo and with his own voice discovered and reaffirmed with astonishment the knowledge that all things are one thing, and that one thing is all things – plankton, a shimmering phosphorescence on the sea and the spinning planets in an expanding universe, all bound together by the elastic string of time. It is advisable to look from the tide pool to the stars, then back to the tide pool again.[73]

The essence of this quote is that we're all connected. It's not a new idea but it's one we frequently forget. As Americans, we are obsessed with individualism, which can make things challenging.

A profound quote that leads me to the next question. What has been the most impactful story that you've worked on?

I've been fortunate enough to be doing this work for 19 years, and I have travelled all over – the US, Central America, Haiti, Africa, Europe and Australia. But it's every project that I work on in real time that excites me the most, because it means that there's evolution in the work we are doing. So, right now, I'm inspired about the project that we've been doing on ocean health. It's a partnership with the social enterprise Woocheen, which is focused on the Tlingit, Haida and Tsimshian tribes of Southeast Alaska, which were formed by the US government into Native Corporations[74] almost against their will, but they have turned this into a positive not only for their own community but for the world.

Woocheen is committed to a healthy ocean and is working on innovation, and my role is to help tell the stories around them. We visited these incredible forests, which have an impact on the community and are important to people's wellbeing and health. All the trees have major spiritual and cultural significance to the Tlingit, Haida and Tsimshian tribes, and are used ceremonially to create artwork, totems, canoes, hats and baskets. Each part of the tree has a purpose, including the tree bark. These communities are revitalized seeing their language acknowledged. While it doesn't sound like it's connected to ocean health or the climate crisis, it is, as there's so much loss when you lose a language, because you lose wisdom and perspective. These languages need to be protected.

These are some of the smartest people I've ever met. Their understanding of the ocean depths, of geology, their local Indigenous beliefs and ideas, enrich the science. There's a clever young Tlingit woman who went on to get a great education at Gonzaga University and entered the science field. She grew up as a fisherwoman, fishing alongside her father in Haines, Alaska, knowing about the real impact of climate change on her community. Now she is marrying her scientific, Western education with her cultural background, bringing the two worlds together. She's going to be the voice for the future, and we made a short film about her that has become a collection of materials. This is one of my favourite pieces of work.

The work we've been creating has been getting noticed, and we have won awards for our films. There's actually a funny story: one of our films that we shot with divers, which is a love letter to the ocean, has recently been nominated for a Webby Award, which we are excited about, but we have found out that our competition is Jane Goodall!

Well, being alongside Jane Goodall is an award in itself!
This leads me to my last question: what legacy do you want to leave?

I don't really think that much about legacy. I am insignificant in this whole equation, and in the spirit of Steinbeck's quote, I'm just trying to contribute my efforts, energy and voice, because it matters; I believe all our efforts create a ripple effect. A hundred million human beings have come before me. Hopefully more will come after me to live in harmony with Nature, and if I played a tiny role in that, then I would be very thankful. It's meant a lot to me to be able to figure out how to make a living – to take care of my family doing the work that I love. This is what I'm most grateful for, although I don't always get it right. There have been projects that we've supported that we thought were fantastic but weren't in the end.

A lot of humility goes into this work, and I believe it's never too late to make things happen. I'm a huge sports fan and no matter how many games you watch, when it comes to the last second, somebody will make an extraordinary extra effort, and perhaps, with a little bit of luck, change the outcome of the game.

KARLA MENDES

AWARD-WINNING BRAZILIAN ENVIRONMENTAL INVESTIGATIVE JOURNALIST

In April 2024, I spoke with the award-winning Brazilian environmental investigative journalist Karla Mendes. Karla is based in Rio de Janeiro, writing for Mongabay,[75] and has been working as a correspondent for international outlets since 2015. Since 2017, she has specialized in covering environmental and land issues. Over her career, Karla has won several national and international awards, including two awards from the Society of Environmental Journalists (SEJ) and the Fetisov Journalism Award. In February 2023, she was a winner of the SEAL Environmental Journalism Awards with distinction for her "powerful work covering the continued encroachment of global corporations into Indigenous Amazon lands."[76] She is also a member of the Pulitzer Center's Rainforest Investigations Network.

What inspired you to become an environmental journalist?

From a young age I was interested in this field, especially investigative journalism, and at journalism school I had this sense of wanting to make a difference in the world and fight for justice. I used to say that I was a "good troublemaker." When I look back at my career, all my life experiences, learning and opportunities have brought me to what I am doing today.

My journey started at the prosecutor's office, working in public relations when I was a student. I learned a lot here and this was where I found my first investigative story. I attended a conference about drug crimes in Belo Horizonte, which is the capital of the state of Minas Gerais, Brazil's second most populous state. At the event a crime story caught my attention, and at the same time the conference was running a writing competition for attendees to enter. I decided to investigate this particular story and I found out that the prosecutor's office would be part of it. I entered the competition and won! It was from 2002 that my career began.

A quick snapshot of how I found myself in journalism: while at the prosecutor's office, I secured a three-month internship at the largest newspaper in Minas Gerais. I thought that after the internship, I would return to my job at the prosecutor's office, but I discovered that I loved working at the newspaper. I was reporting on different subjects, from sports to business and politics. The newspaper decided to hire me, and so I quit my job at the prosecutor's office.

Working at the paper felt right. In 2012, I decided to live in Spain to gain experience as an international business reporter. It was during my time in Spain that I applied for a scholarship at the Inter-American Press Association, and from 2013 to 2014, I went to Nova Scotia, Canada, to do a master's in investigative and data journalism. I was fascinated by investigations, especially data-driven stories. After my degree, I decided to return to Brazil, where I worked for the Brazilian government during the World Cup, where I was part of the media centre, helping international journalists and producing content. Then in 2015, I was hired through LinkedIn by SNL Financial (currently S&P Global) to work on business news for international outlets focused on banks and insurance companies in Latin America.

My turning point came in 2015, when a dam disaster struck in the city of Mariana, in Minas Gerais. It became Brazil's largest environmental disaster.[77] The dam collapsed and destroyed the entire Bento Rodrigues village, killing many. At that time, my friend and I were both bored with work and were watching how this story was unfolding. It bothered us how the press were reporting things, without investigating the root of the problem. So, we decided to do a story independently as freelancers and went to the area. We wrote a series that was very successful – we told the story of the people, which was used in schoolbooks in Brazil.

This experience gave me the bug and I really wanted to be an environmental international correspondent; this became my dream. At this time, I randomly met a Canadian couple at an event who were sat at the same table as me. They were there for their son, who was receiving an award. They told me their son wanted to work in Brazil. Anyway, we kept in touch and then two years later, the son contacted me saying he was moving to Brazil. Long story short, I helped him settle in Brazil. He was working for Thomson Reuters Foundation as the land and property rights correspondent. He knew I wasn't happy at work and I was looking for opportunities, and one came along for us both to work together through the Society of Environmental Journalists. They had a reporting grant for a journalist from North America with someone from the Global South to report from the Amazon. We applied and received the grant. We both went to the Amazon for the first time in 2017 and we published six stories that covered different things – illegal mining, illegal cattle laundering to land conflicts and Nature-based solutions.

After that, the Thomson Reuters journalist returned to Rio, and I stayed on, as I had another story in mind about pirates in the Amazon – it was about the theft of diesel from boats. The pirates story made front-page news in Brazil and won three awards. At the same time, my Canadian journalist friend decided to return home to Canada and recommended me for his position, and I was hired by Thomson Reuters Foundation. I worked for them for a year and a half, but they couldn't renew my contract. During this time, I had a lot of job offers for business reporting, but it wasn't what I wanted to do. I knew I wanted to give a voice to underrepresented people. My time in the Amazon changed my life, and since July 2019 I've been working for Mongabay, a US based nonprofit news outlet focused on environmental news, traditional communities and conservation.

I think it's important for me to add that while I have won several awards and my path might seem easy, there have been challenges during my career. I never took the easy road, even when I was doing my master's at the University of King's College in Halifax, Canada. I decided to lead my investigative project into Canada spying on Brazil, following Edward Snowden's leaks of the US espionage.[78] In 2023, the university gave me a Distinguish Alumni Award and my professor said it was the most ambitious project in the history of the school. But I did it and it was my first investigative story in English with Reuters.

Do you think media reporting of climate change has improved? And if it has, how?

When I started out in 2017, environmental and climate issues were mostly regarded as a 'left-wing subject' by the mainstream media and did not receive much attention. I am pleased to say Mongabay has been doing environmental reporting for the last 25 years! Here in Brazil, the election of Jair Bolsonaro as president in 2018 was divisive – he created a backlash against the Indigenous people, dismantled environmental laws and started to destroy the Amazon. This forced the mainstream media to start to report on these stories, and of course climate change became an emergency.

Today many media titles have created environmental news departments and are giving more attention to this issue, but there are challenges – particularly when dealing with the science, which requires specific knowledge and the ability to translate it to the public. Plus, the advent of fake news has become a real task. Overall, yes, things have been improving, but we need to keep doing better, and by that I mean there's a lot of knowledge about environmental issues and climate change that must be shared widely – not just with young journalists and those transitioning to environmental and climate reporting but with those reporters and editors working in mainstream newsrooms. We need to be open to keep learning.

From my experience, we need to understand how to talk and engage with Indigenous people, so that we understand their stories and do justice to them. Interacting with these communities is not the same as talking to people living in cities. There are a lot of nuances that are very important.

There is an investigative case that I'm now focused on, which is on the Arariboia Indigenous Territory in Brazil and the murder of Paulo Paulino Guajajara, a 26-year-old Indigenous Guajajara leader. He was killed allegedly by loggers in the Arariboia terriority in 2019.[79] Paulo was a guardian of the forest and ten years ago, his community set up a group to fight against illegal logging and environmental crimes threatening Arariboia. It's a complex situation. My current investigation is a follow-up of a 2019 article and a documentary film, I codirected and coproduced with British documentary filmmaker Max Baring for Thomson Reuters Foundation. We did a 26-minute film about the Guardians of the Forest, which won four international awards and is the most awarded project of our careers. However, five months after the release of the documentary film, Paulo was murdered. It was devastating.

When we were filming, Paulo told us that he was being threatened, but we didn't use that interview in the documentary. We have created an epilogue video to the main documentary after his death. Since then, I have closely followed the case and I have published several articles related to Paulo's murder and violent attacks in Arariboia. It has helped create justice for the case, because five years later, the case has not yet reached the courts. This case will be a landmark in Brazil because prosecutors have made the case that Paulo's murder was a crime against the entire community because he acted as a forest defender and was assassinated inside the Indigenous territory, where outsiders couldn't be. The federal prosecutor will use our video in the trial and has said it will help toward getting justice.

My point here is that we need to rethink how we teach journalism, because currently we have the mindset of giving greater recognition to scientists and the government as our sources – giving them more importance than the Indigenous communities who have an intrinsic knowledge of the forests. Because these voices don't have a PhD, they are considered less important, and this needs a discussion – especially as now many Indigenous people go to universities as a way to be accepted and respected. There are so many stereotypes about Indigenous people where we do not recognize their wisdom and value.

Has the media got the balance right in trying to speak to the next generation and their concerns about the climate crisis?

It is key to understand the learning process of the young, especially with the spread of the internet and social media. We know how everything has changed in the way people seek knowledge. I believe it's important to understand our audiences, talk to them and find out their views, how they get content and how they look at it. For example, at Mongabay, we have had lots of discussions so we can really deliver the content that the audience wants and needs. We can't be imposing the items that we want to talk about – there needs to be a balance. Journalists are educators and our mission is to translate the knowledge.

The media also needs to understand how to repack a story once it has been produced, from long written features to video, in order to suit different audiences. Again, here at Mongabay we are going to create a breaking news session, as we see the need. People want things quicker. However, I am a defender of long-form investigative pieces, which are important for legal cases.

Has environmental journalism become dangerous, similar to war reporting? I'm especially thinking of when you're dealing with nefarious actors, some of whom you've already mentioned, but also when you're reporting from regions that have intense heat or are being flooded.

When we talk about floods and fires, for example, you can't just send a reporter without doing a rigorous risk assessment. There needs to be an emergency plan to get the person back safely in case something goes wrong. From my own personal perspective, I have invested in a satellite communicator, and I won't go to the Amazon without it. Every day, three times a day, I send check-in messages with my geolocation. It's important.

In environmental reporting, it's a fight against money, because all of the destruction of Nature is to do with money in terms of supply chains. In terms of wars, many are murdered, but equally some environmental disasters can come close to those numbers too. Things have changed and it's riskier, but we won't stop doing our job. We need to be cautious and of course be balanced.

My last question: what legacy do you want to leave?

I want to make a real difference to help save the Amazon Rainforest and create justice for the communities that are not heard. I also want to leave a legacy about environmental issues and share the knowledge that I have acquired over the last seven years with other journalists. I want to help the next generation of reporters be more informed and prepared to cover environmental and climate change issues.

I had the experience of mentoring a young reporter, which was rewarding. I helped her with insights to not only know how to overcome obstacles to report on the Amazon, but how to approach this region. Reporting in the Amazon is not straightforward – you have to be prepared for your journey. For instance, you need to have purifying tablets for the water. This was advice I gave to a friend who had never been to the Amazon before. She was heading to a place where there was a severe drought. The boat she was travelling in got stuck in the middle of the river because of the drought. They ran out of mineral water, and she told me that is what saved her life, the purifying tablets for the water!

I have been elected to the board of the Society of Environmental Journalists as its first Brazilian and Latin American. I have also been made its diversity, equity and inclusion chair. This is part of my way of giving back to the society, as in 2017 they funded my trip to the Amazon. It's a great organization, where you can talk about the environment and climate change, but it's very focused on the US. I want to help expand SEJ's programmes worldwide and raise more funding because there is a huge need to share knowledge of journalists from the North with the Soth and vice-versa.

In some parts of the world, journalists don't speak English and don't have access to the mainstream media but are reporting on things happening in their country. Two years ago, I went to Angola to give an investigative journalism training and I realized that several of the journalists had been in jail because of stories they published. I want to help these journalists do environmental reporting – it's the most important subject we have today.

CHAPTER 7

FOOD

Food is not only a matter of eating. It is also about the choices we make when we are grocery shopping. Food and climate have a close relationship and as populations are growing, more people are consuming and sadly wasting more food than ever before. When we talk about the global food system, we need to remember that it involves production, post-farm processing and distribution, which are key contributors to emissions. It is estimated that food production is responsible for a quarter of the world's greenhouse gas emissions – you could say we are eating our way to climate change!

Long before food reaches our shops, the process of production releases multiple byproducts that affect the length and quality of life of all species. Human food systems depend on biodiversity to function, and conventional food systems reduce biodiversity – effectively destroying their own foundation. We clear forests to create agricultural space, which results in the atmosphere becoming warmer, diversity decreasing, and soil and water becoming contaminated. We also fortify plants and animals with chemical fertilizers and steroids, which is not good for our own health. Putting this into context, over the past 100 years, more than 90% of crop varieties have disappeared.[80] There is more intensive farming, as farmers have abandoned numerous local plant varieties in favour of genetically uniform, high-yielding ones. Now, 60% of dietary energy is derived from just three cereal crops: rice, wheat and maize.[81]

In the Amazon, for example, trees are disappearing at an alarming rate to make room for soy plantations, yet ironically, forests are indispensable in the fight against climate change because they absorb carbon dioxide. According to the World Economic Forum, biodiversity loss and ecosystem collapse rank among the top five threats to humanity in the next ten years.[82] The demand for food is projected to increase by 60% by 2050,[83] which means the decisions we make today will have an enormous impact on food security and, by extension, the environment, the economy, health, education, peace and human rights.

With the weather becoming more erratic, with less predictable temperatures, we are starting to recognize that climate change, coupled with supply chain challenges, is severely limiting our ability to eat the same foods all year round. Syncing our diets to the seasons, which is what we used to do years ago, is a shift that would not only respect Nature by helping our local ecologies but also help us feel more connected to the food we eat. News headlines in 2023 about widespread shortages of tomatoes and other salad vegetables in UK supermarkets reflected a deeper, darker story of climate change and will become a pattern of disruptive winter weather.[84] However, the UK is one of the most Nature-depleted countries in the world – and the way we produce and consume food is putting further pressure on our local species and habitats.

While this is a complex problem, we need to transform the global food system and act now to rethink our relationships to the way we eat. The way our food is produced and consumed does not have to destroy Nature and habitats for wildlife. We can reduce carbon emissions, cut food loss and waste, and restore Nature, while at the same time supporting farmers and producers locally and abroad to grow enough food for us all. Yes, we can do it all. Our food system can provide sustainable, healthy and affordable food for everyone.

THE ISSUE OF SOIL

You may think soil is boring and just about mud, but it is so much more than that, as life on Earth has always been sustained by a thin layer of fertile soil. Soil is the foundation for agriculture and the medium where nearly all food-producing plants grow. It is estimated that 95% of our food is directly or indirectly produced in our soils.[85] It lies at the heart of the ecosystem, providing critical functions not only for agricultural production but also for plant growth, animal habitation, biodiversity, carbon sequestration, and resilience to droughts and flooding. Yet, the decline in soil health is accelerating many of the most severe challenges that we are facing, including global hunger. Poor soil health contributes to global warming, as it reduces the volume of carbon absorbed from the atmosphere. It also drives biodiversity loss, which impacts the vegetation that provides food and shelter to animal species.

Soil health is defined as the capacity of soil to function as a living system. Healthy soil maintains a diverse community of organisms that help to control plant disease, insects and weed pests. It forms beneficial symbiotic associations with plant roots and recycles essential plant nutrients. It also has a better structure, with positive effects for soil water and the capacity to hold nutrients, which both ultimately improve crop production.

Healthy soil is an important element in the fight against climate change because it can absorb carbon from the atmosphere. After the ocean, soil is the second largest natural carbon sink, surpassing forests and other vegetation. Globally, approximately 75% of terrestrial carbon has been estimated to be stored in soil, which is three times more than the amount stored in living plants and animals. If the soil is covered and has humus (organic matter), it absorbs the carbon from the atmosphere. Conversely, unhealthy soil, which is ploughed and exposed, is a source of emissions of both carbon dioxide and methane. This means that improving the health of soil can play a major role in increasing carbon sequestration and addressing atmospheric carbon. If we fix the soil, we help fix many problems – food security, climate change, biodiversity and ecosystems.

Research published in 2020 suggests that around 24 billion tonnes of fertile soils are being lost each year, and the UN's Convention to Combat Desertification has warned that up to 40% of the global land area is already in a degraded state.[86] This is down in part to a changing climate, but human activity has played a significant role with intensive farming, excessive use of chemicals, deforestation and other forms of land use conversion contributing to the problem. The European Commission estimates that Europe loses 9 million tonnes of soil annually,[87] while according to the UK's Department for Environment, Food & Rural Affairs' triennial report on food security, soil degradation costs the UK around £1.2 billion annually.[88]

For the agricultural sector, declining soil fertility raises a number of issues. It reduces both the yields and quality of crops, eating into farmers' profits, including their ability to produce enough food for the growing population. Estimates suggest that around 95% of food is directly or indirectly dependent on healthy soils, but approximately 40% of the world's agricultural land has degraded.[89] The UN says the world may have agricultural soil only for another 80–100 crops, which means that in 45–60 years there could be severe food shortages.[90] Scientists forecast that worldwide by 2045, we will be producing 40% less food than what we are producing right now.[91]

This is not a world that we have envisaged – one we want to live in or leave for our children. But this is what we are creating. Whether we want to fix or reverse climate change, enhance carbon sequestration, limit rising temperatures around the world, or resolve water scarcity, the link is the need to fix the soil.

A first step would be for countries to switch to something called 'regenerative agriculture,' which includes regular crop rotation, sustainable grazing, and mixed-use farming methods such as agroforestry and planting trees alongside crops. By changing the ways we farm, we can protect healthy soils from damage while restoring degraded soils by growing a diverse range of plants. As individuals, too, we play an important role through the products we choose to buy and the food we choose to eat.

We will need to change the way we farm and potentially the whole nature of the agrochemical industry. We need to improve the ways we produce food – and learn from farmers worldwide who are cutting their emissions, restoring their soils and protecting their local ecosystems.

SUSTAINABLE AGRICULTURE REALLY DOES MAKE A DIFFERENCE TO THE ENVIRONMENT

Sustainable agriculture uses up to 56% less energy per unit of crops produced, creates 64% fewer greenhouse gas emissions per hectare and supports greater levels of biodiversity than conventional farming.[92] However, it may be more costly, as it is more labour-intensive and is often certified in a way that requires it to be separated from conventional foods during processing and transport, and the costs associated with marketing and distribution of relatively small volumes of product are often comparatively high. And, occasionally, the supply of certain sustainably produced foods is limited.

The heavy use of chemicals, medicines and genetic modification allows some foods to be produced cheaply and in higher volumes, so the retail price may be lower. But this is deceptive because it does not reflect the actual costs of environmental damage or the price of the healthcare that is required to treat diet-related diseases.

This does not mean that we have to be vegan, but most of us should eat less animal protein. Livestock production is a major cause of climate change, and even small dietary shifts can have a positive impact.

The other point to bear in mind is that sustainably produced food can be affordable for everyone because as demand for certain foods increases, the costs associated with production, processing, distribution and marketing will drop, which should make these foods less expensive for consumers.

However, there is a lack of understanding about the way that agriculture, the environment and human health come together. Policymakers do not typically consider Nature as a form of capital, so legislation is not designed to prevent pollution and other kinds of environmental degradation. And we as consumers may not realize how our dietary choices affect the environment or even our own health. In the absence of either legal obligations or consumer demand, there is little incentive for producers to change their approach. However, hopefully, from reading this chapter, you will be more aware that you have the power to make positive choices and bring about change.

WHAT WE PUT IN OUR SHOPPING TROLLEY AND ON OUR PLATE

I know there are so many things to think about when we go shopping. Apart from remembering what's on our list, many of us are also trying to shop within our budget and deal with the cost-of-living crisis. And all the good things are expensive! It should not be this way. We should all have the right and access to healthy, sustainable food where we can support farmers, growers and producers. We need to be more aware of the choices we make before we check out at the till.

While writing this book, I stumbled across the term 'climatarian', which means someone who is trying to raise awareness and, crucially, take personal steps to address climate change by changing their shopping and eating habits. I believe we will start to see this term become more mainstream, as fortunately, I believe many of us are already climatarians. For climatarians, it doesn't much matter what you eat – whether it is meat, fish, eggs etc. What is more important is the carbon footprint you put on your plate. The aim is to select foods that have generated the least environmental impact during production.

The term 'climatarian' has a much deeper meaning, too – it is about creating a conscious mindset. Climatarians don't only think about the emissions their food has generated, but also about how they can protect the planet by the way they dress, travel and enjoy themselves. It is a lifestyle change and goes further than recycling or turning off the tap while brushing our teeth – both things we should be doing anyway. Climatarians are the next step up. They want to turn their daily habits toward fighting climate change and reducing their personal carbon footprint on the planet.

CONCLUSION

If there is one thing to remember from this chapter, it is this – what you eat and the way you eat can change the planet. You have the power. We can and must think more deeply about the decisions we make when shopping, using food to bring about the change needed to guarantee a future for our planet and help construct a better, cleaner and fairer food system.

Our main problem is that our unhealthy and unsustainable diet is largely based on meat. Our modern food system has been developed and designed around eating meat, which goes back to decisions made in the 1970s. It is estimated that the world's population will have reached almost 10 billion by 2050. If all these people continue to eat in the same way, as we have done for the past 50 years, it will break our planet. We cannot move forward unless we change the way we eat and produce food. Everything we eat has a consequence. Finding a sustainable way to produce and eat food is one of the biggest challenges for the world in the coming decades, and the choice of eating vegetarian or vegan is, hence, a choice against the present system.

Knowing this helps us reflect and understand the impact of our daily choices and to act with awareness. The change we need starts with us, and our choices are powerful weapons. Our own food revolution needs to start with getting to know what we eat and where it comes from. This will mean better health and better quality.

TAKEAWAY

There are many things we can do. They don't have to be expensive and it doesn't have to be about buying organic. The obvious one is when you are buying your vegetables and fruit, try to buy produce that is loose or not in plastic packaging. Another is to eat fruit and vegetables that are in season in your region. Importantly, it is vital that we all know where our produce comes from – you owe that to yourself – and shop locally as much as possible.

One final thing is to look after the bees and campaign on their behalf. We need to stop the chemical warfare on bees through potent pesticides – sign the petitions!

CHAPTER 8

IN CONVERSATION WITH FOOD EXPERTS

To help us understand food further, I spoke to four experts, asking them to share their knowledge about food, what we put on our plate and sustainable farming – as well as why they think food is important and what difference they want to make. The four are Sarah Bridle, Professor of Food, Climate and Society at the University of York; Kaddu Kiwe Sebunya, CEO of the African Wildlife Foundation; Michael Tingsager, a leading food industry expert; and agriculturalist Shristi Adhikari, who lives in Nepal.

SARAH BRIDLE

PROFESSOR OF FOOD, CLIMATE AND SOCIETY AT THE UNIVERSITY OF YORK

At the end of January 2024, I spoke to Sarah Bridle, who is Professor of Food, Climate and Society at the University of York. Since 2015, Sarah has been researching the environmental impact of the food system, with a particular focus on how our food choices contribute to climate change. Sarah is also researching the potential impacts of the environment on food availability. Sarah coleads the UK Research and Innovation-funded AFN Network+ (Agri-food for Net Zero Network+), which aims to identify the key research gaps holding the UK food system back from helping the country to transition toward net zero by 2050. Sarah also founded the Take a Bite Out of Climate Change project, which provides accessible information to the public on the impact of food and farming on climate change. Finally, Sarah is part of the leadership team of the FixOurFood project, which aims to transform the Yorkshire food system. Sarah has also written a highly acclaimed book, *Food and Climate Change without the Hot Air*, published in 2020.[93]

> Your book, *Food and Climate Change without the Hot Air*, is packed with information about food emissions, such as a latte is ten times worse for the climate than a cup of black coffee. What are the other climate costs of our food and drink choices? And why should we care?

A lot of people are really surprised to find out that about a third of all climate change comes from food. This is actually more than from, for example, transport or heating, which explains why the food system is so important. Most of the contributions from food to climate change are not caused by fossil fuels. Even if we stopped burning fossil fuels, we would still have the climate impacts from food to deal with, and these are increasing because there are more people eating more climate-impactful foods. To put it into context, food alone will cause two degrees of warming by the end of the century if we keep going as we are. We've still got a bigger problem to solve in terms of cutting out fossil fuels, but the food system is much harder to change, even tougher than stopping burning fossil fuels, and it's going to take time to make those changes.

Climate and food are intimately linked. Food is probably the way most people are going to experience climate change, in terms of the food they will be able to buy, because growing food will be impacted by the weather either in their own country or elsewhere, affecting imports from overseas.

Why do we need to change our food systems?

Well, if we want to eat, then we need to adapt to be more resilient to the extreme weather that is already taking place. If we take a look at what's happening right now in the UK alone, we've had a number of extreme weather events in the last few weeks, and other parts of the world have had them too. As we're talking, I can see from my window some of the flooding here in Yorkshire. It's essential that we change and that we really think about the legacy that we're leaving behind with regard to the impact of climate change on the planet. Yes, it is going to be difficult, but we need to reduce the climate impact of our food if we are going to stop our contributions to climate change.

How does regenerative farming fit into this and can it make a difference?

Regenerative farming has started to become a bit of a catchphrase for all the good things that people want to talk about, and it is not very well defined. But there are definitely ways we can change the way we produce food, which will help in terms of addressing the primary places food is produced: farms.

The types of things people are looking at are, for example, having more hedgerows and land set aside for Nature. Both lock up more carbon in the soil, and there are trials going on at the moment to look at how much these measures can help. In terms of farming, there are a lot of other practices that we can look at too, such as covering slurry pits, which contain manure and are a major problem when rearing pigs, chickens and dairy cows. This helps reduce emissions.

There are things we can do in terms of farming. While they are not necessarily regenerative farming, they will have a positive impact. But all of these things will generally have smaller impacts than the changes we can make as consumers in what we eat.

How will climate change affect the food of the future?

The way that climate change is happening means it is causing extreme weather that is affecting larger regions at the same time. For example, we've had various extreme weather events over the last five years that have affected a large part of the northern hemisphere, triggered by the changing disparity in temperatures between the poles and the equator. This has caused weather systems to impact larger regions, and it could knock out multiple bread baskets[94] all at once. This domino effect can cause knee-jerk reactions from governments in terms of reducing the amount of trade, which has the potential to spark catastrophes like we saw happen in 2008, when there were food riots in many countries. This is potentially how extreme events will affect food and it is the one thing that worries me the most.

Extreme weather also has a knock-on effect in terms of what people are choosing to grow, as they know that some crops carry a larger risk than others. For example, soft fruit is vulnerable to extreme weather storms, which can wipe out crops. Plus, there will certainly be some entire regions affected, where they will be unable to produce food due to soil degradation and extreme weather, which could produce a dust bowl.

Something else to consider is that if we ever had government policies to penalize the most climate-impactful foods, then that would affect what's available. An example of this is that people who eat beef regularly, or other high-impact meat products like pork or lamb, could find these items becoming more expensive.

Entire parts of the world might be affected, as the ocean circulation and the jet stream impact climate systems. This could actually make some countries colder, because there's a weather system that is no longer functioning. On the other hand, some places will become warmer – for instance, Siberia might become a good place to grow some things that we couldn't grow there before.

It's not clear how this will turn out for all countries, but overall, it is going to be harder to produce food. On average, the total amount of food produced globally is expected to reduce. An important thing to flag is that climate change affects the nutritional density of crops, with the increased amount of carbon dioxide in the atmosphere. While some crops will grow faster, the amount of nutrition per 100 grams of that crop will reduce, which may have a long-term health impact.

What can we do to eat sustainably?

The majority of people are omnivores, and we know that their meat-based diet is going to be the biggest contributor to climate change, especially if they prefer meats like beef and lamb. One solution is for them to reduce the quantity of meat in a recipe and add more protein-rich foods, such as tins of lentils, beans or chickpeas, which will improve the climate impact per portion.

What research shows is that if you talk about cutting out foods, it can be depressing and scary. A more palatable solution is to include other ingredients to bulk things out or introduce food swaps. We can do this by adding tins of healthy foods, such as pulses or vegetables, which have added benefits for our bodies. This means that you're automatically reducing the amount of meat per portion. It's so simple to do and won't necessarily affect the flavour, plus people who are cooking for others might not really want to serve an entirely different meal.

Another thing that people could look at is airfreighted food. However, this is not easy to do because if you go to the supermarket, you can't tell what has been flown in. So, you need to have some knowledge about food in order to know which products come by boat. Pineapple, for example, is an interesting one, as it lasts a long time on a boat, but if you bought it pre-sliced, then it was probably sliced in the country of origin, because of the labour costs, and would have been airfreighted.

Usually, items that are transported by boat are things like bananas, and these have a lower climate impact than fruit that is flown in. Citrus fruit and apples last really well being shipped. Soft fruits like strawberries, blueberries and raspberries, and also green beans, all tend to be flown when they're out of season, and so do fresh flowers. It's all produce that wouldn't last very long that needs to be airfreighted, and as a result will have a high carbon footprint.

What do you want your legacy to be in this food conversation with regard to climate change?

Being able to sleep at night, feeling I did something useful, is important to me. I also want to be able to help by moving new things along, as we don't know how the situation is going to play out or what is going to work. As we look toward 2050, I want to be able to look back and be able to think that we actually influenced decision-making and that younger generations, as they become voters, will take on board a different set of values to the way that the current world works, which will lead us to a much better place.

But it could go the other way, where we end up going through a horrific decade or two where we experience major food shortages. So, right now, I split my time between working on the climate impacts of food, finding out how to reduce those impacts and determining how to communicate some of these findings to the public, and also looking at how we actually prepare for potential catastrophes in the food system to avert civil unrest.

I want to find new pathways to avert disasters that could arise as a result of climate change and then lead to civil unrest. I want to find out how we can intervene early on to circumvent that happening and how we can respond in the event of a sudden shortage of food. All with the hope that we can live in a safe world for a long time to come.

KADDU KIWE SEBUNYA

CEO OF THE AFRICAN WILDLIFE FOUNDATION

In September 2023, I spoke to Kaddu Kiwe Sebunya, CEO of the African Wildlife Foundation. Kaddu is a powerful voice on the continent, who rallies Africans to lead the fight against the destruction of valuable habitats and wildlife. He has over 20 years' experience in conservation at grassroots, national and regional levels in Africa, Europe and the US. Kaddu has also worked with Oxfam UK, the International Union for Conservation of Nature, the US Peace Corps, Conservation International and Solimar International.

Africa concluded its first Climate Summit in September 2023. Do you believe it was a success? Will it help protect Africa's wildlands and species?

I believe it was a success. While it took time to happen, it shows how Africa is redefining its role. The region has never been given the chance to do so before. If we look at COP27, which was held in Egypt, it was a meeting in Africa, yet African voices were almost invisible. The Africa Climate Summit allowed us to be heard. Africa seeks to be seen as more than a beneficiary of aid-designed programmes; it has always wanted to be a stakeholder in global policy processes. This is a continent that has strongly been pushing to be seen as a leader, and that's the difference and that's critical. Africa wants to be involved in setting the global agenda, and this is also important for our mission here at the African Wildlife Foundation.

At the summit, I saw all types of African leaders – heads of state, leadership from youth and civil society organizations, leaders of rural communities, and leaders from the African private sector. This was key, because in Africa, we need everyone to come together to galvanize political unity, which means success in reframing the narrative.

The summit put Nature at the heart of the conversations, and Nature is at the crux of climate action. We saw Africa discussing its financial needs, with conversations about transforming the global economic system. This was discussed with an African voice and perspective – that's radical! It was successful and really got the right conversation going. Harnessing the power of biodiversity demands a collective effort and dedicated resources. The climate finance solutions we craft must be attuned to the needs of Africa. It is not enough for these solutions to be one-size-fits-all; they must consider Africa's diverse realities.

You're absolutely right. When we think about Africa, we think of aid for food poverty, vulnerable communities and vaccination projects, but really what the world needs to consider is investing in Africa's biodiversity, which will benefit the entire planet.

Absolutely! You know, Africa has about 30% of the world's biodiversity and that is not by accident – it is inherent in our culture, our systems, the way we live, and the relationships that Africans have with local ecosystems; we pride ourselves on our rich biodiversity. However, until now, economic aspirations have mostly been driven by Western policies, which have planned and implemented Africa's economic development and driven the narrative of our livelihoods, cultures and relationship with our biodiversity. But now, Africa is defining that involvement, and the choices we make in that process will determine what's going to happen next.

The biodiversity protection programmes that we have had so far haven't given us the results we want or need. They have directed us to hire the guns; train the snipers to protect the rhinos; build the fences around national parks; hire thousands of rangers. And yet, still, we are failing to protect wildlife in certain areas. That's because these programmes were not initially designed to connect with the local communities and their livelihoods. This fortress-based conservation model hasn't been part of the cultural and social values of Africa. Another point to make is that the climate change conversation and the financial models that are being discussed are using an old playbook of only being focused on protectionism, and about investing in Africa's forests in Central Africa and elsewhere. How will that work? How will it be sustainable when there are people living in these forests? How is it feasible to protect these massive areas?

Africa offers the world a unique path, where development happens in harmony with wildlife and their habitats. It holds 30% of global biodiversity, including almost a third of global fresh water, and our rainforests have now surpassed the Amazon, with the Congo Basin as the world's largest carbon sink.

At the African Wildlife Foundation, we believe that wildlife and wildlands have intrinsic value worthy of protection, and that our wildlife is a treasured resource. The world's clean air, clean water, food security and climatic regulation relies on Africa's wildlands and species, which keep everything healthy. But much of Africa's wildlife and wildlands are in crisis, which is threatening both Nature and the natural resource base for much of Africa and the world's population.

The Western conversation is narrow, concentrating on how trees absorb carbon – trees that have existed for more than 400 to 600 years, that have been protected and managed by Africans during this time, because they are part of our history. We are the natural custodians of these forests. They do not belong to us but to the world – but as Africans we need to take responsibility as stewards of this global resource. Instead, what the West should be saying is, "Let's invest in Africa's prosperity."

Until now, everyone who has protected and invested in these custodian programmes has been driven mostly by international conservation NGOs. Historically, Africa's biodiversity plans have been outsourced to international NGOs, foreign researchers and scientists, mostly Western men, and it hasn't given us the results we need. Africa has suffered from wrong assumptions and stereotypes because the rest of the world has spoken for us and given us the aid they think we need.

But things are changing, and the world is waking up and realizing that these old programmes do not work in addressing the challenges of climate change and biodiversity. The world needs to come and meet us where we are. And thankfully, this conversation is starting. The world has opportunities here.

And of course, Africa needs help, especially with technology, as almost 70% of the technology we need to develop already exists outside the region. So how do we deliver that quickly? We especially need to consider the growing population here, where more than half of Africa's 54 nations will double – or more – by 2050, and the continent will then be home to at least 25% of the world's population, who will be young people. This young labour force will be looking for opportunities and making different choices than their parents, and they will want urban development, like has happened in China. However, the quality of life in Africa is worrisome as unemployment is on the rise. We need to invest in sustainable livelihoods and create conditions where people thrive while coexisting with Nature.

As a global community, we must find a path that leapfrogs Africa's prosperity, so that we don't recreate the same carbon-based industrialized infrastructure the West built upon. We need to build sustainable economies. For instance, how does Africa leapfrog into solar energy and hybrid cars? We also need decisions around energy and the future energy source for Africa.

This will include decisions around food security, and how Africa will feed two billion people in the next 20 years – that's all part of the biodiversity goals and climate solutions that we need.

It's no longer about increasing wildlife management. The COVID-19 global pandemic has already taught us that when we, as humans, locked ourselves away, stayed at home and stopped managing the wildlife, the wildlife thrived without us. During the pandemic, we saw the regeneration of forests in many parts of Africa. So, it's our behaviours that we need to invest in, and I tell those who are propagating carbon markets and carbon systems that carbon is in people's heads. We need to change people's mindsets and aspirations, and how they implement those aspirations for their survival. We need to build a post-carbon Africa.

The African Union has been made a permanent member of the G20. Will this advance the region's climate needs?

This has been exciting, especially for me, my generation. We are excited that this has happened, and we've been asking for this for such a long time and been working hard behind the scenes to achieve it. As Africans, we want to move to a world stage as a continent. Our weakness has been that we've been so divided, which has weakened our voice on the global stage. But now to be a union with the negotiating power of 1.3 billion people – that's the way we can succeed. We are organizing ourselves through our economic discussions and policies to coordinate a trading bloc. We have opened embassies in Brussels and New York, where we want to find mutual climate solutions and benefits for the rest of the world.

A lot of work must be done. It's going to depend on how we show up to the rest of the world, how prepared we are, and how other countries accept and support the African Union. Let's not forget that we are a continent with more than 2,000 distinct languages – we have a third of the world's languages – and that's apart from the 54 countries with different currencies. We need to be joined up in our thinking to be recognized by the international community.

And Africa will take this opportunity – it's a very big step forward. I am also telling African leaders that it is not up to the rest of the world to define us. As the world recognizes our value, they will use us in so many of the discussions between the US and China, between Europe and Russia, etc., and that's fine. That's how the world global systems work, but we need to have our own agenda.

With the right infrastructure, could Africa be feeding the world? If so, what needs to happen?

Look, the way that Africa sees the world is based on a mixture of optimism and reservations. Recent statistics show that about 60% of the world's uncultivated arable land is in Africa, which, with the right infrastructure and technology, has the potential to feed the world – this goes back to what I was talking about earlier.

The reality is that until now, Africa has not been allowed to achieve its potential. We have never received the support or technology to take advantage of our arable land, which can be part of the climate change solution. Enabling Africa to feed itself and realize its potential of becoming a global agricultural powerhouse requires development of large-scale commercial farming using cutting-edge technologies – as opposed to what we are currently doing, with people needing more land to produce a few kilos of wheat or maize or corn, which is highly water intensive. Farming here requires strong and effective support to small-scale farmers to enhance their production and competitiveness in the market.

You have to ask yourself: why is Europe investing in greenhouses to produce food when it could be investing in Africa? The recent *Global Nutrition Report* highlights the economic benefits of investing in sustainable agriculture,[95] and studies show that every $1 invested in nutrition can generate $16 in returns.[96] It's a win–win. I hope that whoever is going to represent Africa puts these issues on the table and demands a discussion.

If you could change one thing across Africa, what would that be?

One?! Oh gosh – more than anything else, it would be to create a profound shift in mindset and a belief in African leadership when it comes to these global negotiations – a mindset of "yes, we can!" We need to believe in ourselves, our systems, our cultures and our societies. This shift of perspective will be a transformative change for the continent. For centuries, we have been encouraged to think we cannot provide solutions to our own problems, but that is starting to change among young people, who now know that Africa possesses solutions to its problems, and to global challenges like climate change and biodiversity.

We need to reframe the narrative that has been driven by others who define our potential through the lens of poverty, decrying that Africans are living below $1 a day. Of course, I am not advocating for poverty, but why don't they say instead, "Africans survive on $1 a day – what can we learn from that?"

Shouldn't we all be looking to live leanly on the planet? How does it benefit the world for everyone to be chasing consumption-based standards of living? GDP is all about production, production and more production; it is about utilization, utilization and more utilization; it is about consumption, consumption and more consumption. Why is that? Why is that seen as the best marker of progress?

The world has a limit and we cannot all live like North America. The planet cannot accommodate that, but global systems are designed to chase wealth. That's what our leaders respond to. I tell you what's funny – in Africa, if you sell timber, you can get wealthy. If you cut down a forest to produce sugar, or if you start to export cars, you will grow your economy. That is how the world is designed. And how Africa is incentivized to approach development within the global economic system – just think about that.

Today the world has bitcoin, blockchain and valid promissory notes that you can cash in a bank. You can walk into a store and buy things on credit with a piece of plastic. But the punchline is that if you are like Zimbabwe with 200,000 elephants, they have no value on the global market. You are a poor country, like the Democratic Republic of Congo, which is a country that is 70% forests, more than any country on the planet, but your wealth in economic terms is determined by cutting down the forest for timber, to produce something like furniture. This is the world we live in; we need to reimagine wealth and prosperity.

We are all Africans; I hope you believe that.

I do!

Africa has the last wildcard for the rest of the world. If allowed, it can save this world – but only if it is given a chance and if the world can listen. I have addressed the European parliamentarians, and they told me that the root cause of the depression in Europe is climate change. To understand this in the context of Africa, let's look at Lake Chad as an example. It is the biggest lake in Central and Western Africa and was previously 72% bigger than it is today, but it has shrunk in my lifetime. This has taken away the livelihoods of more than ten million people, because of the ecosystem services the lake provided for rural life. Those people are now moving to urban areas.

By 2050, a quarter of the world's people will be African. This will shape our collective future, as four out of ten young people will be Africans. This will change population dynamics, as Europe will not have enough workers. Look at Japan – it is the first country to announce that its death rate has surpassed its birth rate, and that's going to happen in Europe. Who's going to work in the industries there?

What do you want your legacy to be?

This is one of the most difficult questions for me. I really hope what I leave behind is Africa speaking with one voice. That we are able to show up in ways that are respected by the rest of the world. I have testified before the US Congress, addressed the EU and been to China – talking to all these different governments, to ensure that Africa is the cornerstone of global conversations because the international stage cannot move forward without Africa.

I have brought my colleagues into the conservation sector with a sense of responsibility because this is an area that has historically been shaped by the West, and as a result Africans have checked out, not being empowered to see conservation as integral to their lives. Instead, it has been the role of the many international NGOs, which have had support and therefore been more successful, which means that their legacy has power. There are also very few Black African CEOs of nonprofits, or charities or NGOs in global conservation. In other sectors we have a couple, such as in the area of health, but in this field we are invisible. Therefore, I take my role very seriously and I lead with purpose, passion and utmost care.

I am also concerned about our young people, who are losing their traditional connection to Nature, so I am driving a big youth strategy programme. Young Africans, who make up 70% of this continent, need to be in leadership positions. They need to be allowed to make decisions and be heard. We need to focus on the managers of these young people too. These are their mothers – women who are helping Africa win. We need to invest in them too for us to succeed. Through our programmes, we listen to the youth and bring their voices to the table.

My legacy is ultimately one of being a connector, of being able to talk to all types of people, from country leaders to sellers on the roadside. I hope that by focusing on empowering Africans at all levels – to define our own conservation agenda and to be the champions of Nature and climate action, harmonizing with Nature on our terms – that we rise fast in the world. Simultaneously, Africa needs to show up with skills, resiliency and clarity on what we want and what we don't want. My legacy is really the deep desire for transformation, where the leadership of Africa resonates with a profound respect for Nature and a commitment to sustainable progress.

MICHAEL TINGSAGER

LEADING FOOD INDUSTRY EXPERT

In November 2023, I spoke with Michael Tingsager, a leading food industry expert and the host and creator of the award-winning podcast Hospitality Mavericks.[97] Michael has been involved in food since childhood and worked at his mum and dad's small restaurant group in rural Denmark. He is behind Pulse Kitchen, whose purpose is to change the world by changing the way we eat; to empower people to cook delicious, healthy meals in minutes to improve their quality of life; and to help transition our food systems to nourish people and heal the planet.[98]

I love Pulse Kitchen's strapline, "Together we can change the world by changing the way we eat." And it has an interesting philosophy, which is "eat like a bear." What does that mean?

This is a philosophy that we as a team came up with, which is based on how bears eat. The interesting thing about bears is that, contrary to popular belief, they don't eat meat all the time – they are primarily plant eaters. They supplement their diet when it's salmon season and will eat meat when there's a carcass left and killed by another animal. Bears are not hunters and primarily source their food from plants, berries, nuts and seeds, which grow in season and are local. Therefore, their footprint on the world is very small and so, when you "eat like a bear," you are eating in a way that's sustainable. This is the Pulse Kitchen philosophy. If you delve into the original eating habits of humans, you see that our diet was predominantly plant based, so when it comes to pulses, it's the healthiest and most sustainable protein to eat.

If we all thought about "eating like a bear," we would probably see some significant, positive and quick changes in the world; it is possible to live without huge meat consumption. At Pulse Kitchen, we take people on a food journey, taking them back to eat what we already have in Nature. This helps us live and eat more consciously and in tune with our surroundings. It is also very good for your body and mind.

Do you believe we can change the world by changing the way we eat?

Yes, I definitely do! There's no doubt about it – we can do this and it's already happening. We're not there yet, but we are all becoming more conscious about what food does in connection to our health and aware about ultra-processed food. This is very much on the food agenda, though it is fair to say that it could be middle-class awareness at the moment.

I have a strong belief that people understand more than we think about the impact that food systems have on the world from a climate and economic perspective. Sadly, the way we have created our food systems means they have become our nemesis, and may well bring about our end, if we don't do something different. However, it's not a black-and-white issue – it's not about "if you don't eat in season or eat less meat then you are evil or if you do this, you are good." It is about thinking about how we can change the world by changing the way we eat.

It's not about stopping eating meat or everyone becoming vegan, because that's impossible. There's lots of global cultural reasons why this can't happen, and we do need animals to be part of the farming practice. Instead, it is about reducing meat consumption and getting the balance right. We need to become aware of how much food we put on our plate, as that has a huge impact not just on our own health but the planet's health too.

A quick question: do you mean we as an international community? Or is it what we do in the West?

While there's definitely a need for change in the West, we are now seeing in the West certain groups of people changing the way they eat because their wealth has reduced and they want to eat healthily but economically. In big countries like India and China, the majority of the population are already eating this way, because it's part of their cultural diet and many of the vulnerable people in these societies cannot afford meat. But I also think this goes for other populations in other parts of the world too, where their income has reduced, so it has become a global thing.

Another point to highlight is that eating is something we all do, irrespective of where we live. And it is one thing that we do try to control – we try to control what we eat, how we eat and where we get our food from, which can feel empowering. I know that sadly some people can't even feed themselves, but if the majority of us start making the right decision, then maybe there is also the possibility of making their lives better.

I quickly want to touch on the food industry itself, as we don't talk a lot about the power of the food industry, which wants to sell us things because they make a profit. I am on a mission, and I want to change this sector from the inside out. I want to help find solutions to our health, climate issues and the quality of the jobs we have created within this sector. I see my job as helping people act and put good, healthy food on the table. I believe pulses are key to making this transition. The interesting thing is that we have pulses in all food cultures, which makes this movement easy to support, as we don't need to change much. The movement would also be great for the soil on our farmlands, as there are so many benefits to growing lentils.

Eating a handful of pulses every day has been endorsed by the blue zones around the world,[99] where pulses are the backbone of people's diets. They do lots of other things as well: they have less screen time and lots of community events – and there's still room for meat.

What is soil health?

Soil health is important for our wellbeing and for the future of the planet. It's now becoming popular in mainstream conversations, but still not enough people are talking about it and there's a reason we need to do so. Often, soil is regarded as dirt, but this is not correct, as the soil is where everything comes from. It has taken me years to understand the power of soil and why it's so important to us. It's not just about farmland, but the quality of farmland. Those who have seen a harvest will have seen some really dark soil, which is healthy soil. Those of us who have seen grey soil will know there's a difference.

The quality of the food and the nutrition that comes from healthy soil – which is the black, brown, really mushy kind of stuff – is high and nutritious. The vitamins and minerals we get out of that food are all the things we need for our body.

We are killing the soil. This started after the Second World War, because we had a hunger crisis, especially in Europe but in other parts of the world too. At that time, we discovered something called synthetic nitrogen, which was used in bombs but could also be used in farming to make things grow faster. Today we know it as fertilizer.

We started using it heavily in our farming practices and over the years it has killed off our farmland. We now have food deserts, like in some parts of the US. But it is possible to bring this soil to life again, by changing our farmers' practices and removing the fertilizers.

We need to bring in farming practices that use crop rotation and don't heavily produce one thing. If we don't fix that problem, I believe we're going to have serious issues around having enough healthy food for everyone, which will result in food wars and hunger. That's the extreme version of what can happen – some say we're very far from that, and others believe we are very close to that scenario.

It has taken us almost 80 years, since the Second World War, to destroy so much farmland and soil. If we continue like this, everything will deteriorate faster and faster. Soil health is critical for the quality of our food and for plant health, which is equivalent to our own health.

As consumers, we need to start thinking about where our food comes from and what's actually happening to it, because this might not be what you think. Lots of farmers want to change things, but they are also trying to run a business, and they need help setting up systems to help them go back to better practices. But sadly, lots of farmers are trapped in the system of producing very, very cheap raw materials to sell on.

I don't believe we should just destroy all the old systems because that will create chaos. Every time you break something down, it has huge consequences for a big group of people. It could be jobs, livelihoods and so on. What I believe we need is to transition faster to achieve better food systems. It is not happening fast enough. How do we adapt our food systems to make a new, better version?

The other thing I want to add is that it's important to have tasty food, and for this we need good soil health, because it gives the flavour to our fresh produce. While there's now more media attention being given to this topic, which is helping raise awareness among everyday consumers, there's still a lot of work that needs to be done. If you think back to just 50 years ago, I believe people were far more connected with where the food came from and how it actually got to the table. How can we help people cook more – take control of their food – so they perhaps choose options that support better health and nutrition? Of course, it's a complicated world and there are budget constraints, but if we understand how to best use that budget, then things change and improve.

If you want to take action, you can start by eating more pulses, because it will drive this transition. No technology will be required, as the pulses will take care of it all. They will fix the soil quality and put the nitrogen back into the Earth.

> You advocate a diet consisting of four food groups that are recognized as being the healthiest and better for a longer life. What are these four food groups? Why is eating this way good for us and the planet?

It comes back to "eat like a bear" again and what you're putting on your plate. Half your plate should be covered with fruit and vegetables, then whole grains such as rice, or whatever carbohydrates you have. Whole grains are the fourth food group and what I have learned is that whole grains have protein in them. If you mix them together with pulses, you get the perfect protein. In the Western world, we have so much protein – much more than we actually need.

It is important for us to understand how to put that plate together. If our foundational plate comprises four food groups - fruit and vegetable, whole grains and pulses, we can then add seeds and nuts. It means we are starting in the right place. It's a very good place for ourselves, and it will start helping the planet and our food systems. I mentioned the blue zones, and there is the Blue Zone Diet. This is what its plate of food looks like – we call it the healthy eating plate at the Pulse Kitchen. It can be enjoyable, because it's also about learning the principles of how you cook with vegetables, which is a skill that I think we've forgotten.

Cooking is so important. We've forgotten how to be in the kitchen, and when you cook, you have a better relationship with your food. It's about falling in love with the process, and everybody knows when a plate of food has been cooked with love. I also think that we in the food industry need to fall in love with serving people in the best possible way.

My last question: what would you like your legacy to be?

That's a very big question. I would start by hoping that I have nudged and will continue to nudge people in the food industry in the right direction. I want to help this sector fall in love with delivering high-quality food to people, and there are no compromises. Actually, I know that's what the majority of people who work in this industry want, but it comes back again to constraints of money, systems and the mindset that "this is the way we do it – it can't be changed." I see it all the time. I believe all the traditional models we've been talking about have to slowly be integrated to pave a better way ahead.

When we start to find long-term solutions to the issues caused by climate change, we will start to solve some health issues along the way, reducing the pressures on health systems. We'll end up with a better food system. And it will improve mental health in general for us all.

If I can get people to believe they have food choices and are in control, that will be rewarding for me, because our food choices matter. It's not relevant if it is one meal a day, one meal a week, one meal a month. The main thing is for people to start to believe they are in control, which will allow them to take other positive actions. This will be enough of a legacy for me, because then I will know there is hope for the planet.

SHRISTI ADHIKARI

AGRICULTURALIST

In early September 2023, I spoke to agriculturalist Shristi Adhikari, who lives in Nepal. Shristi works to empower female farmers in her country. The Youth Ag Summit 2021 recognized her as one of the top 100 global young leaders finding solutions to "how to feed a hungry planet." In 2021 and 2022, Shristi was awarded UN Framework Convention on Climate Change scholarships to attend COP26 (in Egypt) and COP27 (in the UK). In March 2021, she received a grant from the Regen Grant Fund in the category 'Real Food System,' as part of the organization's Top Ten Youth Ambassadors programme, which focuses on youth who introduce a climate change project in their local community.

What do food systems mean and why are they relevant to us?

Food systems are the entire process, from growing crops, to production and processing, to quality control, transportation and marketing – and it doesn't end there. There is another important part, which is what happens when the food is on our plate and food waste. It's not just about the farmers, though of course farmers have a primary role. There are lots of other parts, from the middlemen to us as consumers.

Food systems are relevant to us in different ways, from the families who cannot manage to secure a daily meal in a developing country like Nepal, to those who can have a daily meal on their plate but maybe don't value it, and the food is wasted. This is all part of the food system. We talk a lot about the impact of climate change on food production, but we need to understand that the food system produces a lot of carbon dioxide gas, which is contributing to the greenhouse gases – just one kilogram of food waste can produce 2.5 kilograms of carbon dioxide!

When I was in the first year of my bachelor's degree, I was surprised to see the food waste in my college canteen, especially all the eggshells being thrown away. I decided to do an experiment and asked the canteen to give me the discarded eggshells. Of course, they were surprised, as no one had ever asked this before. I took the eggshells and mixed them with the soil and used this enriched soil on tomato plants. I had one tomato plant using the eggshell soil and another tomato plant using ordinary soil. I kept both plants in the sunlight and after a few weeks when they grew, I measured their length.

The one with the eggshells had grown taller than the one with ordinary soil. This simple experiment showed that food waste can act as a fertilizer.

This approach is a solution to the problem of wasting food whose production has contributed to the buildup of carbon dioxide. I believe it's critical to recognize that food systems are not only about how much you produce or how much you consume, but how you manage the waste.

As individuals, we have a responsibility. Most of the waste is produced from our homes, and that's where we need to manage the problem. The solution can come from us, right from our kitchen table, so, let's do it! We have lots to do in managing waste, and it will help toward reducing our own carbon footprint. That's why the food system is very, very relevant to us.

What are some of the ways that we can feed a growing population?

This was my question too when I attended the international Youth Ag Summit in 2021. I was selected to represent Nepal and it was a big moment for me. The company Bayer hosted the conference and it was supposed to be held in China, but because of the global pandemic, it was virtual. There were 100 global delegates and at that time I put forward my idea for feeding a growing population, which is based on conservation agriculture practices and focused on three principles. The first is minimum soil tillage, which is the agricultural preparation of soil by digging, stirring and overturning; the second is permanent soil cover, which is important in conservation agriculture, as it protects the topsoil from erosion and maintains moisture; and the third is diversification of plant species, which means having a wide variety of plant species in the natural environment. These practices are about investing in soil, which will increase productivity over time – they do not reap instant results. What we need is for these practices to be implemented country by country, and now slowly the government in Nepal is beginning to advocate these methods.

We must not forget other ways to help feed the growing world population, and I do want to flag up food waste again. Currently, approximately a third of the food produced is wasted. If used in another way – for example, as compost for the soil or upcycled for those who need food – it will have a positive impact. I know this may sound like a social solution and not a scientific concept, but this is a conservation agriculture practice.

Another approach to feed our world is a plant-based diet instead of a meat-based diet. I know that in many of our cultures, people enjoy eating meat, and I'm not saying that people should give up eating meat completely – not at all. By reducing the amount of meat in your diet and increasing the amount of plants, you can have an impact. We do need to recognize that meat-based food uses a lot of energy during the manufacturing process. From the rearing of the livestock to its production and manufacturing – the whole process uses lots of energy.

One other idea is to increase indoor farming practices, because feeding a growing population means increasing food production, which means increasing the farming land, but land is becoming limited. So instead of increasing the land, because we don't have enough land space, let's start to focus on indoor and rooftop farming, like here in Kathmandu, where we have increased our farming on rooftops. These small things, which may not sound like a big deal, do make a difference.

I also want to mention climate-smart integrated pest-management practice. Again using Nepal as an example, in this mountainous area we have lots of apple farming that's been affected by climate change. What we did was use climate-smart integrated pest-management practices, where instead of using chemical fertilizers, we used microorganisms as a fertilizer. This is a green fertilizer that improves soil nutrients and crops, making them disease resistant and promoting plant growth, with no pollution to the environment.

Also, intercropping is a good practice. This is where you grow two types of crops in the same field, such as apples along with potatoes. It includes tree management, which is essentially pruning trees by cutting away the unnecessary branches that may hinder the trees' development.

So different actors have different roles to play, and we have various methods to increase food production for the growing population.

On that topic, because we've talked about different actors, what are the climate challenges that female farmers face - particularly the female farmers you've been working with in Nepal?

I think what most people don't know is that more than 70% of farmers here in Nepal are female farmers and are automatically impacted and more exposed to climate change.

In 2022, I was assigned as an intern in the mountainous region of Nepal in a place called Mustang, which is famous for its apple farming. I found that the farmers were facing lots of challenges due to the changes to the climate, from rising temperatures to irregular rainfall. Every year there was something, such as flooding, landslides or even droughts. In fact, about a month ago, half of the houses were swept away because of the floods. It affected the apple production and a lot of the apple yield was of low quality, because of the insect pests eating the apples.

Added to this, as I mentioned these farmers are predominantly female, and apart from being on the farm, they also handle the household activities and the children. Plus, many of the men from these families are migrating toward cities or going abroad to find better employment opportunities. These female farmers have a huge burden and a double responsibility.

Moreover, they have no skills and don't know what climate change is in scientific terms, but when I asked them, "Do you think there is heavier rainfall every year?" they said, "Yes, we know the rainfall is getting heavier." If you asked them, "Is the temperature increasing?" they said, "Yes." If you asked them "Do you see these changes impacting your production?" they answered, "Yes, they are." And when I asked them, "Do you know the solution, or what is your adaptation strategy?" they didn't know and replied, "We are growing apples in our own way and we don't know anything, but we want to be educated!" Therefore, these female farmers need a proper and sustained education programme.

Do you believe female farmers are being heard in the current climate conversation? If not, what is needed to drive awareness?

The first thing that comes to mind is the UN's COP events, which are important conferences. I participated at COP26, in the UK, and COP27, in Egypt. The first COP was in 1995, before I was born, and this year we will have COP28. So far, from the first to the 28th COP, there have been only five female presidents. So, how can we expect female voices to be heard equally?

But maybe to a certain degree, our voices are being heard, because lots of people are talking about gender and climate, and people are realizing that women are more vulnerable to climate disasters. However, at COP27, only 38% of the participants were female and, to me, this shows that there has not been enough participation from women in the current climate conversations.

I belong to SHE Changes Climate, where we campaign for the equal inclusion of women at the top levels of all climate negotiations, and for the implementation of the updated Gender Action Plan from COP25 in 2019.[100] At COP27 in 2022, SHE Changes Climate worked toward its global mission to ensure all delegations, for all climate negotiations, have at least a 50% representation of women at their top levels now and in the future, and we suggested that COP adopts a copresidency approach. This is because we are more powerful when women and men lead together to build a movement for collaborative climate action and systemic change.

In September 2022, we sent an open letter to the COP27 presidency and leadership team, calling on them to deliver greater accountability and transparency on male–female parity on the Egyptian COP27 leadership team. Our letter was supported by over 700 female and male environmental leaders worldwide. We recognize it's difficult, and it takes time to be heard, but we all need to keep taking steps forward.

Do you think COP is important and is it really making a difference?

COP gives people a platform, gives hope, allows for networking and creates positive channels. Plus, it's a high-level climate discussion with world leaders. However, my participation has been as an observer – I am not involved in the negotiations, even though I have first-hand knowledge and experience of what is happening on the ground. I do believe it is important to have people like me in the room to be heard and help make the changes that are desperately needed. Being at the side events at COP does not allow things to happen.

It is important to be in the room – to be able to speak and tell the leaders what we need. If I'm representing the voices of Global South female farmers, I should be able to represent their needs. Instead, in my experience, what you have at COP is people from 190 countries just sitting around like it's a shopping mall. It seems that climate has become more like a brand, where you go to COP to post some pictures on social media. It is a very big platform to attend but we need to utilize it.

You're full of passion and still starting out on your journey, so this might be a difficult question, but what legacy do you want to leave?

Legacy is a very big word and I have never thought about it – but there is one thing that I will say, and that's wherever I go, whatever I do, big or small, what is important is tomorrow's generation. The next generation might not know my name, but I hope they will see my work ten years from now and that it will have made a difference in the field of agriculture. I want the work that I do to inspire the next generations, and for them to do better than me. I believe your work should always be your identity.

When I was about eight years old, I used to ask my father, "Why do people write books about others?" My father would say, "Because they have done some remarkable work." From then on, I always wanted someone to write about me. My father would say, "Do good work, and one day people will write about you." That has always had an impact on me, that I should do something to be an example for the upcoming generation. So, being interviewed at the age 25, by you, is like a dream come true.

I think another important thing to add about my legacy, being a girl in a patriarchal society where people always expect a son as the firstborn, was that I was the first granddaughter in my family. My grandma has always been proud of me, especially when she saw me attending international conferences, and that has had an impact. I want to show that a girl can do the same things as a boy; that too would be my legacy.

CHAPTER 9

INDIA

You are probably wondering why I have a whole chapter dedicated to a country in a book about climate change. Well, it's for a few reasons. This is a country that has a population of 1.4 billion people, which is now the biggest population in the world, overtaking China. This is a timely reminder of the growing influence that India and its activities exert on the rest of the world, and not just because of its size. India is under no illusions about the threats it is facing because of global warming and has been slowly taking on a global role in the Earth's fight against the climate crisis.

Just to note, I am not backing one political leader or party over another. I know that there are both good and bad things happening. I am not focused on that. Instead I am focused on India's role – especially as I have a theory, which is that India has a lot to offer the world in this fight against climate change, offering real opportunities, solutions, hope and leadership, including a voice for the Global South.

EMERGING INDIA – MOTHER INDIA

Historically, India has remained the hub of climate protection and environmental sustainability. Its traditional literature and practices have always taken a holistic view of natural resources – and this is Bhārat Mātā (Mother India), which is a national personification of India (Bhārat) as a mother goddess. I believe India is looking outward, taking this role to the world, continuing her legacy to become Mother India to the world, helping us reconnect to Mother Nature. India has frequently been acknowledged for its cooperation and efforts to promote climate change mitigation and environmental sustainability. This has been done through policy measures, facilitating dialogue between nations and taking decisive steps to encourage renewable energy, incentives for the production of solar technologies, and ramping up the production of green hydrogen. Mother India is emerging as an inspiration for countries around the globe, particularly on how economic development and conservation of the environment can go hand in hand.

I think it's important to note that while this is a nation that has broken free of its colonial past, its colonial legacy is alive in the present. The colonial grabbing of land not only dispossessed people of territories and resources but also altered what were previously sustainable local ecosystems. From the late 1800s, oak and deodar forest areas were cut down by the British for commercial purposes for more than a century, which in turn resulted in more intense and frequent wildfire events in India's Western Himalayan regions. If that wasn't enough, the British colonists reorganized the agricultural system: India's land, previously used for low-scale subsistence agriculture, was now used for cash crops (cotton and tea). The Indian domestic economy and manufacturing base were destroyed and replaced with an economy geared for export to international markets.

India is not preaching anything that it is not doing itself. It is keen to nurture itself and is conscious, progressive and aspiring. Sustainability has always been a core component of the national culture, where Indian philosophy and values have underscored a sustainable way of life. These values were reinforced when India took up the presidency of the G20 at the end of 2022. The theme of its presidency – 'Vasudhaiva Kutumbakam,' which means 'The World Is One Family' – is drawn from the ancient Indian Sanskrit text of the *Maha Upanishad*. It affirms the value of all life – human, animal, plant and microorganism – and their interconnectedness on planet Earth and with the wider universe.

Vasudhaiva Kutumbakam is a saying that resonates on a human level with us all, and the principles offer a roadmap to a better future for all. By promoting unity, cooperation and mutual respect, we can work toward resolving conflicts and reducing inequalities. Vasudhaiva Kutumbakam fosters a world that is more peaceful and inclusive, and in which, importantly, we live in harmony with our ecosystems. There is also LiFE (Lifestyle for Environment), an initiative by the Indian government focused on environmental, sustainable and responsible choices, both at the level of individual lifestyles and at the national level. The hope is that it will lead to globally transformative actions resulting in a cleaner, greener and bluer future.

In April 2014, India became the first country to make corporate social responsibility (CSR) mandatory, following an amendment to the Companies Act, its business incorporation law. Since then, other countries have followed suit, including China and Indonesia. Through this law, Indian businesses can invest their profits in areas such as education, poverty relief, gender equality and hunger remediation, as part of their CSR compliance. All businesses (national and multinationals) with annual revenues of more than 10 billion rupees (£93 million) must give 2% of their net profit to charity. The Indian government believes the law will release much-needed funds for social development, and the general consensus has been that it's working. This legislative change has made corporate India wake up to its wider social responsibilities, and the domestic press has reported positively on its impact.

This idea of Mother India is further reinforced by the Energy World, which said that "India has become the fastest in renewal energy capacity addition among major economies that had added over 100 gigawatts of renewable energy capacity by the end of 2021 with the vision of 500 gigawatts by 2030."[101]

This is a nation that now has the lowest cost for large-scale solar power in the world and is poised to transform from a net importer of energy to a net exporter of energy.[102] India is a global leader in renewable energy, with the third-largest production of renewable energy in the world, the fourth-largest installed wind power capacity and the fifth-largest installed solar power capacity.[103] Moreover, today India has the lowest cost for setting up renewable energy capacity and its cost of green hydrogen is touted to be the most competitive globally in the near future.[104]

The energy transition holds huge significance in the new world order and has the capacity to influence and determine geopolitical change. Mother India has tremendous potential to lead the world in green energy and forward the cause of global good, in addition to generating green jobs. Clean energy and closing the energy access gap are good business. They are the ticket to growth and prosperity. By choosing a path where the economy and ecology can coexist happily, India has been able to protect the environment without blocking a large number of infrastructural projects. This urgency to become self-sufficient, as well as meet the energy needs of not just its own people but the global community, is about doing the right thing and I believe it will propel India further on its way to becoming a global superpower. As a global family and village, we should come together to learn from each other, and good lessons can be drawn and implemented from both ancient wisdom and scientific fact.

CHALLENGES OF CLIMATE CHANGE

At the time of writing, the World Bank's latest India Development Update (April 2023) noted that although significant challenges remained in the global environment, India was one of the fastest-growing economies in the world.[105]

Most of India forms a peninsula, which means it is surrounded by water on three sides. The world's highest mountain range, the Himalayas, rises in the north, while the southeast is bordered by the Bay of Bengal and the southwest is bordered by the Arabian Sea. Its terrain varies widely, from the Thar Desert in the west to jungles in the northeast. A fertile area called the Ganges Plain covers much of northern India. The nation's terrain is as diverse as its culture, which is a land of 22 recognized official languages. Known as one of the oldest civilizations in the world, acknowledged for its culture, history and heritage, today it has the world's third-largest economy in purchasing power, and its recent growth has been a significant achievement. India's official name is the Republic of India, or Bhārat Gaṇarājya, and since independence in 1947, it has had an agricultural revolution, which has transformed it from chronic dependence on grain imports into an agricultural powerhouse and now a net exporter of food.

However, with its vast size and ecological diversity, India is already experiencing many of the worst impacts of climate change. Floods and droughts are becoming all too frequent and severe, causing major damage to food systems, local economies and human health. Climate change hits the most vulnerable hardest and is undermining the country's progress in bringing millions out of poverty. In June 2023, temperatures in several parts of India soared to over 45°C. In a little over two decades, the country's climate is estimated to exceed survivability limits. Its water crisis continues to escalate, with experts warning that India's groundwater table risks steady depletion over the next two decades – this would have a cascading effect on irrigation, agricultural production and livelihoods. Therefore, with such a large and still industrializing country come challenges. Where in spite of the fact that the nation consists of over 17% of the world's population, this is a population that only accounts for only about 5% of global emissions, yet India is the world's third-largest emitter of carbon dioxide.

While its per capita greenhouse gas emissions are among the lowest in the world, it is the third-biggest generator of these climate-altering gases. And while it may be the third-largest economy in the world, it has the greatest number of people living below the international poverty line.[106] It is a country trying to quickly achieve equitable economic growth to meet the changing needs and lifestyle aspirations of its 1.4 billion people, while also hitting national and global climate change targets. This great landscape is facing a dark challenge, as this is one of the world's most climate-vulnerable countries. Climate change is already affecting human health, wildlife, food production, clean water access and the economy at large, and the country is experiencing higher temperatures every year.

By 2030, over 160–200 million people across the country could be exposed to lethal heatwaves annually, and around 34 million people will face job losses due to a heat-stress-related productivity decline. Currently food losses due to heat during transportation are worth close to $13 billion annually.[107] India's dependence on an increasingly erratic monsoon for its water requirements makes the situation more difficult. The climate crisis will intensify this pressure on water resources, even as the frequency and intensity of floods and droughts in the country increase.

One of the most pressing environmental issues in India is air pollution. According to the 2021 World Air Quality Report, India is home to 63 of the

100 most polluted cities in the world, with New Delhi having the worst air quality in the world.[108] Moreover, even though since 2015 the number of people working in renewable energy in India has increased fivefold, there is an access rate of 95%, with 64 million Indians still being without access to electricity today. Plus, subsidies for fossil fuels are still some seven times higher than subsidies for clean energy. There is still work to do and opportunities to be grasped.

India has been trying to face up to its problems. It has been at the forefront of driving global action on climate change and emerged as a key player in shaping the 2015 Paris Agreement, part of the UN Framework Convention on Climate Change. It has used Indigenous technology to optimize its resources and promoted green energy to reduce carbon emissions. At COP26 in 2021, India pledged to reach net zero emissions by 2070.[109] This was one of the most important announcements and it did not go unnoticed. Critics wanted to see India make a stronger commitment. But we need to remember that India is on a growth trajectory.

THE ROLE OF INDIA'S YOUTH

The youth of India have immense potential and are already playing a key role in shaping the future. There is no denying that young people everywhere, not just in India, are among those who will be most negatively impacted by climate change, and they need to be involved in policies and discussions. They are needed to lead the way in promoting progressive ideas and climate justice projects to address the kind of future that they want for themselves. They are a critical and dynamic demographic of stakeholders who have a prominent role to play in achieving a just transition to a sustainable future.

Regarding the UN's Sustainable Development Goals, today's youth will influence the development of the goals, and they will be the ones to determine whether the 2030 Agenda for Sustainable Development is successful. In India, this younger generation must forge a cohesive voice in the debate over the country's transition to sustainable energy sources.

India's youth is one of the country's strongest assets and is strengthening the foundations for its bright future. According to projections from the UN Population Fund, India will continue to have one of the youngest populations in the world until 2030.[110] They are the future leaders and bring many benefits for economic development. They are more plugged in to the world than their parents and elders: half of Indians aged 15 to 24 have access to the internet via a phone, computer or other device.[111] They are vibrant, with an untapped potential for creativity, innovation and resilience. With their fresh perspectives, innovative ideas and boundless energy, they have the power to drive positive change in every aspect of society.

In the report *Rising to the Challenge: Youth Perspectives on Climate Change and Education in India*, published in 2021, 64% of the respondents said that they could explain climate change, while 70% were worried about the future effects of climate change. Another 84% stated that they would be keen to act to address climate change if they were given the needed support.[112] The youth in India are already responsible for a sizeable portion of jobs in the renewables sector, and they are emerging as a key source of talent for reaching energy access, renewable energy and energy efficiency targets. Mahatma Gandhi said, "Be the change you want to see in the world," and India's youth are already inspiring transformative action and bridging the gap between intent and impact.

Both the mood and style of India exude youthfulness, where the youth are leaders and not followers, and where it is essential to find solutions to overcome challenges and for the country to set new challenges for itself. This is a country with big ambitions. It has set a target of building a $5 trillion economy and becoming the third-largest economy in the world.[113] Alongside building its services and IT sectors, India knows its responsibilities toward the future mean it must work on the challenge of climate change. It recognizes that it has to set targets and achieve them in a timely manner.

CONCLUSION

Going back to my theory, India's geopolitical role is changing. India has emerged as one of the strongest global voices on climate change and has been at the forefront of driving global action on climate change. Renewable energy is growing faster in India than in any other major economy, and data shows it's on track to meet its emissions reduction target.[114] It has used Indigenous technology to optimize its resources and promoted green energy to reduce carbon emissions. Its youth are its powerhouse, galvanizing the country to be proactive in finding climate solutions, despite not being a major contributor to the crisis, and its announcement that it will establish a National Green Hydrogen Mission is noteworthy. It has also cofounded the International Solar Alliance with France, and in doing so is leading the global movement toward solar power, with a focus on promoting energy access and transition.[115] Already, the alliance has

110 member countries and is pursuing nine programmes promoting 10GW of off-grid and grid-connected solar projects in developing countries.

However, there is no denying that there are challenges and problems. India has severe air and water pollution, growing biodiversity loss because of development, waste management issues, water shortages and growing food shortages. Many will argue that India is not doing enough. A fine balancing act is needed as the country stands on the precipice of massive economic growth while seeking to meet its ambitious climate goals. It is crucial that India ensures its economic growth is balanced with social and environmental considerations; this is a nation situated on the front lines of climate change, where policies are not only about reducing greenhouse gases but also about providing people with a better quality of life.

TAKEAWAY

This simple takeaway is drawn from Gandhi, who is widely quoted as having said, "The future depends on what we do in the present." This takeaway requires us to build an understanding of emerging India, so we can be informed.[116]

A second takeaway is to use a minute of every day to be mindful about the consumer choices that you make. Can you buy items with less plastic? Do you need to drive or can you walk? Do you have your water bottle? Being mindful allows us to connect with ourselves and with the planet.

CHAPTER 10

IN CONVERSATION WITH VOICES ON INDIA

To help encapsulate the huge opportunities here, along with the impacts of climate change, I held conversations with some of the best minds in India to discuss the country's exciting opportunities and explore my theory. You will discover Sunita Narain, a leading Indian environmentalist and political activist; Sanjoy Roy, innovator and entrepreneur in the arts; Prachi Shevgaonkar, youth activist, trailblazer and founder of Cool The Globe; and Shombi Sharp, an American diplomat with the UN and UN Resident Coordinator in India.

SUNITA NARAIN

ENVIRONMENTALIST, ACTIVIST AND DIRECTOR GENERAL OF THE CENTRE FOR SCIENCE AND ENVIRONMENT

In February 2024, I spoke to environmentalist and influential political activist in the Indian green movement Sunita Narain, who is the Director General of the Centre for Science and Environment (CSE), a think thank based in Delhi. Sunita has held this role since 1982, building CSE into a significant independent institution that advocates for real change in India's environmental policies. Her work saw her named one of *Time* magazine's 100 most influential people in 2016.[117] In the same year, she appeared alongside Leonardo DiCaprio in the documentary *Before the Flood*, talking about the impact of climate change on India's monsoon and how this has affected farmers.

> During Prime Minister Narendra Modi's ten years in power, he has established India as a climate leader in the Global South. But his government has been criticized for diluting environmental protection laws to benefit business and perpetuating coal mining. Do you think India is positioned to become a world leader on climate change?

I do think Prime Minister Modi is very serious, and from what I hear, he definitely has the right intentions about moving India in this direction, but as you have mentioned, there are challenges. These challenges are not new to India and are the same challenges faced by other countries, where the route to what we call 'environmental sustainability' in the current pattern of growth, while paved with good intentions, has tough roadblocks.

The fact is that right now, India is dependent on coal – we get almost 80% of our energy from coal. To think that India can get out of coal while at the same time it needs to double its energy consumption between now and 2030 – that's a very tall order. It's not being done anywhere in the world. Countries like the UK have only moved away from coal because they have gas, and even now the UK is talking about going back to North Sea drilling. And I have just read about the farmers' protest in Europe, which has meant a dilution of the EU's environmental climate goals.

So, it is tough, and I think we should not make light of this because it's very easy to dismiss India and say, "Oh, you know, India's not serious," because it is serious! I think Prime Minister Modi is serious, but the situation is tough, and we need growth and development.

Now, you asked about the dilution of the environmental laws, and there is no doubt that we are seeing a swing in the pendulum right now. It's true we have not found a balance in the environmental laws of India, particularly in the regulations that were designed to shape decisions so as to achieve a balance between growth and the environment. Things have become cumbersome, complicated, corrupt and even abused. I wouldn't be a truthful environmentalist if I didn't say that to you or if I claimed that everything is okay. Over the last seven years, we have seen processes deteriorate so that the parliamentary committees have become faceless, deciding which projects are to be implemented, which projects won't be done, stopping projects. In the last government, there was a lot of stoppage of projects, but then those decisions were overturned and the projects went through. Even under the United Progressive Alliance, the maximum number of clearances were given.[118] But they were given with lots of conditions that were impossible to meet.

I believe that the environmental impact assessments of the clearance of forests are critical because they help determine how to mitigate the harm a project is doing and help improve a project's design to ensure that it is good for the environment and good for people. But today, because of the backlash against these systems, it is fair to say that laws are being watered down. While I'm not happy about this, I understand why the government is frustrated. They have inherited systems that are holding up growth.

I think it's important for India to now find balance again – I know we will, and we will find a way to protect the environment. The purpose of these regulations is not just to say "no" to projects. They are designed to enable careful decisions to make sure that projects are good for the environment and good for development.

Research shows that as much as 90% of the country will be in extreme heat and vulnerable danger zones. Do you think India is fully prepared to deal with climate change?

No way. Who can deal with this kind of extreme heat that we are talking about? The CSE has recently published a report on India's extreme weather events, and you will be shocked to find that there is one extreme weather event a day in India![119] That's extreme heat, extreme cold, landslides, extreme rainfall and even combinations.

Climate change is breaking the back of countries all over the world, and whether they accept it or not, even the rich are being affected. Look at California, which has experienced severe flooding: nowhere is immune from climate change. So, a country like India is really very vulnerable, and it's no fault of ours. It is important to know that the poor in the world are suffering today because of the emissions that have been released into the atmosphere, which are forcing the weather patterns to change. These are emissions that have come from the developed world and China. We need to make that clear – that the vulnerability of countries like India is not our fault. It is not because of us.

This heat is hard to endure and in 2022, here in India, we had this horrendous long period of extreme heat. I had lots of people calling me, asking, "How are you coping?" Well, quite frankly, my response was, "How can you even ask me this question?! I live in a house with air conditioning and I work in an office with air conditioners. I am protected to some extent, but have you thought of the farmers and labourers who are exposed to this heat without air conditioning? How are they managing?!" We need to put that human face on the environmental impacts of climate change and understand the impact on the poor.

We also need to understand how to cope, which means returning to old wisdoms that have worked well. We already know how to build for heat in our country. For instance, in the state of Rajasthan, the houses are built for heat, and modern science is now proving that these old systems and architecture are what is now required. In the past, people understood their local ecosystems. They built according to the orientation of the sun, they planted to avoid the extreme heat and they made sure they had bodies of water nearby. We really have to get back to that.

We have been mapping Indian cities in terms of where there are heat islands and it's not rocket science. Heat islands are where there are high-rise buildings, maximum concrete, the least amount of green, the least amount of water, and buildings wrongly built with glass and not bearing in mind the natural elements.

Therefore, keeping climate change in mind, there's a lot we will have to do, as we are already at a 1.1°C rise. We have enough emissions in the atmosphere to take us to at least 1.3 or 1.4, maybe even 1.5°C. We are close to that furnace and it's time we planned for it. That's something the Indian government is talking about – changing our building codes, talking about how to save energy by regulating the temperature in our air conditioners and talking about past architecture. But my complaint is that we're not doing it at the scale or the speed that is needed. That's really what we need to talk about.

The Indian government is aware and understands the crisis, and that we have to build differently and that we need to protect the poor. The government has included heatstroke in its disaster management code and is tracking the number of deaths that happen as a result of heat, but a lot more needs to be done.

You've touched on this, but is there anything to add about the consequences of India's development as the country gets hotter? I say this thinking about the disparity between the rich and people living in poverty.

People living in poverty don't have the luxury of cooling systems and will be more exposed, more vulnerable. However, there is no doubt that the poor in this country have actually learned how to live with heat better than the rich have. If you go to villages, you will find that they don't have air conditioners, but they have learned to build courtyards and have green areas. But I don't want to sound complacent or glib, saying, "Oh, the poor will cope with it." They can't, not at the scale we're dealing with – and in fact, they're going to be more exposed because they will be out in the fields. It's going to be very tough. I don't want to paint a doomsday scenario, but the reality is that it is going to be hard.

What are your hopes regarding India's fight against climate change?

My hope is that we will work on a strategy of benefits and deal with the issue of climate change, but what is also important is sustainable development. We need clean air in Delhi and across India, and to get clean air we need two things: first, clean fuel, and second, clean mobility. Those are the two biggest things.

Clean fuel means moving away from coal, which means we need to move either to gas or to electrification, where the thermal power plants are cleaned up at source. Clean mobility needs to be at a scale like we have never seen before. We have such horrendous air pollution and congestion, and we need to make sure we can provide for 100% of Delhi to be connected by a clean public transport system that is convenient and modern, and that the rich will use and the poor can afford. That's the challenge.

If we do that, then we can deal with the problem of climate change, because coal is what leads to climate change. So, we get out of coal, not only for climate change but to get the best benefits for us. We reinvent mobility, which means it will be good for us and good for climate change, because as you know, transport-related emissions are the biggest contributors to climate change today. These strategies need to be deliberate and scaled up. They have to be based on our core benefits: What is good for us today? What is affordable? And what is inclusive? Because if it is not affordable or inclusive, it can never be sustainable.

You've already created such a big legacy. What would you like your legacy to be?

I am not important enough to leave a legacy – we are all here to do our work. I am not talking flippantly. I believe in keeping your head down and doing the work for society and in the interest of the public, all with the hope that it will make a difference.

But you know, sometimes, and I have to be honest, I think, "Oh God, in Rio at the 1992 Earth Summit, it seemed so much more was possible." If only we were able to turn back the clock. I'm thinking about it and as I look to the future, I know it is going to be so much tougher, so what kind of legacy can I really talk about?!

We say to people that we have tried, we have done our best and we will continue to keep at it, but there are going to be very difficult times ahead. We all need to understand, it's going to be very tough.

I find that we tend to paper over things. I've seen this so many times. When people ask me what I think has gone wrong over the past decades, my answer is that we've just thought we could be genteel, that we could talk nicely and that somehow something would happen. I think now it's time that we called a spade a spade and put stronger strategies in place. That is going to require us not to give up. It will need us all to drill down to make sure we're focused on the need for change at scale.

SANJOY ROY

MANAGING DIRECTOR OF TEAMWORK ARTS

In August 2023, I spoke to Sanjoy Roy, Managing Director of Teamwork Arts, which produces over 33 highly acclaimed performing arts, visual arts and literary festivals in 40 cities across the world, including the iconic annual Jaipur Literature Festival (JLF) and its international editions. He is a founder trustee of Salaam Baalak Trust, which provides support services for street and working children in Delhi. Sanjoy works closely with various industry bodies and the government on policy issues in the cultural sector in India and has lectured and collaborated with leading international universities.

JLF has always included climate change panel discussions and in 2023 it announced that the event would be working toward becoming more sustainable and plastic free. What motivated JLF to do this? How easy will it be to do? How will you motivate JLF audiences, who are an international crowd, or are they already motivated?

JLF is part of Teamwork Arts, our production house, and pre-COVID we decided to see if we could show that our festivals could become zero waste and carbon neutral. We also wanted to see if others in our industry could learn from us and if we could become a model for others to follow. We chose our Kabira festival to be part of this experiment. It takes place in Varanasi and is not the easiest place in the world to work in, but we decided if we could create any change here, in the heart of India, even a 5% change, then a 1% change would be equivalent to a 90% change. If you are able to get something right in Varanasi, then you can succeed anywhere.

At the festival, we were clear about what we wanted to achieve and collaborated with an organization called Skrap, which did our waste management and audit. Also, as a global adviser on the well-known Earth Day, I wanted to make the initiative carbon neutral and offset the travel miles of our visitors and artists. We've now been doing this for a while, and in 2022 we signed an agreement with the UN which said that everything we do, we will try to make waste neutral.

Then we did a conference in 2022, for the Event and Entertainment Management Association – which covers all events, from weddings to tourism, in India – and we decided to do an audit, and it was amazing! On the first day, we asked Skrap to manage the audit and to present the findings at the end of the day. It was approximately a 300- to 350-people conference, and we also collaborated with a local NGO to ensure that all the food waste was donated. At the end of that first day, while I can't remember the exact numbers, the audit for 300 people showed that over 6,000 small bottles of plastic water had been used and that between 800 and 1,200 kilograms of food had been wasted. We presented the audit findings to the conference attendees the next morning, announcing, "This is what you've wasted – this is the food wasted from your plates." It had an immediate impact. On the second day, when Skrap did the audit again, only 440 plastic bottles of water had been used, with very little waste, while the food waste was, I think, reduced to 40 or 60 kilograms.

From India, we have tried to create this awareness in other places where we run events, such as Texas and Florida. Wherever we host our festivals, we want to create change and, of course, in some places there's more resistance. For instance, in America, there's more pushback, as down South they don't think that climate change is real. However, I do find that people listen if you explain it to them. But it's not about making people feel guilty – it is about asking people to take responsibility for their actions. For example, if you're picking up a bottle of water, remember, there are so many people in the world who have no access to clean drinking water. It's about being respectful, finishing the bottle of water or hanging on to the bottle of water. If we go back to Varanasi, we now steer clear of plastic, and we give everyone who attends a copper flask when they arrive. It's a new thing, where we ensure there's clean drinking water available for refilling at different places. We also started an initiative called Be Inspired, which is about looking to the future using technology. It is a project we do with the UN, where we show that you don't need plastics, because there are so many alternatives available, and while some of these new solutions are expensive, it's about reuse and collaboration.

You asked me when we started doing things around the climate. Well it was pretty much right at the beginning, when we started in 2006. We used to think that the great disaster movies would make the climate crisis sexy, and people would start to make a difference. But that's not been the case, and in spite of all those blockbuster films with big stars, nothing has changed. The climate crisis even today is still not sexy enough for people to think that they can make a difference.

Every individual can make a difference and our team efforts across all our platforms focus on how we do that – how do we make this issue sexy enough, especially for young people? How can we get them to adopt these new standards and see how, by small actions such as switching the lights off in their rooms when they leave, they can have an impact? Giving people the facts about what they are helping to save and making them conscious does make a difference. For example, this young lad, who at the time would have been about

14 years old, had seen some of the work that we'd been doing. One day, I met him in Delhi, and he said, "I've come up with this idea, to move away from plastic straws and to use paper straws." It was a brilliant idea, because at the time there was a report that had come out about how plastic straws were endangering our rivers and oceans. I introduced him to restaurants and general managers of hotels and his idea was very successful nationally. This was a young person, not an NGO, but he wanted to make a difference by doing something specific. So, when people say, "Oh, you know, government has to do it," I respond, saying, "No, it's not about governments, it's about you and me. It's only when you and I make that effort will we feel the impact."

At JLF, we have a series called "The Urgency of Borrowed Time" that looks at climate change – water, energy, recyclables or plastic – to create awareness of the innovations, along with a call to action. There's so much that can be done and it's our collective responsibility to make it happen.

I want to add something about JLF. For Jaipur to become zero waste is a very different challenge compared to the festival in Varanasi, where we deal with approximately 10,000 to 15,000 attendees. At JLF in Jaipur, we are talking about hundreds of thousands of attendees. It will take a while before we're able to say that Jaipur is a zero-waste and carbon-neutral event.

Plus, in Jaipur, the city itself doesn't have a process. We work with the local government and tell them that daily they will be picking up tonnes of waste, which we will have segregated. However, the funny thing is that after we at the festival finish segregating all the waste – for example, by separating out what is recyclable – we find that the local authorities throw everything we have segregated all together. When our team tracked the waste collected, there was no segregation. So, while it may sound like waste segregation is happening, it's not. We are now working with the city to raise awareness that waste segregation is good not just for us but for the city.

It's really a process of getting people to understand. When we make these announcements, we do so to start the process of change and insist that everybody who works with us, such as hotels, takes on these green commitments. To their credit, they get on board to do what's needed. We can't track it all, but at least we can make that bit of difference and open up their minds to the possibility that sustainable good practices can be done.

Following on from this, is the international audience that attends JLF more conscious?

In some countries, there's total buy-in because people get it – they've been doing it and they have systems in place. At the British Library, we've been doing things together for a while, so there's no problem. In other places too, such as New York and Boulder, they understand the need for better practices. Or in Florida at the Mind, Body and Soul festival that we host, people there get it and everything that they do on the campus is green. But in places such as Texas, there are no green systems. It's really a political question of whether you engage with waste management or not. The politics does not allow people who are on the right to say, "This is a problem, and we should do this." It's pretty much divided along political lines. In Democrat states, there's more a possibility of our efforts being successful than in Republican-dominated cities or states, because they're in denial about climate change! They don't care about how you dispose of packaging or how do you deal with plastic goods.

However, there are different degrees of success. Australia's great. Hong Kong is getting better, even though it's quite a difficult place in which to raise awareness, as Hong Kong in itself is a challenging environment. But then in places like Singapore, it's easy.

Do you think India has a global role of influence in making climate change matter in other countries and driving change?

I don't think India has any choice anymore in the matter, even though its contribution to climate change is still pretty low on the scale. However, the very fact that we have 1.4 billion people, and that climate change is going to impact places here, means we need to get our act together. Otherwise, millions, hundreds of millions of Indians will be subjected to climate disasters, which is already starting to happen. I don't think it's a question anymore of "should India?" or "does India?" – India has to lead in this area and needs to shame the Western developed world, saying, "If we can do it, why can't you?!"

The good thing is, even though there is some degree of greenwashing, we can see by and large there's a greater understanding of climate change in India over recent years, especially in the bigger Indian cities. Here in Delhi, or Gurgaon, where I live and work, you now need to have a certificate of possession, and you cannot get one without ensuring your house is connected to a solar grid and that you're generating your own power. Plus, you have to ensure you have water vats to collect rainwater. You cannot get a certificate anymore without these key things, and that includes segregating your waste. However, we have so many cities and towns that have a low level of understanding.

You also have to remember: when 400 million people still don't have two regular meals a day, waste disposal is the last thing on their list. Plus, their contribution is so minimal – they're not ordering from Amazon or needing to recycle plastic packages. Many don't have electricity or air conditioning systems.

They don't have any kind of carbon footprint and are pretty much at the bottom of those contributing to global warming.

You can't expect them to have an input without education, and awareness of these things is key. Technology has driven change, and renewable energies in India – whether it's solar or water or wind, including oceans – are gaining traction. Plus, families are becoming more aware and making their own hydroponic gardens, looking at ways to save energy by creating rooftop gardens – the challenge is how do you make more people aware?

Going further, could India become Mother India to the world on climate change?

I think we need to separate the political rhetoric from reality. While some of the political announcements have been well meaning, it doesn't necessarily mean that they have translated into action, or are what they were made out to be.

The monsoon we had in 2023 lasted 45 days, with 145% more precipitation than in 2022 in key areas, especially in the north of India, with hundreds of homes being lost, bridges being swept away, highways being destroyed and landslides. We live in a very precarious part of the world, especially the Himalayas. There had been reports of places sinking over the past two decades, but nothing was done, and now the land has sunk and most houses have been split wide open. So, it's not that the authorities didn't know that there was a problem, and they continued to advance development. An eight-lane highway has been created, in the full knowledge that perhaps it wouldn't stand the test of time when it comes to Nature, earthquakes, floods etc. Now large parts of it have been washed away. When you look at this kind of disruption, remember, you're looking at disruption of money and wealth, because this is all ultimately taxpayers' money.

I think the key thing is how does the government invest resources and use them in the most efficient way? I don't think that's something that we've been doing; instead, we've been making progress focusing on things being shiny, and the bigger the better. We know that that's not the need of the hour. In the 1960s, 1970s and 1980s, big dams were needed, but now we are seeing that they aren't necessarily the solution, as smaller traditional dams and ways of holding water are more sustainable. Regarding forestation programmes, we have these great laws, yet at the same time we are seeing key parts of forested places being delisted and opened up for development. Similarly, tribal areas are typically very rich in mineral wealth, which is part of tribal life, and we are seeing changes to the laws that protect these tribal lands. They are being opened up for extraction, pretty much in the way that China has done to Africa.

These are some of the factors that I don't think quite fit with the larger messaging that India has been announcing at the COP events. I'm not an expert on climate change by any degree, but going back to the original question, I don't think there is any doubt that India should and could be a forerunner in showing the way forward, particularly when it comes to the Americas and Europe, encouraging them to catch up with what we are doing. We are leapfrogging them, using new technology. America should be able to do the same thing that we're doing, especially given that they have made a huge contribution to global warming, including their contribution to all the energy waste. It's a nightmare, even though they have a smaller population.

It's now easier for India to implement good practices in every place, in every construction, in every city, in every town, in every village, as we're becoming a much more developed economy and developed country. Plus, I think the way we look at a developed economy in terms of GDP per capita needs a new approach. In India we need to consider – can GDP carry more people with us? Can we lift more people out of poverty? Can we bring about a level playing field for everyone, including those who are not just disenfranchised but are pretty much at the bottom of the economic ladder? They cannot catch up until and unless we have very clear policies in place.

Are more fiction books being written where climate change is the plot? And, if there are more fiction books being written, are there more stories from Indian writers about climate change?

Let me qualify that by saying that in all our Indian traditional texts, from stories of the Panchatantra[120] and every traditional text across languages and philosophy in Tamil, Malayalam and Bengali, there have always been stories that have focused on climate change. If you look at Hinduism, in the context of its philosophy, every vehicle of our gods is an animal, and these animals are protected by traditions that are meant to be inclusive. If you visit Varanasi today and walk along the banks of the river Ganges, you will see that the older buildings built about 300 years ago were built with bays for birds to nest in.

We've evolved from an animistic philosophy or tradition; it has been built into our culture and has been very much part of the Indian pantheon of mythology around the climate. For instance, the South Indian festival of Olam, where you use rice flour to create a pattern on the ground, is done because the rice powder feeds the ants. Therefore, climate change and our relationship with Nature exist across Indian literature and present in today's stories. We are seeing more inclusion, and I think a lot of stories have been set against the backdrop of devastation, which climate change impacts.

People like the Amitav Ghoshs of the world today have taken the climate crisis as the key issue around which they write and have been able to popularize it by selling hundreds of millions of books.[121] We are seeing this across the literary spectrum, not necessarily in English writing in India, but certainly across the length and breadth of writing that's coming out of regional languages because everything is based in that village, in that town, in that city, where you know those stories are true. The stories are true, because of the devastation that the river does when it floods, or the drought that envelops and impacts that family. It's part of their lives.

What past and modern-day writers excite you?

I read a lot. *(Sanjoy swings his laptop camera round to show me stacks of books.)* This is my reading for this month, and I read about six books at a time. I find time because I love reading. I don't watch television. I enjoy reading more nonfiction than fiction, and when a book is recommended, I read it.

There's a slew of amazing writers across the spectrum. Of course, you know the well-known ones like Amitav Ghosh and there's Tarun Tejpal's book *The Line of Mercy*, which talks about people in prison, where you get the very context of humanity.[122] People like Gopal Krishna[123] and also Rajmohan Gandhi,[124] who write about Gandhi and his letters to his own father – again, they open up a whole new spectrum of thinking. There are the wonderful works of many women writers that are coming out, which are pivoting our understanding of the way women see the world.

Then all of the work on transgender issues is so fascinating. People like Anosh Irani all the way from Canada, who writes about transgender in Bombay.[125] The book is called *The Parcel*.[126] I asked Anosh, how did you get this story? I wanted to know, because I've worked closely with street children, and he said, "I spoke to a few people, but this was a story that had come to me, and I put it down." This story is so real and shattering. It totally changes your mind.

Today, more and more translations are coming out, such as of Manoranjan Byapari, who was a refugee just before the Bangladesh war.[127] As a child, he had a rough life, living in a refugee camp around Bengal, which he left to become a Naxalite.[128] It's a long story, but he is arrested and lands in jail, and the jailer takes a shine to him. He starts learning to read and write. He goes on to read about 200 books while he's in jail and when he is released, he is given a rickshaw as part of his rehabilitation programme. While he's pulling the rickshaw one day, a lady gets into the rickshaw, and he asks her the meaning of this complicated word in Bengali. This lady answers him, giving him the meaning and asks him, "How did you come across this word?" He replies, saying,

"I'm reading Mahasweta Devi's book."[129] She then asks him about his story, and he tells her about his life. They reach the destination, and as she is about to get off, she says to him, "Show me this book." So, Manoranjan Byapari pulls it out from under the seat and shows her and she says, "I am Mahasweta Devi!" Mahasweta Devi then says to him, "Let me help you publish your first article. "Fast forward and he's written his first book and comes to JLF to release it.

My last question: what legacy do you want to leave?

I think legacy is a big, onerous term. The reason we think we have made a modicum of difference is that, today, there are over 300 literature festivals around the world – from the Bay Area Book Festival in Berkeley to Australia to the length and breadth of the Indian subcontinent – that say they owe their inspiration to JLF. So many platforms have been created that will hopefully give a voice to local writing and enable younger people to have access to an array of writings across languages and across dialects. That's something we're certainly very proud of, including putting out considered information, as opposed to what you see on WhatsApp, where you push back against the ignorance from which hatred and violence arise. By doing this, maybe one can make some kind of difference.

There's a story that explains this. I always like to stand for an hour every day welcoming people to the festival, and in the early days, the gates opened at 7.30 am. At that time, this man and a boy walked through the gate and because it looked like they didn't belong, they were stopped. As I happened to be there, I went up and I asked if I could help. And the man replied, "You know, I sleep on the pavement of the road opposite, and I know that I'll never be able to afford to send my son to school, nor will I be able to afford to buy him a book. But I thought that if he heard a story, it would change his life forever and I hear you tell stories here, so I brought him."

That was a realization that perhaps what we were doing was changing lives. Similarly, some years later a tall, well-dressed gentleman in a starched white outfit and turban came and said, "I am from a village 40 kilometres away," which is pretty much in the boonies. He said, "I love everything that you all do, and to attend the festival daily, I stay at the railway station in the waiting room. I used to be a schoolteacher. But I have been so inspired by everything that you've done, that I've set up a little library in my village, and I read to the older population, who are unlettered. My library is also open for the children." The next time he attended the festival, he came with nine or ten other villagers, so they would open libraries in six other villages, where they would share books.

When you look at any kind of legacy, these local efforts are what will bring about change. As we know, it's not about one SDG[130] or two SDGs – all the SDGs are linked. It's actually SDG 17, which is about collaboration – until we look at collaborating across sectors and with each other, across state and national and international boundaries, it cannot happen. We need to ensure that individuals are connected into a worldwide web, at the local level, district level, city level, state level and national level, which then starts making this larger impact that the world needs.

The climate crisis is not a distant problem anymore. It's today. It takes generations for us to adapt as human beings, and humans are very adaptable. But everything from food to water – all of this will be impacted. All of these policies that the world continues to make, despite realizing the impact of climate change, are ridiculous. We're not telling the right stories. People like Amitav Ghosh are giving us a sense of what the story is and what we need to be aware of, into the future.

Politics has to change. People need to be empowered to make the right choice. This is what JLF is for – to present different perspectives and get people to understand that there is no one truth, that there are many truths, and they all stand side by side. When you make an empowered choice or decision, that's how change will happen. We've entered this strange era where we don't want to ask questions – we're too afraid. We're not holding people accountable. We're not holding ourselves accountable. We need to provoke thought and ask questions. Be true to yourself. Do what you have to do. Get on with it.

PRACHI SHEVGAONKAR

FOUNDER OF COOL THE GLOBE

In February 2024, I spoke with the very inspiring Prachi Shevgaonkar, who is a media professional, climate activist and founder of the award-winning climate action app Cool the Globe. Prachi was the youngest and first Indian citizen to be appointed to the advisory board of the Climate Leadership Coalition, alongside Esko Ahoa, a former prime minister of Finland. Google made a TV campaign inspired by her journey of building her app. Prachi is a TEDx speaker, an adviser to Tata Power, and a founding member of the Global Youth Council, formed with the president of Colombia and Nobel Peace Prize laureate Juan Manuel Santos to address existential threats to the global community. She leads the Next Generation India Fellowship by the UN Foundation and the Council on Energy, Environment and Water, aimed at empowering youth to take up high-impact careers and shape the world. Prachi represented India at COP27, where she received the COP27 Young Scholar Award. She has also received the Young Changemaker of the Year Award from the Indian government.

What motivated you to become a climate champion?

It goes back to when I was eight years old at school and my teacher asked us to write a letter to our future selves. I mention this letter because when we go on to talk about legacy, we'll see it is relevant to my journey. This letter was about where we wanted to be in the next ten years, what we would want to be doing and who we would want to be. I wrote that letter and completely forgot about it. A few years went by, and I had enrolled in a computer engineering college. It seemed the natural thing to do, as everyone in my family is an engineer, including both my parents. But deep down I had this nagging feeling that there was something else for me to do. It was at this moment that I received the letter I had written at eight years old, as my schoolteacher posted it to me, and when I started to read it, it was a big wake-up call. In that letter, my younger self had written about making a difference and changing the world. I was inspired by those words and my dreams at that time and decided to go on a quest to figure out how I could make a difference through my career. I decided to take a gap year.

I had to get my parents on board and decided to give them a presentation; it was the first presentation I had ever done, and I had to convince them to allow me to take a gap year and drop out of computer engineering in the first month of college. College is a big thing for any Indian family and by the end of my presentation they were just as excited as me! I made a list of people whose work inspired me in fields that I thought were impacting India, and I included issues that I cared about. I wanted to shadow social entrepreneurs working in different sectors and travel across India. As a result, I travelled with farmers in Maharashtra for four months, spent some time with waste pickers on the outskirts of Bangalore and then worked in education with children, where I helped document the dreams of children.

While I had, of course, heard about climate change, I did not see how it was really affecting me, or anybody around me. But when I started to spend time on the ground, I witnessed so many climate events happening to people, and this had a profound effect on me. For instance, there was a young girl I met who had to drop out of school because her house only got water for an hour in the afternoon. Nobody else in her family could afford to stay at home during that time except for her. I discovered that her town had a drought. All these experiences showed me how extreme weather events can be, and when I started to connect the dots, I understood what it meant to that clever young girl who had to skip school to stay at home to fill buckets with water. This was when I realized that climate change impacts our education – it impacts our political, economic and human rights.

There's another event I remember from my travels when it rained one night like I had never seen before. I sat scared under the safety of my roof, but many people lost their homes that night. In the morning, as I went on a walk to see the aftermath, I saw dead cattle lying on top of a car, and next to them, I saw this old couple of vegetable sellers, trying to retrieve their only source of income – their vegetable cart – which had been destroyed in the flood.

There are so many other people facing and dealing with climate change in India. It made me think – if I, as an educated person, did not care, then what would happen in 30 years?! We need ordinary people to care. I asked my father for help, as I felt overwhelmed, and it seemed that this big issue was beyond my control. Together, my father and I came up with an idea to start small and with ourselves, looking at how to reduce our own carbon footprint by 10%. We started researching what activities made a difference, and crucially how to calculate the carbon dioxide emissions from our daily sustainable actions.

It was interesting and it became a game that I started to play with my family. And it felt good that I was doing something positive. I was enjoying it so much – my friends, neighbours and people around me started to take notice and wanted to be involved too, and that was when I started to look at how I could harness this interest to become global. This was how the idea for the app was born. It was to bring people together to start taking climate actions in their daily lives.

I was at college at the time, working on building this app, which I launched by the time I graduated. When we launched the app, we started making simple videos on what everyone could do and surprisingly people picked it up. I also realized that most people want to do something – they just don't know what. Through the app, we were giving them solutions and giving them something they could do at their own level. People started recording their climate actions on the app and telling others about it, and it had a ripple effect, where one climate action inspired ten others. Slowly this app became more than an app – it became a citizen-led movement for climate action.

Who were the people on your list that you wanted to follow?

First there was Dnyaneshwar Bodke, who was from my home city of Pune, who had started to work on an acre of barren farmland. He quit his job to start farming, which was crazy to everyone because farming was no longer profitable.

However, he was able to solve the agricultural challenges related to climate change by starting polyhouse farming to minimize the effects of the weather and made a good profit in just a year.

People started to hear about his success and wanted to know how to do it too, so he created the one-acre farming model called the Abhinav Farmers Club, with around 250,000 farmers from across India. I travelled with him across Maharashtra, where his mission was to create a movement, as a lot of farmers were disheartened and feeling the negative effects of climate change, where their efforts were going to waste because things were beyond their control. I saw how he inspired them and, most importantly, I saw how he built a movement, and that's what made him a change-maker. Watching him inspired me and I took a lot from his leadership: I didn't just want Cool The Globe to remain an app, but for it to become a movement.

The second person was Nalini Shekar, founder of an organization called Hasiru Dala, which, among other things, was helping waste workers to become entrepreneurs. Nalini encouraged me to spend time with the local community, where I met lots of inspiring people. I must have visited all the landfills in and around Bangalore, along with all the waste segregation centres. I learned that change-makers are in every corner of India, from all walks of life, from the 75-year-old woman who was the pillar of her community to the 18-year-old climate refugee who I met from Bangladesh – there was a flux of refugees coming from Bangladesh to India because of extreme weather events. The first day I met her, I walked with her for five kilometres to the nearest school. This young girl was already married and had a young daughter. She went to the school to see if her daughter could be enrolled, but as they were refugees, they did not have the necessary paperwork. This young woman could not speak any of the local Indian languages, but she didn't give up. For the next two months, every day, she would walk to the school, sit at the doorstep and demand that her daughter got a place. Finally, they found a solution for not only her daughter but for everyone else from her community, so they could have a place in the school.

This showed me how you have to fight for the most basic things. When you hear about the thousands of climate refugees around the world every year, you don't realize that they could include an 18-year-old girl having to fight for something as basic as getting her daughter enrolled into school.

Also, there was the time I spent with the IDEA Foundation in Pune, where I was documenting the dreams of children – what they wanted to do and what they wanted to become. I visited the slums and talked to children, and I realized that 90% of these children were going to end up dropping out before they could even get to higher education and that so many of these dreams were not going to be met. However, the fact that they had dreams meant something.

What do you think is India's role?

India is a young country and because of my work, I get to speak to a lot of young people. I visit about four colleges and schools every month, talking to them about taking up high-impact careers and mobilizing them for climate action. I have noticed that these young people really want to make a difference, which is what I think sets our generation apart. There is a real sense of growth here and it is what I love about being a part of this new era. The last generation dreamed about going outside of India for success – that's not the case anymore, as my generation wants to stay and be part of this growth. They see it not just as a sense of responsibility but an opportunity – an opportunity to make an impact and to leave our mark in the world. We find ourselves at the cusp of our youth in perhaps some of the most defining decades of human existence. Our actions today have the potential to impact generations to come.

There's a huge opportunity here. India has an abundance of sun, and we have a One Sun, One World mission[131] to connect the world with an interconnected solar grid. In the next few decades, we have to build a new world that's carbon neutral, that operates on renewables and that's rooted in sustainability. The country takes this seriously and is starting to build structures and economies that are aligned with this vision. We are going to be leaders of tomorrow.

Shifting to solar gives India an opportunity to be the new energy capital of the world. India has started Mission LiFE,[132] which underpins the fact that sustainability has always been part of our culture. Wherever I go, I meet so many young people excited about finding the solutions to climate change. It's a thriving space. The role I see for India is one of immense opportunity, to become a leader of this new world that we are building, and I see signs of that already happening.

What do you want to change globally?

When building the app, I spent many hours researching sustainable actions and how to integrate climate actions into daily life. I would scour reports by many recognized organizations, which was helpful, but at the end of the day, I realized it's actually very simple. Whatever you learn from the scientists' reports is the same thing that your grandmother has been doing all along – you just have to look two generations back, and you will learn all about sustainability. It's been central to our culture for many years. We don't have to reinvent the wheel; we just have to take the simplicity back. If there was one thing I could change, I would really like the rest of the world to shift its perspective on how it looks at climate change, and not see it as a burden or a responsibility, or something you have to do out of guilt, but as an opportunity to create a legacy to grow in a way that's sustainable and profitable.

With the influence of social media, technology and mobile phones, do you think the climate is high on the agenda of many young people?

Absolutely! When I first started Cool The Globe, I honestly did not think anybody would care or use it. I thought the only users would be me and my father! But then we saw the responses from young people, and it was something I could have never imagined.

At the start we made videos with my friends. It was a youth-led climate change campaign that went viral. We started being approached by young people from around the world. I remember receiving an email from a nine-year-old, along with emails from 40- and 50-year-olds. Everyone asking how they could be involved. The email from the nine-year-old girl was asking what she should change in her life to fight climate change. She was straight to the point – she wanted action and decided to start cycling to school. She recorded saving 60 kilograms of carbon dioxide emissions on the app by doing this for a few months, three times a week.

This is a theme that I've noticed with all young people. They are doers, they take things seriously, they are extremely knowledgeable and aware, and they ask tough questions. I am more nervous speaking to schoolchildren that I am with leading policymakers or journalists, because these young people will ask tough questions, and after the session, they want to know what next, what they can do and how they can be involved. This is a clear difference that I'm seeing in this age group. Another young person said that they had started an initiative to upcycle school uniforms and recorded saving 500 kilograms of emissions on the Cool The Globe app.

This enthusiasm snowballed with young people from around the world wanting to be spokespeople for the app, and that's how we started an ambassador programme. We have a girl from Pakistan and another girl from Africa. They made their own videos, started doing lectures in their schools and in their communities about the app, and started getting people to use the app. Today, we have 110 countries involved on the app. We have reached citizens around the world, and this is because of young people who wanted to spread the word.

Another big thing I'm noticing is that being conscious about sustainability has become cool, and to me that's the biggest reason for hope – it is the cool thing to do. When something becomes cool, then you know it is going to get big. Plus, these young people influence their parents, changing their mindset. Younger people make climate action exciting for everybody in the family, where it becomes a fun thing to do together – it becomes a moment of togetherness. Young people do not nag or guilt-trip their families to take climate action. Instead they inspire the family to join in, which is important. That's why we need more young people, as they bring the right energy.

At such a young age, you've already created a legacy. What else do you want to do and what legacy do you want to create for yourself and the planet?

Growing up, I was very inspired by what I used to read about the freedom fighters in India – it's what everybody grows up reading. I was motivated also about scientists and innovators, and I used to think that I had been born in boring times. But I now realize that I and the rest of my generation are living in the most important decades of all human existence. Working on climate change is the way to create the biggest legacy and make the biggest impact.

I have been heavily inspired by India's struggle for independence – particularly by Mahatma Gandhi's philosophy of ahimsa, which means nonviolence. There are very few people who can make extreme sacrifices and not everyone is in a situation to be able to take extreme measures. Through nonviolence, people can be involved in this struggle with this same spirit and values. India's nonviolent struggle for independence has instilled in me the belief that real change takes place when ordinary citizens come together to take small actions in their day-to-day lives. It is the same belief with which we are now building Cool The Globe's movement for climate action.

Individual actions by global citizens can create a ripple effect for the larger systemic changes needed to fight climate change. So, my personal mission in this is to make climate action easy, rewarding and measurable for ordinary citizens, and get global citizens to ask the same question that I asked myself when I started this journey – "What can I do about climate change in my own life?" That's the legacy that I want to create – empower people to believe that, in the face of something as big as climate change, our actions matter and we can make a difference.

SHOMBI SHARP

UN RESIDENT COORDINATOR IN INDIA

In December 2023, I had an insightful conversation with Shombi Sharp, who is an American diplomat with the UN and has been the UN Resident Coordinator in India since November 2021. Shombi has devoted more than 25 years of his career to promoting inclusive and sustainable development internationally and, prior his first UN appointment, as Resident Coordinator in Armenia, he held a number of leadership positions with the UN Development Programme (UNDP). He has been UNDP Resident Representative in Armenia, Deputy Resident Representative in Georgia, Deputy Country Director in Lebanon, Regional HIV/AIDS Practice Team Leader for Europe and the Commonwealth of Independent States based in Moscow, Programme Manager for the Western Balkans based in New York, and Assistant Resident Representative in the Russian Federation.

Originally from the US, Shombi began his development career with the international nonprofit organization CARE International in Zimbabwe. He is a published author of works in health economics, has been a USAID (US Agency for International Development) policy champion and has received a nomination for the UNDP Administrator's Award.

Did you have a connection with India before starting your post in 2020?

Other than a lovely week in Goa as a tourist many years ago, I really had no prior connection with India before my appointment and was thrilled with the opportunity for such a new experience. I started my development career with CARE in Zimbabwe and then joined the UN after graduate school. Most of my UN career has been in the 'post-Soviet space,' with two postings in Moscow, including a regional position, as well as postings in Georgia and Armenia. In between, I spent four years in Beirut. Having thoroughly enjoyed my adventures in Africa, Eastern Europe, Central Asia and the Middle East, I began to set my sights on Asia, which I saw as a gap in my personal and professional edification. I had imagined, however, that I might first 'ease in' by way of a smaller country, but being here has been an excellent surprise!

I recognized from the beginning that in such a diverse and complex new setting, the learning curve would be steep. I've often described it as resembling the Himalayas – as you reach one peak, gain a level of comfort in one area, it's only then that you see the next higher one ahead. That keeps things exciting, and I take solace from my Indian friends, who freely admit even they have not figured everything out.

On a personal note, I've been pleasantly surprised by how at home my name feels here, both in sound and meaning, perhaps more than anywhere before. I've even been told it sounds Bengali. People have always been curious where my name is from – I was born at a time of social upheaval in America, and my mother, an artist and musician, wanted to give me a completely unique name. My first name, Shombi, actually carries the Sanskrit sound 'om,' signifying breathing in the energy of the world around, with 'bi' meaning pausing for the stillness of being, to contemplate and cleanse. My middle name, Dwah, then signifies breathing out to return a more purified energy to the world. I was surprised to learn only recently that Dwah sounds just like the Hindi word *dua*, meaning 'worship' or 'blessing.' I never expected to be thinking about my own name in such new ways. This is part of my personal experience in India that I will definitely take with me when I leave.

Your name certainly vibes with India's spirit. Tell me about your climate work here.

Frankly, I can't think of a more important calling and a more exciting place and time to be engaged in climate action than in India. Working for the UN more broadly is the best job in the world for me! Every day, despite our imperfections and failures at times, we're striving to make positive change – and that's what gets me out of bed each morning. The successes and lives touched make it all worthwhile. Now, all roads have come to this point, where the climate stakes couldn't be higher, and India is playing and will play an increasingly central role.

We're already at the midpoint of the 2030 Agenda for Sustainable Development, and the 'halftime talk' that took place in New York in September 2023 at the UN General Assembly SDG[133] Summit and delivered a distressing message. Only 15% of the global SDG targets are on track, with almost a third having come to a halt or in some cases even having reversed in the face of what's been called a polycrisis – a host of mutually reinforcing challenges, from pandemic, war, shocks to food and energy security, suffocating debt and economic distress, to shrinking civic space, pollution, biodiversity loss and the climate crisis, which is likely the greatest existential threat of all. It is very easy to feel overwhelmed by all the negative news, but we need to stay aware and awake, searching for multipliers to let us act at scale. And that's what's so important and exciting about being in India. We estimate that upwards of 25% to even 50% of some global SDG targets will need to be met here. While it will not be easy, with government data pointing to SDG Goals 2, on nutrition, and 5, on gender equality or *nari shakti*,[134] as areas for particular investment, there are many reasons to be optimistic, with major efforts being made across the board, including on food security and women-led development.

UN Secretary-General António Guterres made this point on one of his recent visits to India, noting that India is the country that can make the global SDGs a reality, with the potential to impact progress more than any other country.[135] India is the largest country in the world now, with the greatest youth generation in history – more young minds than any country has ever had before to tap into solutions. India, mid-transition, is delivering development at scale, lifting hundreds of millions of people out of poverty.

I grew up with the slogan "think globally, act locally." But in India, I like to say, "You can think globally, act locally – and impact globally." The way that I see things moving forward, India will be a bright spot when we take stock of the world in 2030.

If we look at the world right now, there are few world leaders taking the lead on climate change. Do you think India is in a unique position to bring countries together to talk about this crisis, especially when the world is so divided right now?

Yes, definitely! India used its G20 presidency to demonstrate exactly that. There was a lot of doubt about whether India would be able to deliver a successful presidency and achieve a consensus, especially following the pandemic and with the continuation of the Ukraine war and its many consequences. The world was and is perhaps more divided than it has been since the Second World War. Certainly, multilateralism is facing extreme pressures. But I always said that India had a better chance to deliver at this point in history than perhaps any other, even though it clearly wouldn't be easy, and it really did come down to the wire.

This is a nation that is uniquely placed, with strong bridges of trust and goodwill in all directions – east and west, north and south. India is comfortable in all settings, from the G77 to the G7. It has the fifth-largest economy in the world and may have the third-largest economy by 2030. This is a country doing remarkable things, from landing on the moon to developing world-class technologies. At the same time, India is also a middle-income country that has the very real experience of addressing development at scale for its own population, meaning it understands development challenges and solutions, from water and sanitation to energy access and other areas. India has also long been a voice for the Global South and a provider of South–South cooperation, development assistance and solutions that are practical and appropriate for the Global South. By straddling those two worlds comfortably, and articulating clear intent with strong political support, India brought inclusive, authentic leadership, along with a lot of solutions, to the table under the mantra 'Vasudhaiva Kutumbakam' – 'The World Is One Family.'

Regarding the climate crisis specifically, again the matter is incredibly urgent. This year looks to continue the trend of record-breaking temperatures, some say the hottest in 100,000 years. And India is a country already taking large-scale action.

At COP26, India set out ambitious commitments to be met by 2030, from 500 GW of renewable energy capacity and 50% of energy from renewable sources, to reducing the carbon intensity of the economy by 45%. Further, India updated its nationally determined contributions in 2022.[136] The contributions will be challenging to meet; however, I don't think there's a place in the world right now where you see more exciting changes in terms of investments and policy around renewable energy, such as solar and green hydrogen, including electric vehicles. My favourite game is to spot the new blue-coloured electric three-wheeler auto rickshaws popping up around Delhi, which really didn't exist when I arrived two years ago. They're going to be everywhere in a couple of years from now, and the government is rapidly putting in place a charging station infrastructure to help expedite the transition, as well as innovating with complementary approaches like battery swapping. These are ideas that can help other developing countries also to make the transition.

India is moving forward on the energy transition quickly, and the private sector is very much on board. India is already fourth in the world in regard to renewable energy capacity, and I understand there have been upwards of $200 billion of multi-year commitments from the Indian private sector in renewable energy. These include moon-shot aspirations for green hydrogen breakthroughs. India is accelerating the transition to a green economy not only to meet climate commitments and ensure energy security but also to tackle pollution challenges and provide decent jobs at a faster rate.

We see a similar pace in urban growth. As the Minister of Housing and Urban Affairs, Shri Hardeep Puri, has noted, India will be adding something of the equivalent of a new Chicago every two years and, if I'm not mistaken, 60% of Indians will live in cities by 2050. When you project these development trends onto India's aspirations of becoming a developed country by 2047, you recognize these are big numbers. The math is pretty clear that without significant increases in technology and financing, and without domestic alternatives, even coal will remain a declining but not insignificant source of power for a while, in addition to the rapidly increasing renewable energy sources such as solar and hydrogen.

It's not about where India is right now, because where India is right now is not the problem and has not been. Home to one sixth of humanity, India has contributed only around 4% of historical greenhouse gas emissions. Clearly, nobody can point a finger at India in terms of how the world got to where it is.

It is often mentioned that India is now the third-largest emitter behind the US and China, with an 8% share of annual global emissions. But we must again put this into the context of its population of 1.4 billion people. When we talk about human development, or indeed the right to development, per capita measures are what matter and allow us to compare meaningfully across countries. In this case, India still emits less than half the global average, not to mention many times less than countries like the US, Russia, Japan, China and the EU member states. What India's per capita emissions will look like down the road – say ten, 20 years from now, or by 2047, when the prime minister's vision foresees India reaching developed nation status on its 100th year of independence – is a different matter. That's why India is trying to change the dynamic and move toward renewables as quickly as possible. Amitabh Kant, G20 sherpa, talks about India's efforts to possibly become the first country in the world to industrialize without carbonizing, and that's something to be optimistic about.

The Indian government also put forward a new dimension of thought and action when Prime Minister Narendra Modi launched Mission LiFE,[137] which is about lifestyles for the environment, together with the UN secretary-general. LiFE aligns well with the SDGs, especially Goal 12, shining a light on how each of us has an individual role to play as responsible consumers and actors – how we can nudge people to make sustainable choices, businesses to produce sustainably and governments to adopt sustainable policies.

In a sense, the world changed between COP26 and COP27 due to the energy insecurity generated by the Ukraine war. We saw some high-income countries suddenly returning to nonrenewable fuel sources, even coal, which was a shock for many of us halfway achieving the 2030 Agenda! The explanation was that citizens needed to heat their homes in the coming winter. Of course, that's a valid argument, to which the developing world replied, "Okay, this is what we've been talking about. Your temporary crisis is the reality for much of the Global South, who haven't yet fulfilled their right to development and have a lot of houses with heating and cooling still to build." At the same time, the appetite among low and middle countries to develop in a sustainable way is enormous but requires financing and technology.

At the end of the day, we're all in the same boat. We have to understand that the dramatic differences regarding historical contributions to the global carbon budget can't be ignored, and that the high-income, developed world still has a significant way to go in meeting its legal and moral obligations, to walk hand in hand with the developing world. We must ensure together that all nations enjoy the same right to development, and that it is done in the most sustainable way possible, on the back of green economies. We haven't gotten there yet – we've just barely met the $100 billion annual commitment[138] and some may disagree with those numbers, which is why the UN secretary-general has said that we need an SDG rescue and stimulus plan of $500 billion a year of additional spending. It could also be several trillion when climate is included. At the G20, India made the case for similar numbers in its *Triple Agenda* report, also known as the N. K. Singh and Lawrence Summers report.[139]

This is why we need India's new kind of multilateral leadership, which embraces multilateralism and is keeping all of us honest on what needs to happen for climate justice. India also reminds us that we need to place equal emphasis and focus on adaptation measures, like providing disaster-resilient infrastructure and tapping into a green transition, because we don't have any time to wait and the reality is that those countries that contributed the least to the problem are already paying the highest price.

India has its own climate challenges, with warnings that it could face multiple climate-change-induced disasters in the next two decades unless greenhouse gas emissions are drastically reduced by 2030. Is it possible for the Indian government to reverse a potential climate catastrophe?

Yes, I think so. India is one of the most vulnerable countries in the world, with large coastlines that could disappear and where farming in the Himalayan region has been exposed to flooding and heatwaves. Over 80% of Indians live in districts vulnerable to climate risks. This year alone, we've faced hundreds of climate-related hazards of different levels, which is why there are big investments being made in disaster risk reduction.

Another important element to consider is disaster-resilient infrastructure, and again this is where India has been showing leadership and is moving the needle globally. For instance, India is invested in the International Solar Alliance, which is focused on financing renewables, and it is also part of the Coalition for Disaster Resilient Infrastructure, a multi-stakeholder global partnership that aims to build resilience into systems to ensure sustainable development. Again, India has demonstrated dramatic progress, for example in early warning systems for cyclones and hurricanes all along the entire coast of the country, where we've seen the loss of life reduced dramatically. When we look at cities in the high-income world that are impacted by climate change, the impact tends to be more financial than in terms of loss of life, because those communities and cities have resilient infrastructure with early warning systems, good roads, strong buildings etc. It may not be sustainable for the long term, but right now, this infrastructure is providing people with resilience and shelter. India is saying, "The world needs that – the developing world needs the same."

Looking at agriculture, there's a lot of work still being done in terms of adapting varieties and looking at different commodities and different cropping patterns. India has been a huge proponent of millets, and it was India's initiative to make this year, 2023, the International Year of Millets. We know that millets are a superfood, not only nutritionally – they are also resilient to climate change, with much lower water consumption than wheat or rice.

Overall, India has made important progress, but we just don't know what's going to happen with climate change. It is nonlinear and impossible to predict. I do believe that India is moving quickly in the right direction in terms of its response to the climate crisis. There's so much happening, which makes it fascinating – the pace of change is phenomenal.

Do you think India will stay on track if it has a change of government?

We in the UN in India are, of course, apolitical in this sense. I would say there are many fundamental longer-term processes well underway that will span multiple governments ahead, from relatively high-growth, economic resilience and major investments in renewable energy and the green transition, to a world-class digital public infrastructure and very favourable demographic and gender dividends to leverage. From auto rickshaw drivers who are out there increasingly adopting electric mobility to the private sector making big bets, the green transition is becoming a national movement.

I have a theory that India could be a strong, authentic leader for the world.

I have a similar hunch. India is really positioned to lead with authenticity and with credibility in so many of these areas for the Global South. It's not the only voice by any means, but it is an important one, showing the way in terms of technologies, applications, digital public infrastructure and much more. Plus, the UN has a strong presence here with one of the largest country teams in the world in a development setting. However, in terms of per capita metrics or the vast human and material resources that India has at all levels, we must work with government and other partners to achieve impact. We are proud to collaborate with India's big flagship missions that are lifting people out of poverty, and we are growing our partnerships.

For example, we have a brand-new collaboration with the Gates Foundation, which we've engaged with under the leadership of the Ministry of External Affairs to support Indian cooperation across the Global South. As we have an operational presence across much of the country, we have a good idea about what's happening in the Indian development space. Part of our role is to increasingly help identify Indian development best practice, and take it to the international level, to other countries for their benefit. It's no longer the old model of development – it's really a two-way partnership now.

Plus, India's digital public infrastructure is highly advanced, even more than where I come from in the US in many respects. Here you can pay a coconut vendor on a street corner using UPI digital payments.[140] A good example is how India has empowered its population to be digitally banked, in just a couple of years. When Queen Máxima of the Netherlands, the UN secretary-general's Special Advocate for Inclusive Finance for Development, visited here, she was very impressed. The technology solutions coming out of India are relevant for any country, including high-income countries, and India is putting forward a different kind of model for digital infrastructure that is democratically accessible to everybody.

I think with changes in technologies and the fruits of these investments, the speed of change is going to pick up each year. I will not be surprised if longer-term commitments on the energy transition are brought even further forward in the near future. The long-term story is always harder to predict for policymakers, but the more important story is the investments being made across society here now, as they are going to really change the frontier of what's possible.

How has India changed you personally?

India is larger-than-life, off-the-charts fascinating in every dimension that makes a place and a people interesting. And I'm only half way through my posting, having travelled to 'only' 14 out of 36 states and union territories, so there's a lot left to experience. But if I had to put it into words, I would say India has taken me out of my comfort zone to grow in directions and at distances I never imaged possible, to gain confidence and even more curiosity about the world.

It goes without saying that India offers a seemingly limitless palette of colours and flavours – human and geographical diversity that has to be experienced firsthand to comprehend, with a millennials-old civilization that has given so much to the definition of humanity throughout history. While everybody, no matter where they've lived, will arrive with some idea about Indian culture and philosophies, given the country's global cultural and diasporic reach, it is a true privilege to be able to dive deeper, to really begin to grasp why, as the famous slogan coined by my friend Amitabh Kant goes, it really is "Incredible India."

My favourite part of the job is travelling around the country, going to the different states and into villages to meet with communities and learn about the projects the UN supports. I once did a homestay in the Rann of Kutch, in the middle of May, to help launch a joint UNEP,[141] ReNew Energy and SEWA[142] training centre for women salt-pan workers transitioning to the solar industry. It was blazing hot and we ended up sleeping outside under the stars as villagers do, together with our hosts. It was an absolutely wonderful time, a special human connection. You know, it's much easier to connect with people in India at all levels than in many countries, which makes all the difference in our expat lifestyle.

I feel I have opened my mind in spiritual ways, too. India makes you think about the universe and your place in it, with so many directions to turn for emotional nourishment. I think I've also become more thoughtful and self-aware as a global citizen. A lot of people feel that when they come to India. Your eyes are opened in ways that you never could have imagined. And I've been living in different countries outside of my home country for most of the last 20 years, so I've had lots of experiences to compare.

Although we've talked about how challenging the world is right now, where there's so much to be distressed about, I have a new sense of hope and optimism since coming here. This young generation have such incredible energy and ideas, I believe they will help solve the climate crisis, and other challenges.

This leads to my last question: what would you like your legacy to be with regard to climate change?

That's a big question. I think my legacy is simply the privilege to serve in a position that has some influence in such an importance place at such an important time in history. It's a daunting obligation and opportunity to help the UN system be the best possible partner for India to make the green transition, to help with resilient infrastructure and access to livelihoods, and other measures for the people of India to achieve the SDGs on time and in full. I hope that I can play a tiny role in this incredible story and be remembered as somebody who 'walked the talk' – took LiFE to heart. And as a small symbol, I'm hoping to be the first diplomat with an Indian-made, fully electric vehicle – that would be really cool with UN plates!

Perhaps I could conclude with my favourite film dialogue. Speaking in front of 18,000 people at the International Indian Film Academy Awards 2023 in Abu Dhabi as part of a partnership to enhance sustainability in the industry, I invoked Shah Rukh Khan[143] from the film *Om Shanti Om.*[144] "Kehte hain agar kisi cheez ko dil se chaho toh puri kainaat usse tumse milane ki koshish mein lag jaati hai." This means "If you really desire something from the heart, then the entire universe will work toward getting you that." This is a fitting way to sum up my feelings.

CHAPTER 11

ART AND MUSIC

I have a confession to make: I wrote this chapter first. I think it's because music and art have the power to move us, keep us spellbound, inspire us, make us remember things forgotten and help us consider possibilities. They speak to us all, irrespective of language and region, and this book is about change. And maybe – well, perhaps a big maybe – it's because my first name, Sangeeta, means 'music.'

Art and music are all around us. Nature creates her own melodies with birdsong, the rustle of leaves, the buzz of bees and sea waves. All these sounds and landscapes have the incredible power to move us and create wonder within us. Imagine a world where none of these natural sounds or scenic views – which have inspired so much of our culture throughout our civilizations – existed. Instead, think of a world where we are living in the "Sound of Silence," as in the title of the Simon and Garfunkel song, or against a ravaged *Mad Max*-style backdrop. Sadly, that's the way we are heading with many species under threat, including what once used to be the ubiquitous summer bees.

Art and music, at first glance, do not seem to have much in common with our ecosystems. But there are many areas where artists and musicians have made significant contributions to making our world more conscious and sustainable. Importantly, an awareness of sustainability in art and music runs through all genres and generations and is inclusive of all. Art and music will always transcend culture and differences in language and customs. Nature is inseparable from art and creativity. Images have the power to get the message across and musicians are the voices of awareness.

Did you know that one of Dave Matthews's earliest songs, "One Sweet World," inspired a Ben & Jerry's ice cream flavour that has raised tens of thousands of dollars for an environmental coalition? Or that for her second album, Miley Cyrus wrote "Wake Up America," a rock song about going green. Songwriters and artists are increasingly treating climate unease as a part of life and creating achingly honest artwork that's opening our eyes and inspiring us to ask, "What are we doing for our planet?"

INDIGENOUS ART

Indigenous communities have always known that art connects us to the natural world. But advanced economies have lost this connection and wisdom. Indigenous art is where it all began, as the natural world has been a source of inspiration since time immemorial, going right back to prehistoric cave paintings. Indigenous peoples have long collected environmental data. Today scientists are cataloguing these observations, learning how these communities are being affected globally. Many of us, when we think of climate science, think of satellite observations and temperature records. But other types of data exist, provided by Indigenous communities who have long lived close to the land – who have depended on deep knowledge of their environments to survive.

Anthropologists and climate researchers working for Western institutions are increasingly turning to these communities, seeking their wisdom and observations about the world around them. Scientists are learning that they have been cataloguing in their own way, often in their own language. This is data at a hyper-local level – insights that Westernized climate science might miss about how the changes are affecting people. There is now a growing school of thought that Indigenous science is real science.

A great example of the importance of Indigenous art is that of the Tlingit, who live in what are now Alaska and British Columbia. The Tlingit, whose name means People of the Tides, have a strong history, and some believe their origins date to as early as 11,000 years ago. Their art is reflective of their culture, ancestry and collective histories. As in many styles of the northwest North American native cultures, creatures from Nature and mythology are displayed in various states of realism. The Tlingit are known for amazing artwork, especially their totem poles, which are works of art carved from the trunks of local trees and are distinctive in their features, showcasing animals and mystical symbols that are important to their spirituality. The figures featured on totem poles are comparable to family crests, featuring animals – such as bears, killer whales and eagles – that tell the tale of a clan's history and mythology. These animals would have assisted in the survival of the clan or contributed to a major discovery in their legends.[145]

However, climate change threatens the loss of the Tlingit culture, and as humans, we need to rethink our relationships with the nonhuman world. We are losing our human connection to Nature's landscapes and beings. We need to remember how we stand in relation to and as a part of the Earth.

ART ACTIVISTS

This is where art activists come in. Many contemporary artists have become climate activists, using their work as a platform to raise awareness and imagine a more sustainable future. This type of art takes many different forms, each offering a unique medium for expressing the urgent need for action. These forms include visual storytelling, geospatial maps, visual arts, performing arts, film and media, street art and installations.

Artists have the ability to depict landscapes altered by global warming, melting icebergs or the devastating impact of natural disasters. They can serve as powerful reminders of the consequences of our actions, using their work to mobilize support for climate action, issue a a rallying call for peaceful protests and marches.

In Nairobi, Kenya, for instance, there are several meaningful pieces of street art that promote an understanding of climate change. There is a mural, located in a low-income area in Nairobi, which expresses a vision of the city as sustainable and green, using images of trees, solar panels and bicycles to promote conservation. The mural is named after Nairobi's other name, The Green City in the Sun. Paintings, sculptures and other artistic expressions have the power to evoke emotions, spark introspection, and create a deep sense of connection to the Earth and its ecosystems. By fostering this emotional connection, art becomes an essential ingredient in climate storytelling.

ART AND CLIMATE SCIENCE

All art forms reflect culture and society, and artists often engage with climate change by using environmental themes in their work, helping to integrate climate consciousness into cultural discourse. Collaborative art projects involving artists, scientists and activists can bridge gaps in understanding and communication between different sectors of society. We are seeing a closer relationship between artists and scientists, where scientists are looking to these storytellers to help translate scientific findings into actionable messages.

Climate art can provide impact beyond scientific knowledge. Historically, media coverage has focused on the ecological aspects of climate change, from the out-of-control forest fires to the cities under threat of falling below sea level to the crops that have died due to drought. However, artistic statements can comment on other, equally detrimental issues tied to climate – from mass migrations to disease outbreaks, economic disparities, and other sociocultural and economic troubles.

Creating and appreciating art is a communal activity. Climate-related art projects can bring communities together to work toward common goals, share ideas and discuss solutions. This fosters a sense of belonging and much-needed collective responsibility.

THE MUSIC INDUSTRY

The same can be said for music, another form of art that can connect us to Nature and all its beings. Music helps us relax and destress, and the sounds of Nature are known for their therapeutic benefits.[146] The early morning birdsong known as the dawn chorus is the most wonderful sound, or think of the sea waves, the chirping of insects – these are all rich, natural sounds that nurture our wellbeing.

In the last year of writing this book, so many initiatives were launched using the power of music in climate action. One was Music Declares Emergency, which is a group of artists, music industry professionals and organizations that stand together, declaring a climate and ecological emergency and calling for an immediate governmental response to protect all life on Earth.[147] They believe in the power of music to promote the cultural change needed to create a better future.

In fact, music and advocacy have a long joint history. Music can tap into the emotional and cognitive motivators of human behaviour, fostering a deeper connection to environmental concerns and inspiring positive change. A growing number of musicians are using their talent and celebrity status to shine a spotlight on climate change, pollution, species loss, plastic pollution and other environmental threats. The live music industry influences the hearts and minds of people around the world, offering the opportunity to inspire and inform us about how we can all live better.

However, concerts, festivals and tours can also contribute to the climate crisis, increasing emissions through fan and artist travel, energy consumption and the mass production of merchandise. Even vinyl and streaming have an impact on the planet. Vinyl is a form of plastic made from PVC (polyvinyl chloride) and, as such, is derived from fossil fuels, including crude oil. And guess what? Vinyl records are pretty much impossible to recycle. A single record can take up to 1,000 years to fully decompose in landfill. The vinyl manufacturing process also consumes large amounts of energy and often uses something called ozone-depleting, solvent-based ink to print the cover art.

But solutions are being found. There is Deepgrooves, a vinyl pressing plant in the Netherlands that operates on green energy, and RPM Records offers sustainable production practices. When it comes to greener music generally, in the UK, Ninja Tune is one of the country's best-known independent labels and has made environmental sustainability a priority, divesting its funds and pensions from fossil fuels and installing renewable energy systems at its London headquarters.

But don't think you're doing your bit by streaming, as that too comes at a cost. According to a joint study published by the University of Glasgow and the University of Oslo in 2019, "The transition toward streaming recorded music from internet-connected devices has resulted in significantly higher carbon emissions than at any previous point in the history of music."[148] In response to this, companies are looking at solutions to help minimize the carbon footprint of audio and video streaming. Spotify, Apple, Amazon and Netflix are committed to reaching net zero and belong to DIMPACT, which brings together researchers from the University of Bristol. DIMPACT has developed a tool to measure, understand and ultimately reduce the emissions of serving digital media and entertainment products, demonstrating that technological advancements can align with environmental responsibility.[149]

Music festivals have become a multi-billion-dollar industry where waste is a serious issue. Major US festivals such as Coachella and Desert Trip generate around 100 tonnes of solid waste daily.[150] Thankfully, more and more festivals are going green. In Norway, Øya Festival has strong green credentials: food and drink are served in plastic-free packaging that's 100% compostable.[151] And Italy's experimental and sustainable Terraforma focuses on land restoration.[152] Glastonbury boasts one of the largest solar panels in the country, as well as 1,300 recycling volunteers.[153]

No one, including me, wants to stop going to live performances, and there are ways to make festivals and live tours more sustainable. All musicians across genres have an important role to play in progressing environmental advocacy and really tackling this crisis. They need to work in collaboration with their record labels and other musicians.

MUSIC FANS

Another study by the University of Glasgow found that 82% of music fans are concerned about climate change and expect the music industry to do more.[154] The UN Environment Programme global campaign Act Now – Speak Up is spurring systemic change in everything, including the live music industry, to limit global warming. It has outlined the steps we as individuals can take to engage in environmental advocacy, suggesting that music fans encourage artists, concerts and festivals to reduce their greenhouse gas emissions.[155]

Concertgoers can ask artists to stop flying on private jets, instead using low-emissions transport. Festivals and venues could be asked to switch to renewable energy and use energy-efficient facilities. And fans can also demand organizers only partner with companies that have signed on to the Race to Zero, the UN-backed global campaign rallying organizations to take "rigorous and immediate action to halve global emissions by 2030."[156]

TEN GREAT SONGS

I felt this chapter would be incomplete without mentioning ten great songs about the environment and climate change. I suspect some of this music will be a surprise. It may make you listen again to the lyrics and see each song in a different light.

JONI MITCHELL - "BIG YELLOW TAXI" (1970)

Who can forget Joni Mitchell's catchy "Big Yellow Taxi," written in protest about chemicals and pesticides. It is a form of an environmental ballad.

MARVIN GAYE - "MERCY MERCY ME (THE ECOLOGY)" (1971)

Years before global warming became a hot topic, Marvin Gaye wrote a song about the environment and our obligation to care of the Earth. "Mercy Mercy Me (the Ecology)" described his thoughts on environmental issues at the time.

THE BEACH BOYS - "A DAY IN THE LIFE OF A TREE" (1971)

A haunting environmentalist strain runs through the Beach Boys' 1970s composition. It is about a tree thinking silently but singing out loud about all the bad things that were happening to it.

REM - "FALL ON ME" (1986)

This song was one of REM's early compositions about the environment. The lyrics sum up the ongoing desire to avoid the seriousness of environmental issues that face us.

THE PIXIES - "MONKEY GONE TO HEAVEN" (1989)

This song by the American alternative rock band references environmentalism.

JOHN DENVER -"EARTH DAY (CELEBRATE)" (1990)

Denver has an enduring legacy as an advocate for environmental causes.

MICHAEL JACKSON - "EARTH SONG" (1995)

Michael Jackson wrote the lyrics to this song and sings about the devastation that we have caused to the Earth from destroying the animals to the cost of war to pollution.

CHILDISH GAMBINO - "FEELS LIKE SUMMER" (2018)

The lyrics of this song caution against our harmful actions negatively impacting the climate. The music video allows us to comprehend Gambino's complex and interlinked messages about climate change, race and politics.

BILLIE EILISH - "ALL THE GOOD GIRLS GO TO HELL" (2019)

This track toys with the idea of personal responsibility and climate change.

THE 1975 FEATURING GRETA THUNBERG - "THE 1975" (2019)

This song doubles as a political manifesto, featuring climate activist Greta Thunberg, who ends the song with a rousing call to action.

CONCLUSION

Humanity needs to engage emotionally and empathetically with the climate crisis in order for lasting change to happen. Art and music can help create the emotions that we need to feel in order to act. The challenges facing our planet take us beyond the usual human scale of our day-to-day lives, relationships and worries. It can be emotionally difficult to connect to the crisis, but art and music can help us do so. We need to be able to express ourselves, and these creative mediums unite us with our spirit and with Nature herself.

Art can create a personal, even emotional connection to the scientific data. Sharing people's lived experience of climate change creates a level of understanding that motivates shifts in attitudes and actions in response to the challenges the world faces. There is a leading role for creative expression in achieving this, where artists and musicians can create ways of seeing and feeling that were often not there previously. They give visibility to new or different ways of looking and hearing. If we are to tackle the climate crisis, we will need to see, hear and feel differently.

Across the creative sector internationally, there is a huge amount of work being done to deliver projects in a more sustainable way, including to influence wider social transformation.

TAKEAWAY

"If music be the food of love, play on," said Shakespeare. Find a place to sit – an easy one would be your garden if you have one, or stretch your legs and go somewhere different, such as a meadow or field. Then sit and listen to the sounds of Nature. Listen to the beat of the planet and connect to it.

Then think of one thing you can commit to doing for the rest of your life, in order to keep those living sounds alive and thriving. Perhaps you could drive less, walk more, use public transport, do a litter pick-up or use less plastic. Do just one thing to be the main performer in this greatest and oldest band of all time.

CHAPTER 12

IN CONVERSATION WITH PEOPLE FROM MUSIC AND THE ARTS

For this chapter I spoke to three musicians and artists and one person who works in the culture industry. The four are Ricky Kej, international Indian composer and environmentalist; Janina Rossiter, artist, author and 'artivist'; Stevie Kalinich, American 'peace poet' and songwriter; and Claire O'Neill, co-founder and CEO of A Greener Future.

RICKY KEJ

INTERNATIONAL INDIAN COMPOSER AND ENVIRONMENTALIST

In July 2023, I had this email exchange with Ricky Kej, three-time GRAMMY Award winner, US Billboard number one artist, and internationally renowned Indian composer and environmentalist. Ricky has won over 100 music awards in 20 countries. He serves as UN Goodwill Ambassador for the UN Convention to Combat Desertification (UNCCD), UN High Commissioner for Refugees high-profile supporter, Global Ambassador for Kindness at the UNESCO Mahatma Gandhi Institute of Education for Peace and Sustainable Development, UNICEF celebrity supporter and ambassador for the Earth Day Network. His vast repertoire of work includes 24 studio albums released internationally, over 3,500 commercials and eight feature films, including the natural history documentary *Wild Karnataka* (2019), narrated by Sir David Attenborough.

What role do you think music plays in connecting us to Nature, and is it a universal language?

Indeed. I believe music is the most universal language there is. There is a rhythm to the way our hearts beat. There is a rhythm to the rain, and there is a melody in the wind. There are even research materials that say plants grow better when they are exposed to pleasant music!

Music is the most natural, organic presence within all of us. If we tap into this, we can all see that music will help us connect effortlessly with Nature and with each other. I firmly believe that music is capable of uniting life – not just people – for it is within us all.

At the end of the day, how did music start? Music started off as sounds from within Nature – sounds of the animals, the birds, the winds, the rivers – then we humans started to imitate those sounds and make them more pleasing to our ears. Then we took objects from Nature and created our own musical instruments

– like boxes of seeds, bamboo flutes, animal skin for percussion instruments – and it is only for the last maybe 1,000 years that music has actually become academic with notes and scales and raags.

What special sounds and notes do you think Indian music brings to help us connect to the planet?

If you read up on the connection between Indian music and our faith and lifestyle, you will understand how highly it is placed in our culture. For example, the notes in Indian classical music are Sa, for Agni Devta; Re meaning Rishabh, for Brahama Devta; Ga meaning Gandhar, for the goddess Saraswati; Ma meaning Madhyam, for the god Mahadev or Shiv; Pa meaning Pancham, for the goddess Laxmi; Dha meaning Dhaivata, for Lord Ganesha; and Ni meaning Nishad, for the Sun God. They are believed to symbolize gods. Music is part of India's life and heritage.

Our instruments, too – the sitar, mridangam, tabla and konnokol – have all been developed in harmony with Nature and are part of our lifestyle. This divinity of music is something unique to India. More than just an art form, I think this approach to music that we have can help us apply it as a universal healer. This is also why, for me, music, Nature and humanity are all so closely connected, and I propagate one with the other.

On a more practical note, Indian music has always been about 'feel' and 'improvisation.' So, any art form that relies on the expression of an individual artist based on their mood, time of day, and life experiences will always have a deep connection with our planet.

What inspired the collaboration with Stewart Copeland to make your album *Divine Tides*? And how did you approach making this music?

I had been working on a follow-up to my GRAMMY Award-winning album *Winds of Samsara* and had catalogued some of my favourite ideas. Recordings were delayed because of my relentless touring schedule, and when the pandemic hit, it presented an opportunity for me to spend time in my studio and kickstart this project again. I reached out to Stewart Copeland of The Police and was thrilled when he said yes to making this album with me. I have always relied on technology for all of my recordings, and Stewart also uses technology a lot and has one of the most amazing home studios. That helped us record seamlessly during the pandemic. Stewart and I recorded our portions individually, and it all came together superbly. We are thrilled to have created an album that celebrates life and will create a wave of much-needed positivity in our audiences.

Stewart has always been my musical hero, and I have been a lifelong fan. Working with him was like attending the best master class imaginable. Stewart is not just the founder and drummer of one of the biggest-selling bands in history, The Police, but he also regularly composes for operas and orchestras, and has written for over 50 Hollywood movies, including the Oscar-winning *Wall Street*. Despite reaching the pinnacle of success, he is constantly evolving and learning by exploring new sounds, traditional music instruments and rhythms. We constantly threw ideas at each other, adapted sounds and crafted this album piece by piece. All of the songs have strong Indian roots with a fusion of the West, and the entire album celebrates the magnificence of our natural world and the resilience of our species.

Staying with the success of *Divine Tides* and its GRAMMY win in 2023, what did it feel like to have Indian music stand up against mainstream Western music? I'm especially asking as *Divine Tides* won in the same category as albums such as *Aguilera* by Christina Aguilera and *Memories... Do Not Open* by The Chainsmokers.

It was a great feeling to see Indian music, primarily created in India with Indian musicians, compete against mainstream Western artists and not only get nominated but also win a GRAMMY. It just shows that our music is getting its due recognition on the international stage. I have always felt that if we crave international recognition, then the best way to go about it is to stay true to ourselves, dig deep into our roots, figure out what it is that makes us uniquely Indian, draw on that and create music. Aping the West and trying to beat them at their own game never works; it is just not who we are.

Who or what inspires you to create the music you make? Do you draw on your Indian heritage for creativity?

I am an Indian and will always remain an Indian. My permanent home is India. So whatever I am is because of this great country, and it definitely has the largest influence on my music and creativity. No matter how Western I attempt to make a piece of music, it will always automatically transform into being Indian by the end of the creative process, because that is just who I am.

Who would you like to work with that you have not worked with yet?

My dream is to collaborate with as many traditional, Indigenous musicians from across the world as possible. This has already been set in motion with a few collaborations with tribal musicians in India, but it is something I want to pursue on a much larger, global scale. There is so much to learn from these amazing people – music and so much more.

You have already created a strong and wonderful musical legacy. What's next?

My next goal is always to benefit the planet through my music. As you know, in December 2022, I was given the title UNHCR Goodwill Ambassador. This year I was honoured as a UN Goodwill Ambassador for the UN Convention to Combat Desertification to raise public awareness about the challenges of land degradation, desertification and drought. These are the causes to which I have dedicated my life and my music. I do not have any large overarching goal, but the plan is to take things as they come and try to solve one problem at a time through music.

What would you like your legacy for the planet to be?

A helpful human being. A musician with a purpose. As much as I would like to call myself an entertainer and performer, I believe in the responsibility that comes with being an artist. I hope to inspire every artist to be more than just an entertainer. I think now, more than ever, artists have the limelight they need, and they have platforms where they can stand tall and share their thoughts with people who will listen. I believe that with all the problems we face in our world, our biggest threat is that we constantly wait for someone else to make a difference. The only way we can bring about meaningful change is if we change ourselves. So I also hope to inspire my audiences and all of us to be the change we want to see in this world and empower all of us to believe that the small, incremental changes that we can make within our own lives, within our own tiny capacities, actually matter.

JANINA ROSSITER

ARTIST, AUTHOR AND 'ARTIVIST'

In April 2024, I spoke to Janina Rossiter, artist, author and 'artivist.' Janina creates art to raise awareness of environmental issues and uses her art as a way to communicate – a visual language that anyone can understand. She is an Amazon best-selling and multi-award-winning author and award-winning artist who brings her passions together in her work: painting and illustrating children's books. Her children's books focus on plastic pollution and endangered sea creatures, helping empower young children to protect our wildlife and make a difference. She is also an environmental speaker, having visited many international schools.

What or who has inspired you to create art that gives Nature a voice?

I have had a deep connection with the elements of Nature since childhood, especially water, as I was a competitive swimmer from the age of five. I love water in all its forms – the sea, ocean, rivers – and regard it as a safe space. It is where I go to destress and forget the world.

In my 20s, I was living in Hamburg, Germany, and I felt disconnected from Nature. It was when I met my husband and we went to the Auvergne in France that I reconnected. The Auvergne is magical – everything is alive with insects, butterflies and snakes. I found it exhilarating and I loved the natural world around me. It was at this time that I noticed how children respond to Nature and don't always see its wonders. Instead, when they see an insect, they want to squash it. This observation made me want to help give children a different relationship and reaction to the beauty of Nature and its creatures.

When my first child was born, I was working in Paris creating product designs and it wasn't fulfilling, but I did have this desire to write children's books, which I started to do. It was fun! I created a little penguin character called Tovi the Penguin, and I self-published my books. As my daughter got older, my art technique also developed. It became reflective of the ocean colours. I started to use fluid ink, which took me back to my love of water, which I wanted to explore more. My defining moment came in August 2018, when my daughter and I visited the Aquarium de Paris. That day the aquarium was running an educational show about ocean pollution. My daughter was immediately engaged, and I felt proud – she wanted to protect the sea and its creatures. That evening, I had an epiphany. I was going to start writing children's books about ocean life, connecting them to environmental topics.

When I started researching ocean pollution, I discovered how badly affected the rivers were too, especially in Asia. I was shocked and sad. There were beaches in Mumbai where you could no longer see the actual beach! I learned that we in the West were shipping our supposedly recycled rubbish to be dumped in parts of Asia. Our system was messed up – we had no real idea about what happens on the other side of the world and that we were washing our hands of reality. Sea life doesn't have a choice or a voice. Sea creatures live in the ocean, and we use it as a dump. That is how my book *1,2,3, Who's Cleaning the Sea?* was born. The book motivates children to be engaged. I visit classrooms and it really works, because children want to help, they just need the conversation. I'm very proud of the impact this book has had and the change it is making.

This leads to my next question: how can art inspire a shift in conversation to get us thinking about climate change?

Art is a great way to access emotions, whether as a child or as an adult. When I work with schools, I hope the children will become so relaxed about the subject of art that they will create what they feel and put their emotions into their artwork.

Sadly, our societies put a lot of pressure on us to work in the corporate world, particularly artists, where we become disconnected from our spirit of creativity and are always asking, "What do we do next for money?" Many artists become graphic designers, working commercially, instead of being artists. But I believe artists give a lot of hope to future generations and we are just as important as other professions.

I think it is important that we try to live by example in order to inspire and encourage others, rather than telling people what they should do. I believe we all have the right behaviour within us – we are not born polluters. However, we are conditioned by what we see, by who raises us. If we create the culture that raises people to take care of the environment, then I believe we will be better off.

Through my art, I want to make a difference and educate everyone about plastics, the truth about recycling and the environmental relationship we have with the climate. When you ask, "Where does our oxygen come from?" people will generally say the Amazon Rainforest or trees, but very few will mention the ocean, the whales or the plankton. The ocean is part of our lungs. Therefore, I believe art has an educational role. It is a fabulous way of understanding how we feel and see the world. Change does not start with blaming others – it starts with how we want to change the world and how we would like to see it.

I see myself as a climate art activist. I think about what I want to communicate and how I want people to react to it. My art is more than a decoration to be placed in a corner – it is evocative and inspires people to think and act.

For instance, the artwork I was commissioned to create for ChangeNOW Summit 2024, in Paris, had a message about our ecosystems. I wanted the two trees I painted opposite each other to show how our world works, and that the Earth's natural system is shifting because of climate change and that we are losing important elements.

What do you feel is your most impactful piece?

I think my mangrove has been my most impactful piece. It was the winner of the Sketch for Survival 2021: Wild Spaces - Explorers Against Extinction. Then in November 2021, it was exhibited at the Explorer Against Extinction gallery in the VIP lounge of COP26, in Glasgow, UK, which was just amazing. Plus, the mangrove piece became globally significant, as the chancellor of Germany, Angela Merkel, along with Dr Nigel Clarke, a Member of the Jamaican Parliament, decided to stand in front of it, and it was then captured in a photo by the international media.

I created this piece originally to support the NGO The Marine Diaries to raise awareness of how important mangroves are, and how they are a key weapon in the fight against climate change. Yet they are in decline, and according to UNESCO's current estimates, we have lost half of all mangroves in the past 40 years. These areas are being destroyed, sometimes because people have no other choice to support their families. It's really important to protect the mangroves, but they need to be planted in the right way, as many of the mangroves that are being replanted don't survive. This is where education and local knowledge play an intrinsic part.

On a personal note, I felt my mangrove piece was a turning point for me as an artist, and that I had made an impact and was being recognized for my art.

What is the one thing you want people to feel when they see your work?

There are different things that I want people to take away when they view my art, but essentially, I don't want to upset people by creating stark images. Instead, I want to foster a connection between people and the issues affecting our planet, using my artwork, using the beauty of Nature and its elements. Saying that, I do have some pieces that are a little more shocking, but overall, I like to create poetic, transformative pieces that people can interpret how they want. My purpose is to reach people's hearts and create the connection. When I work with children, it is important for me to not let them feel upset or devastated, and my work here is to inspire these young minds and to nurture their creativity.

I am of the view that when we continually see lots of traumatic images, we start to switch off. This means we are no longer reaching people, and instead we become immune to these upsetting images. Therefore, it is important for my artwork to foster this deeper connection to our emotions because we need these reactions to care and feel.

What legacy do you want to leave with this climate conversation?

It's complicated, because I never thought about leaving a legacy. I started my art activism because of the guilt I felt. I do have a mission, which is to connect the dots between other activists and artists who are trying to make change. I believe that by working together and highlighting other people's work, we make positive impact happen faster. I want my work to be a catalyst to create action for the good of our ocean and for it to build an awareness of plastic pollution.

I know I cannot stop climate change, but I hope through my books I am able to help the next generation to have a different mindset – one that encourages them to protect the ocean and to recognize how important marine ecosystems are in fighting climate change. I want to give the ocean a voice. I see lots of people saying "school education is important," and they create these wonderful school projects, but afterwards, nobody follows up with the children or guides them on to the next steps in the conservation. This is where I hope I am making a difference.

STEVIE KALINICH

AMERICAN 'PEACE POET' AND SONGWRITER

In June 2023, I spoke to the American 'peace poet' and songwriter Stevie Kalinich. Stevie has worked with nearly all the great music legends, and if he had a resume, it would read like America's Hall of Fame (a monument that honours US citizens who have achieved distinction or fame, located in New York). I have known Stevie for years and his work has always been purposeful. It focuses on world peace, humanity and Nature, reminding us that the climate crisis cannot be resolved without peace in the world, and that all these challenges that we are facing as a species are interlinked. Through his work, he has become known as the 'peace poet' by his fans and collaborators. When I spoke to Stevie, he was 81 years young, still collaborating and working, showing us that we are never too old or too young to start making a difference.

You have worked with so many great names from the music industry, from the Beach Boys to Randy Crawford, from Mary Wilson of the Supremes to Diana Ross and many other greats. What has been your favourite musical collaboration?

I loved working and collaborating with them all, for different reasons. Let's first talk about Dennis Wilson from the Beach Boys. It was my first real partnership and where I became known – it was on the *Friends* album in 1968. I had two songs with Dennis, "Little Bird" and "Be Still," and I loved working with him. We were dynamic – I would write the words first, and then Dennis would do the melodies. It was collaborative and energetic, and we worked closely. Dennis had a soulful approach to his music, with lots of emotion and feeling. Also, at that time, I was in love, so those songs were also love songs and being in love added to this musical collaboration, making it an amazing experience.

You know me, I have had so many memorable collaborations, such as the one with Brian Wilson, who touched my soul, and we did "California Feelin'." Then I worked with Paul McCartney on "A Friend Like You" – another incredible experience. Another inspiring partnership was with the late American singer-songwriter P. F. Sloan, who wrote the iconic protest song "Eve of Destruction." Sloan had a strong influence on my work, and we were close friends.

I have to mention my work with the late Keith Reid from Procol Harum, which was tremendous, along with my work with Jon Tiven and Steve Cropper called "Explosions of Love," which is a very touching song. And of course, how can I forget Brian May from Queen, and another collaboration with Frank Black from the Pixies – both wonderful beings.

It is important to mention that when you are collaborating, writing and composing, you create work from the state of consciousness that you're currently in and experiencing. People don't often talk about that but it is relevant. So, when I was in love, it infused the way I wrote "Little Bird."

Nature and world peace have been at the heart of your poetry and songwriting, creating important messages in your work. How easy or difficult is it to put these messages into your work? Do the words come first or the idea?

Usually, the words spring from an inspiration that probably was created by an idea. It could come from something you said, or it could be something I learned when I was with you. Writing my poetry is also the way I grow, and I have been interested in world peace since I was four or five. As I got older, I realized I wanted to create world peace.

And then when I hit my late teens and early 20s, and Brian Wilson met me, he said he believed in it too, and was so, so supportive. We thought, let's try to write a record that could create world peace, which as we know is not possible – how could we create that kind of change?! We were naive and young then. But while we didn't create world peace, what we did do was put a ripple out.

Humanity has to go through many more changes in consciousness. Sadly, there is so much disparity in the world, where some people have everything and others nothing. It is this inequality that causes disharmony and I want to bring peace to all of us. I believe peace starts with inner peace, and inner peace must be translated. It's not enough to write a beautiful song or a poem – we need the action, otherwise we will destroy the planet. We need to learn to collaborate to create good and I hope my work will be a tool to wake people up to do good and act.

I believe my work has a place and is desired by people. I am also living proof that you don't need drugs to be creative. I never did that stuff. I just felt high on life. I could go on a trip and look at a drop of water and be inspired. Dennis would say, when he would get some LSD, to look at that drop of water, for the experience. I see the beauty in everything that Nature has created.

Do you believe musicians can help protect Nature through their works?

I think musicians can help protect Nature, but not just through their musical work – through a collective effort that is action, which is about planting trees and protecting the planet. While writing a song is beautiful, it takes more to create change.

We need action and neither is it about becoming famous, even though a lot of us go through that desire. But we need to grow up and wake ourselves up. We need to think and say, "Hey, I'm doing great for myself, but how can I do better for the planet?" I believe it's our individual duty and a responsibility. We need to learn to care and listen to others, and it may sound idealistic, but we can't just think of ourselves – that thinking will never solve the world's problems.

Stevie, what would you like to see more of from songwriters and musicians and poets?

(Stevie ponders a moment.) I don't know if you can demand it. But what I would like to see is far more action from my industry, making a difference in local communities and in people's lives. The wealth gap is unfair and unbearable. However, if you don't feel that calling, just do the best you can and put it out there.

I also think it's important not to make people feel guilty, as there are people who might not care as much as you do.

You helped write "Little Bird" by the Beach Boys, as you've said. How did Nature inspire this song? What's your favourite line from this song?

Well, I mentioned that I was in love when I wrote this song, and I was sitting at Dennis Wilson's piano on 14400 Sunset Boulevard. Dennis was upstairs taking a shower and I happened to look out the window, and there was a little bird with a red breast. It was a robin perched on a tree branch.

I felt inspired and I pulled out a notepad and started writing the words. And I thought, if I could only understand that one line of what the bird knew – then I would know the secret of all creation! That one line that I wrote for "Little Bird" was a powerful message from divine grace, which has been the cue to my life.

I wrote two songs during that time, "Little Bird" and "Be Still" for the Beach Boys. These were my first two songs and I love the lyrics, which are very simple, not complicated. Very much like grace and Nature.

The fact is that "Little Bird" was my first song where I was in tune with grace and Nature. I've written a lot of weird songs since then. I'm trying to get back to the purity of my first lyrics.

California has changed in the years you have lived there, and now is severely affected by climate change. Has this influenced your work? Do you worry about the future health of the planet? Did you ever think this would happen in California?

If I am honest, I never thought of the climate in the beginning. But I must tell you, I was drawn to California's beauty and climate. Coming to California from upstate New York, with the freezing snow, getting asthma every year and then living in California, becoming healthier, seeing oranges grow on the trees – that's why I think the beauty and the sunlight of California came through in the lyrics of "California Feelin'," plus I was in love! It gave me hope for the future of mankind.

"California Feelin'" – I felt it, with the feeling that I could do anything, that I could come from a little town in New York and write songs. I still feel that when I go out in the sun. I still walk almost every day. I'm almost 82 and while there are so many problems in California, including the pollution, I think there is still hope.

But I think it is important to say that album could not have been written now, as it was inspired by what happened at that time in history. It's not something that you could sit down and write today, because the world is different.

What would you like your legacy to be? What footprint do you want to leave behind?

I care about people and the planet. I want to help humanity. Am I still a selfish person? In a lot of ways, yes. Do I still want to be recognized? Yes. But I want to overcome myself and get rid of my ego and let the divine consciousness or whatever we want to call it – God or Krishna or Grace, whatever – live with action and humility. I'm still learning.

I think I have lived through the songs I have written and the poems I have created. I want to feel that I have made a difference through my life's work, and that it will help people try to do better, be better beings. That would be the footprint I would like to leave behind.

CLAIRE O'NEILL

COFOUNDER AND CEO OF A GREENER FUTURE

In October 2023, I spoke to Claire O'Neill, cofounder and CEO of A Greener Future (AGF). AGF was founded in 2006 and today is a leading authority in sustainability and event management. Claire is internationally recognized as a key voice for sustainability in the live events and entertainment industry, regularly speaking alongside heads of industry, activists, scientists, and UN agency and government officials. She has trailblazed best practice including the Greener Festival Award, Green Touring Rider for Arcadia Spectacular's shows, and the Green Artist Rider with Paradigm Agency – which aims to help artists and encourage better collaboration with promoters, productions and venue, and inspired the new platform, A Greener Tour, which has led to the creation and implementation of the Greener Arena Certification.

What impact has AGF made since its launch?

There have been a number of different threads of work since we first started. When we first began, the goal was to raise awareness about sustainability within festivals and then among their audiences. We've assessed, certified and advised thousands of festivals, events and venues – and trained hundreds of sustainable event auditors and managers worldwide. Seventeen years later, we can see that awareness has been raised. People are now mindful of what that they can do to help improve things.

Following on from festivals, we decided to include all players within the live sector – tours, arenas, venues, suppliers etc. We've done a lot of groundwork and the engagement has been positive. Through the AGF sustainable certification process, we have been able to approve festivals, events and venues globally. In more recent years, we've been able to launch the world's first Greener Arena Certification, which looks at operations, how touring productions interact with venues and how we can make touring more sustainable through collaborations. We've also started to work on the supplier side, looking at the entire ecosystem of the live sector to understand how we can all be pushing in the same direction. We have made a lot of progress in the last five years, especially since the global COVID-19 pandemic, where now different elements of the sector work together internationally.

Why is there now more collaboration – what's changed?

People want to make change. It reminds me of that funny meme that says, "Who wants change?" and everybody puts their hand up; then there's the question "Okay, who wants to change?" and a few hands go up; and then "Who wants to lead the change?" and nobody puts their hand up. So, while there's definitely an appetite for change, there are still challenges in working as a collective, in what's traditionally been a competitive space.

It takes effort to pull together and the global pandemic has helped, because while it did set us back in some respects with regard to operations and loss of people power, it also forced disparate parts of the live sector to collaborate in a way that it hadn't before, with a more united voice to lobby governments along with a will to work together. I think, as we approach the second half of the decade in which the Intergovernmental Panel on Climate Change report said we need to make critical changes to curb our emissions by 2030,[157] people know time is running out. This urgency is forcing people to collaborate better, where there's more joined-up thinking across sectors – energy companies, transport companies, local authorities, governments, institutions, research institutes – all in partnership with the live music and live sports arenas. This will lead to innovation and that's quite exciting!

It also means that not every organization involved has to go away and do the same piece of work. A good example of this is the collaboration for the European Green Festival Roadmap,[158] which is creating a sustainability action plan template. Previously everyone had to do things from scratch, but now you can use open resources, which allows us to make things happen quickly.

Is the music industry keen to act to fight climate change? Do we need to see more involvement from bands and musicians or are they reluctant to be seen to support climate change?

I think it really varies. On the one hand, it is about making the music industry sustainable, by looking at our venues and how we produce festivals. Then there's the question how does an artist make money in their career? What does their success look like? Unfortunately, traditionally, the more success an artist has, the more trucks they need on the roads and the more they will need to fly. My view is that this onus should be more on the industry itself. It should be implementing frameworks so that when an artist is brought into this industry, they're guided into a sustainable way of sharing their music and connecting with their audiences. This also comes down to how artists are able to make a living in the industry and how deals are structured with record labels, promoters, agents, streaming platform, and so on.

Artists can certainly influence this too, and there are platforms such as Music Declares Emergency,[159] EarthPercent[160] and others that have created a safe space where artists can speak out as a collective. However, the majority of artists are obligated to what the festival organizer is doing, particularly if they are starting out, as they don't have a lot of influence to drive change. However, at the other end of the scale, there are established artists who can shape what happens on the operational side of their tours and festivals.

Artists and bands do have a voice and a platform with their fans. It doesn't have to be about the climate – it could be other passions that they care about. Being in a high-profile position, they can help change hearts and minds. We've seen this throughout history, where music has gone alongside cultural shifts. This is what we've been doing at the moment via the Justvote24 campaign, which is leading up to the UK general election in 2024 and is focused on getting people to vote. The election in 2024 will be a critical one, determining policies for the next five years, and this will impact people's entire future in relation to the climate. This is why we are using the platform of music to engage with as many different people as possible, to encourage them to take control of their future and to have a say. This is just one small example of how an artist can create change. This is a campaign that wants to bring in the music and sports sectors to use their platform to help make a green transition for the sake of all of our futures.

Similarly, there's an organization in the US called HeadCount[161] doing the same thing, as there is an election coming up there too. There are lots of countries in election years with the same challenges. We need to make the green transition case and counter the dangerous rhetoric and culture wars that are being created by populist governments and media outlets. They are muddying the waters by spreading misinformation and inciting division. It's a pity that we have to spend energy and time on things like this when there are so many other things to be working on in what is already a challenging transition for humanity.

This is why we need to use the platforms that we have to make sure that we don't mess up this pivotal moment, because no matter what policies we put in place as an industry or business, if we have governments in power that are not committed to or investing in green energy in a country, or not supporting sustainable agriculture, or not investing in sustainable transport networks, etc., then our policies and initiatives are just not going to work.

Tell me about the AGF initiative with the UK's O2 Arena and The 1975 to host carbon-removed events and what it means.

We've been working with the O2 Arena in London for a few years, looking at their carbon analysis and how to reduce emissions throughout the venue. I'm really impressed by the work they've done. There's also an organization called Levy that operates food provision as part of the Compass Group, and then there's Peppermint Bars & Events, that runs some of the bars. We have worked with them all and they each have their own net zero strategies, where they are moving toward reducing emissions and protecting biodiversity. We've decided to work directly with bands to remove carbon at their gigs, and in this case it's The 1975. To do this, we are also working with carbon removals specialists CUR8.

We have moved away from discussing "offsets," as there have been so many bad examples and scams. At AGF, we've never recommended offsets. Instead, our complete focus is on reductions because there is now too much carbon in the atmosphere for us to avoid its worst impacts. Therefore, for the purpose of carbon accounting in relation to residual emissions, we only work with carbon removals, as it is fast, durable, evidenced and reliable.

If we want an event to have a net zero carbon balance sheet, the residual carbon has to be removed, not just prevented. The University of Oxford provides guidelines that can be described as a sort of scale, where at one end there is the avoidance of carbon and at the other end is its removal.[162] The avoidance might consist of, for instance, protecting the rainforest or replacing a piece of kit so that it doesn't have emissions. These are important measures, but not for the purpose of dealing with residual carbon emissions from a balance sheet perspective.

On the other hand, carbon removal involves sequestering[163] carbon from the atmosphere. So, the difference is, if I take a flight, which emits a ton of carbon into the atmosphere, and then prevent someone else from taking a flight in the future, there's still the ton of carbon in the atmosphere from my flight. Whereas if I emitted the carbon via my flight and then I removed it, I would be back to zero.

This led us to thinking: how quickly can we remove the carbon? While it can be done by tree planting – which is great, as it adds to biodiversity, assuming it's done in the right way – it will still take time for that tree to grow, potentially 30–50 years. The speed at which the carbon is reduced is important, as we don't have that amount of time. There are various types of removal, such as direct air capture, which is pretty much instant and durable, and takes the carbon out of the atmosphere and puts it into a rock formation.

Other means of removal include enhanced rock weathering, which is a natural process where carbon in the atmosphere binds to rocks. It's a long-term solution for carbon storage. Or there is the carbon removal process, where rocks are ground into a powder that can be scattered onto fields as a natural fertilizer. This speeds up carbon sequestration and prevents the use of chemical fertilizers. Or there is a process where you heat up organic matter to produce biochar, which can enhance the fertility of soil. There are some reforestation projects specifically using biochar.

In the case of The 1975's gigs, we use a combination of these different methods – new forest growing, direct air capture, biochar and enhanced weathering. It's a way of balancing the risks, because if you invest in one thing, then you need to be able to adapt to the various regulations and structures around it. Plus, while the definition of net zero at the moment is to reduce your emissions by 90% and then the last 10% are removals, the music industry isn't anywhere near reducing its emissions by 90% and this would be difficult to do. So, we are focusing on the removals alongside the reductions.

The other thing that's interesting with The 1975's gigs is that we will be assessing the actual carbon emissions for each gig as they're happening. The O2 will cover the cost of removing emissions related to energy in the building, while Levy and Peppermint Bars & Events will remove the food and drink impacts, and the band itself will remove emissions related to the touring production. The audience will pay an extra 90p on each ticket, as agreed by The 1975. This will be for the purpose of carbon removals of audience travel. With 90p per person, we should be able to remove the whole of the emissions from the gig.

Why was The 1975 chosen?

The idea could have worked with any band or musician, but we knew that The 1975 have been committed to this approach, as they have been reducing their emissions during touring and production and would be on board for doing more. Another factor was where their tour fell in the calendar for the O2. The 1975 team is willing to put their necks out and say, "Okay, we're going to try this." What I always find funny is that when you do nothing for sustainability, you don't get any flack, but as soon as you do something, it's not good enough.

What could we as festivalgoers and concertgoers be doing better when we attend events?

One of the main things is how we travel to events and festivals. It should be as low in carbon emissions as possible, and if driving is the only option, then make sure that you are car sharing. The other thing is what you eat. We did a study of various events and found that the food and drink emissions were almost on par with the audience travel emissions. Audience travel made up around 40%, and food and drinks made up a third. We found if people chose plant-based meals instead of meat and dairy, then it reduced the emissions by 30%!

Last question: what legacy do you want to leave in this climate change space?

I think it would be to help us as a society to have pivoted or transitioned to a green economy, where we have created a way of working that enables us to have so much more fun and access to everything that we might need. I think that is happiness.

We've started to create regenerative cultural events. It's not just about being sustainable. It's about far more than that. Wherever we go, whether it's for music or entertainment, it's about ensuring that we are leaving places more biodiverse, abundant and cleaner, and better than when we found them. While I say this through the framework of festivals, events and entertainment, I also mean as a species, where we start to do what I think we're meant to do, which is to care for things, make things better and create, instead of taking and depleting.

I am not sure if this is a legacy, but it is my hope. I would like to see a world where all the troubles since the Industrial Revolution, including colonialism and the suffering that's followed, wouldn't have been in vain. Where in the end, we respect and revere Indigenous wisdom, along with the incredible things that have been created through technology. Where we can communicate to come together, and we haven't lost what's really important. I don't know if that's my legacy, but it's certainly my hope.

CHAPTER 13

BUSINESS

We need to remember that there is no business without the planet, and the current economic order is failing us. The world is on track to get hotter, and if it does, we will see a significant drop in food production, an increase in urban heatwaves, longer droughts, fiercer hurricanes and more devastating wildfires – actually, this is already happening. These scenarios threaten businesses, livelihoods and economies. Those businesses that continue to dismiss the issue will be badly handicapped relative to those that are now implementing strategies to reduce risk and find competitive advantage in a warming, carbon-constrained world. We know that climate change is now a fact of political life and is playing a growing role in business competition.

Companies need to act now. Those that persist in treating climate change as a side issue rather than a business problem will risk the greatest consequences, as the effects of climate on companies' operations are now so tangible and certain that the issue is best addressed with the tools of strategy, not philanthropy.

There is no one-size-fits-all approach to combatting climate change. Each company's approach will depend on its particular business and should be baked into its overall business strategy. For every company, the approach must include initiatives to mitigate climate-related costs and risks in the value chain. CEOs need to start treating carbon emissions as costly, because they are or soon will be, and companies need to assess and reduce their vulnerability to climate-related environmental and economic shocks. Implementing best practices in managing climate-related costs is the minimum required to remain competitive.

All types of business will need to evaluate their vulnerability to climate-related effects, such as regional shifts in the availability of energy and water, the reliability of infrastructures and supply chains, and the prevalence of infectious diseases – something that the global COVID-19 pandemic taught us. For some, but not all, the approach to climate change can go beyond operational effectiveness and become strategic. In the process of addressing climate change, some companies will find opportunities to create solutions to enhance or extend their competitive positioning by creating products to address climate issues more effectively, or by innovating in activities affected by climate change to produce a genuine competitive advantage – such as sodium-ion batteries, electric cars or recycled fashion.

One thing I sometimes find, when I am speaking to the business sector, is a disconnect with their awareness of the importance of including diversity, equity and inclusion (DEI) within the climate change conversation. There does not seem to be enough understanding of how climate change poses the greatest threat to those least responsible for it, including low-income disadvantaged populations, women, racial minorities, marginalized ethnic groups and the elderly in our societies.

CUSTOMERS & DEI

Let's start with customers who today expect transparency, responsibility and action from the brands and companies they buy from and are voting with their wallets. In this digital world, where 'authenticity' is the buzzword of choice, businesses must keep up with growing demands for ethical behaviour and transparency in everything from employee rights and gender discrimination to the supply chain. This sea of change for ethical products and the rapid rise of the vegan consumer have been driven by social media – #vegan has more than 130 million posts listed on Instagram as of July 2024.

Sustainability will continue to be a key factor impacting shopping behaviour, and consumers want more information to help make better sustainable choices. For example, increasingly, consumers are choosing paper and metal straws over plastic ones, along with organic products and cruelty-free brands. Consumers across all age brackets are banding together to fight climate change and, in response, many companies are going green or making zero-waste, package-free products their value proposition in a bid to attract environmentally conscious consumers. Being ethical and pro-planet also nurtures brand loyalty.

At the heart of this climate change conversation is DEI and employee well-being. We know that companies are committing to ambitious net-zero targets, but the question is, how are they going to achieve those targets in practice? While investment in data, infrastructure and technology is vital, we should not neglect the importance of people. Organizations will only be able to meet their targets if they invest heavily in their teams. Green skills are in short supply and businesses will need to take responsibility for equipping their workforce with the necessary skills to create green economies.[164] And from a talent perspective, it's going to take more than skills. Organizations will need to focus on their DEI strategies if they are to empower their teams to help solve the problem of climate change. Research has shown that diverse perspectives lead to greater innovation and problem-solving, both of which are critical for the systemic transformations needed to address climate change.[165]

Plus, a key component of sustainability is the ability to embrace diverse communities and the unique voices they support – with growing challenges related to climate change, resource scarcity and population growth, it is more important than ever that we work together to create a more resilient world.

DEI has also become important to customers, who are looking to their favourite brands for action against systemic racism. Yet one of the biggest challenges brands have when it comes to producing effective inclusive marketing

– particularly for minority audiences – is the lack of cultural intelligence they have about the audience they are trying to cater for and target.

Moreover, companies are just as accountable for the health and safety of their employees and communities as they are for their bottom line. I have observed when employees feel secure and actively empowered to bring their full selves to work, a business thrives. But all too often, this is not a reality for workers, and unsafe and unequal working conditions continue for many people around the world. Businesses have a unique and powerful role to play in both upholding fundamental rights and charting an innovative and inclusive path toward the future of work.

BUSINESS LEADERS

Where business goes, others will follow. Business leaders will need to first look at and understand their own activities relating to the climate and then how authentically they are delivering their business. CEOs cite government regulation as the most important accelerator of the transition.[166] The right policies and incentives can overcome major barriers to the transition cited by business, such as lack of infrastructure and poor commercial viability. Yet policy signals are not coming fast enough. Research shows that business is the best implementation partner for governments around the world as they strive to hit their climate targets.[167] National and local governments can and should turn to business to help transform their climate commitments into tangible actions. Climate change requires action across national boundaries, as the impacts of climate change are already displacing people both within countries and across borders.

However, to understand its impact, a business will need to assess its value chain: logistics, operations, marketing, sales, after-sales service – everything needs to be forensically examined. Leading boldly and placing stakeholder engagement at the heart of corporate governance models is the right thing to do – and also the best way to drive shareholder value for the long term.

THE WORKFORCE

Businesses that want to stay competitive in the hiring market and recruit the best talent need to understand that the pandemic changed the future of work dramatically. People want a better work–life balance, consisting of hybrid working and employers that offer stability and good pay. Globally, today's workforce want different things, have different priorities and higher expectations for the actions of business when it comes to social purpose, accountability and climate change. They also want to work for companies that uphold these values and are doing their bit. This means businesses and brands have to evolve and innovate to stay relevant, attract quality employees and retain top performers in the new millennial marketplace.

People are motivated and more willing to go the extra mile to make their company successful when there's a higher good associated with doing so.[168] In such cases, it's no longer just a job. Work becomes meaningful and this makes us more competitive.

Being purposeful, ethical and pro-planet has many benefits.

First, it inspires better citizenship behaviours and improved employee relationships. If employees think their employer is doing the right thing, they are more likely to do the right thing themselves. When organizations implement best practices in corporate social responsibility (CSR), employees are more likely to engage in cooperative behaviours toward their coworkers and the organization, such as going out of their way to help their teammates. It also promotes a higher-quality and closer relationships between employees.

Second, it brings about better employee affinity with the business. When employees feel that their organization is socially responsible, they experience a greater sense of identity with the business or brand they work for. These days, social responsibility can be more important than financial success in determining how much employees identify with their workplace.

Third, it leads to increased retention and organizational commitment. Feeling positively about their organization's CSR initiatives has been shown to increase employees' intention to stay with their current employer and their overall commitment to the organization.[169] Commitment includes a huge range of positive attitudes, including how much employees like their organization, make personal sacrifices for the organization, and see their own future and success tied to the organization's success.

Fourth, it attracts talent. Along with increasing current employees' commitment, being ethical and pro-planet can make a firm look progressive and more attractive to applicants and prospective employees. In the age when we want to work for 'high-impact' organizations, being ethical may help companies attract top talent over other organizations.

Fifth, it means better employee engagement and performance. Employees have been shown to be more engaged and perform better when they feel good about their company's pro-planet involvement. By making employees aware of your company's efforts to give back and celebrating these efforts, you can help employees become more actively engaged with their work and do better work overall.

Sixth, it increases creativity. When companies are doing good by the planet and being purposeful, it can increase employees' creative involvement, including generating new and practical ideas, and enabling original and creative problem-solving. When companies express their values and passions, employees may be inspired to develop new and better ways to do their work.

GREENWASHING

Greenwashing is a term that we have all probably heard. It means when a company makes false claims about its purpose and has business practices that are deceitful and unethical, misleading investors and consumers.

The path for companies to overcome greenwashing is easy: they need to be authentic. Don't claim to care about something that you don't actually care about. Companies have a history of manipulating the public by claiming that they are leaders in an issue that people find important. Fortunately, these companies commonly get caught in their lie – but often not before thousands of people have been duped.

Global challenges, ranging from climate, water and food crises to poverty, conflict and inequality, need solutions that the private sector can deliver. This represents a large and growing market for business innovation. In the rush to transform business models and systems for the future, integrity and values will have a huge role to play. I explore the relationships between CSR, PR and greenwashing more fully in my book *Corporate Social Responsibility Is Not Public Relations*.[170]

BUSINESS AND ACTIVISTS

Following on from chapter three, 'Global Leadership', business engagement in protests is important to dispel the myth that activists are only interested in gluing themselves to roads. It is becoming increasingly popular for companies around the world to encourage their employees to support climate activism. One example is Ben & Jerry's closing for the day to support the global student strikes for climate change in September 2019. This American ice cream brand has a long history of participating in political protests. During the US mid-term elections in 2018, it released a flavour called Pecan Resist consisting of chocolate ice cream with white and dark fudge chunks, walnuts, pecans and fudge-covered almonds. It has also thrown its weight behind the Black Lives Matter movement with its Empower Mint peppermint and fudge variety.

In another example, outdoor clothing company Patagonia sued the Trump administration in 2017 and has also become involved in politics, endorsing candidates in 2018. And in 2020, the company added anti-Trump tags into some of its clothing as a protest against the administrations actions on the environment.

Meanwhile, the British handmade cosmetics brand Lush says, "We can't keep quiet about the things we care about. Sometimes it is anger at how animals are treated, or sadness about the treatment of fellow humans and panic over the progress of climate change and our fragile planet."[171] It runs campaigns about these issues through its shops and website, collaborating with activists, grass-roots charities and campaign groups.

Brand activism can help build loyalty and cultivate lifelong customers. When people associate a brand with values they support, it creates an emotional tie that goes beyond product quality or price.

SMALL BUSINESSES AND CLIMATE CHANGE

I meet many small business owners who think they are not part of the climate change conversation, or that it's a challenge that only impacts big brands. This is a misconception, as small businesses are particularly vulnerable to climate change and need acceptable weather conditions to function properly. Nearly every company has a carbon footprint, and the good news is that small businesses can be at the forefront of reducing their carbon footprint. Big companies with large value chains use smaller firms for things like raw materials, packaging, production and marketing, and all of those things have a carbon footprint. Therefore, a drive to reduce emissions could help small businesses land bigger clients. Small- and medium-sized businesses have an opportunity to disrupt their competition by demonstrating to larger corporations, that have their own sustainability goals, that they are committed to reducing their emissions. By acting quickly to eliminate their carbon footprint, a small business may appeal to larger companies seeking additions to their supply chain.

Perhaps one of the biggest considerations any company can make is where it banks. As I am writing this, in September 2023, *The Guardian* newspaper has published a story exposing how Europe's banks helped fossil fuel firms raise more than €1 trillion from global bond markets.[172] Businesses are often surprised that the larger conventional banks are still funding fossil fuel companies, which is effectively bankrolling the climate crisis. There are lots of things small businesses can do to be part of the solution, because the bottom line is that all types of business, irrespective of sector and where they are located, have a responsibility when it comes to climate change.

There are companies that have led the way in showing kindness and humanity, demonstrating that there is a better way to do business. Small- to medium-sized businesses are the backbone of most economies around the world, and they can be more innovative than larger organizations, implementing ideas faster and pivoting easier than many big companies. Now is the time if you are about to start a business to think about whether you are solving a problem, whether you are ethical and whether you will be doing right by the planet. Or, if your business already exists, then you have the opportunity to improve what you are doing, make it better and do better.

THE BUSINESS OF WAR

Wars like the one in Ukraine and the one between Israel and Hamas harm the environment in ways that could jeopardize public health and devastate biodiversity for years to come. War is destruction, resulting in widespread toxic substances, dead wildlife and an atmosphere choked with fumes. Bombings and other methods of modern warfare directly harm wildlife and biodiversity. The collateral damage of conflict can kill up to 90% of large animals in an area.[173]

Using the Russia–Ukraine war as an example, these two countries are among the world's most important suppliers of key staples and fertilizers. By causing disruption in the supply of these commodities, the war is driving up global food and fertilizer prices. In the UK, we have seen the cost of living shoot up rapidly. Nearly 50 countries depend on Russia and Ukraine for at least 30% of their wheat imports, and of these, 36 source over 50% of their wheat from the two countries.[174]

The effects of war are pollution - the contamination of bodies of water, soil and air, making areas unsafe for people to inhabit, where the deteriorating environment threatens people. Another aspect of war is that it fuels the climate crisis, as it props up the global fossil fuel industry by locking in oil, gas and coal demand. Militaries consume enormous amounts of fossil fuels, which contributes directly to global warming. If the US military were a country, for example, it would have the 47th highest emissions total worldwide.[175]

The climate consequences of war and military occupations are poorly understood. However, a report by the Initiative on Greenhouse Gas Accounting of War – a research collective partly funded by the German and Swedish governments and the European Climate Foundation – has produced the most comprehensive study of the climate cost of the Russia-Ukraine war. It analysed the Russia–Ukraine war and found that the first 24 months of Russia's full-scale invasion saw the release of 175 million tonnes of carbon dioxide. This exceeds the annual emissions of a highly industrialized country like the Netherlands, putting 90 million new petrol cars on the road, or building 260 coal-fired power units of 200 MW each.[176]

There are other effects of conflict too, including the mass movement of refugees, which has huge effects on the environment. Land may also be either destroyed or rendered uninhabitable by landmines. All of this puts pressure on scarce land resources. As the climate crisis intensifies in the years ahead, sadly more and more people will be forced to leave their homes. So, how will countries cope with this influx of refugees? Will the sharing of already scarce resources lead to conflict? Occupations can be relatively short-lived or can last decades. While states have an obligation to protect the occupied population, their environmental responsibilities are less well defined. Occupations can hold back sustainable development by limiting access to materials or technologies, or by acting as a barrier to investment and development. Preexisting environmental programmes and projects may be curtailed or replaced by an incoming administration.

The business of war detracts from the fight against climate change, as money is pumped into warfare rather than climate solutions. We need love, not war.

CONCLUSION

We are seeing the rise of conscious consumerism, where many of us are making better and more informed decisions about what we are buying. This has a ripple effect, helping to bring about positive change in society, the economy and the environment. However, we are still being outpaced by war, greedy corporates and unethical companies that are destroying the planet, all contributing to the climate crisis.

We all need to be more mindful and start to think about the companies that are behind the products and services that we are buying from, and we need to prioritize sustainability, human rights and social responsibility when we shop. We all need to be aware of how our purchases impact our planet and inhabitants. Choosing to buy from brands that have authentically green commitments must be at the top of our priority list. One option is to buy fair-trade goods that ensure the workers behind the products receive fair wages, which helps alleviate poverty and provide better living conditions. Or we can shop locally, which helps support small businesses, which often set higher standards for ethical practices than larger companies.

TAKEAWAY

The obvious takeaway is for us to try to buy less, upcycle, recycle and buy vintage. But to truly make a difference, boycott companies and brands with questionable unethical behaviour, such as animal testing or environmental degradation. By refusing to buy from these brands, we send a powerful message that we want better from them and that they have to do better. Support local independent artisans when you can; they provide local areas with job opportunities and positively contribute to local economies, which encourages local communities to prosper. These art forms are a link to the past and keep traditional crafts alive; let's not lose our various heritages.

And here's something for all types of businesses to do. Buy more green office supplies, reduce waste, reuse and recycle. One of the easiest and important things all organizations can do is improve energy efficiency, switch off lights when the office building/premises are closed. Continue to encourage remote working and, most of all, empower all your teams, getting them ready for the future, investing in green skills.

CHAPTER 14

IN CONVERSATION WITH BUSINESS LEADERS

To give us an in-depth perspective on climate and business, I spoke with four different types of experts: Yamide Dagnet, Director for Climate Justice at the Open Society Foundations; Jim N. R. Dale, founder and Senior Meteorological Consultant at British Weather Services; Nicholas Janni, award-winning author and leadership practitioner; and Malin Cunningham, founder and owner of Hattrick, a communications agency.

YAMIDE DAGNET

DIRECTOR FOR CLIMATE JUSTICE AT THE OPEN SOCIETY FOUNDATIONS

In early January 2024, I spoke to Yamide Dagnet, Director for Climate Justice at the Open Society Foundations (OSF). Yamide has more than 20 years of deep, multiregional expertise on climate justice and experience in the private, nonprofit and public sectors. She was recognized by *The Ecologist* as one of 25 female climate leaders shaping 2019.[177]

Prior to working at OSF, Yamide worked as UK Policy Lead and Negotiator on the UN Framework Convention on Climate Change (UNFCCC) measurement, reporting and verification framework. She has also been UK Deputy Focal Point for the Intergovernmental Panel on Climate Change; a reviewer of countries' national policies under the UNFCCC; and France's focal point for the EU neighbourhood policy and twinning program. She has served as the Director of Climate Negotiations at the World Resources Institute in Washington, DC, focusing on the equitable implementation of the 2015 Paris Agreement and the UNFCCC. Yamide recently cofounded Allied for Climate Transformation by 2025, a consortium that amplifies the voices and priorities of vulnerable countries and communities to guide ambitious and just outcomes in UN climate negotiations.

What is a 'just journey' toward climate change, and what is required to create shared prosperity for all?

It is a journey that embraces everyone – a conscious attempt to leave no one behind. I know that the phrase "leaving no one behind" is overused, particularly within conversations about the Sustainable Development Goals, but it's an important one. It ensures justice for all, allowing us to envision a future that looks prosperous for everybody. To make it happen, we need a holistic approach from governments – one that involves all ministries and departments, together with their stakeholders, to help fulfil the promise of the 2015 Paris Agreement.

Climate change is impacting us all; no country is immune to it, and it is affecting all sectors, from trade to health and food at national, city and community levels. It affects our livelihoods; exacerbates inequality and water and food scarcity, resulting in more conflicts; and undermines energy security. It is for these reasons that we need every ministry – whether agriculture, energy, trade, finance, defence or education – to work together.

Climate is a security issue and will create more mobility and forced migration within countries, between countries, between regions and across oceans. This has cultural implications. For instance, countries threatened by disappearing underwater due to rising sea levels – like the small islands, particularly atoll nations – are worried about the fate of their cultural heritage, their statehood and the need to reimagine a different type of democracy when their citizens are forced to leave.

Nongovernmental stakeholders, such as the private sector, from insurance companies to financial institutions and different industries, have an opportunity to be energy efficient, leaner and more effective by imagining how to do things differently, how to use technology and align better with Nature to produce less emissions and be more resilient. This requires engineers and architects to rethink the way they design homes and other infrastructure to ensure they are resistant to floods and to minimize the disruption that could be caused to supply chains.

We need all stakeholders involved in the design and implementation of climate measures – economic and industrial, including marginalized communities – if we are to use this as an opportunity to reduce inequality. Research shows that to get effective climate measures, we need to address inequality, and that climate actions can result in reduced inequality if they are codesigned with all stakeholders. We need to hold all industries and businesses accountable and be respectful of the rights of all communities. We need an intergenerational and gender-sensitive approach, involving the youth, along with women, as well as Indigenous people. It is going to be imperative to include all communities in debates and implementation plans so they can see how they can shape a climate-proof future.

This includes the role health ministries and the whole health sector should play. In addition to the physical impacts, we should note the rise of mental illness due to increased levels of anxiety, especially in the younger generation, who are concerned about how climate will affect their future. Let us also flag more threats from zoonotic diseases, including infectious disease, exacerbated by changes in biodiversity, a rise of vectors such as mosquitoes and the risks emerging from the thawing of the permafrost.

Indigenous communities are vital because they possess a lot of ancestral knowledge, which holds some of the wisdom and solutions – such as about resilient and energy-efficient architecture and the circular economy – needed to tackle climate change. This could help us align Nature with technological solutions. This is a conversation that will be important for the private sector, to prevent greenwashing and 'techwashing.'[178]

A just transition requires humility and efforts to recognize and minimize unintended adverse effects of climate measures. Let's take the 'renewable energy revolution,' as it has been called by the Intergovernmental Panel on Climate Change, as an example. This is driven by reductions in the costs of production, making it a more profitable investment than fossil fuels. We need to be careful that the dash to renewable energy and electric vehicles doesn't result in more deforestation and land-grabbing. Electric vehicles require batteries made of rare critical minerals such as lithium, copper, nickel and manganese. It is estimated that the demand for these minerals will increase six times by 2040 and there's concern that the supply may be insufficient. While it is vital that we understand how much critical minerals will be required, we must avoid the same mistakes witnessed with oil and gas.

Most of these critical minerals are found in the lands of Indigenous people, who will need protection as their land rights become threatened. The current supply of these critical minerals is geographically concentrated in the Global South – for example, in Chile, the Democratic Republic of the Congo, Zambia, Zimbabwe, South Africa and Indonesia. This means we need to make the mining industry better by minimizing waste, labour abuse and local corruption. These are regions that are often in conflict and prone to climate disasters. Therefore, this new quest for critical minerals must become an opportunity to help move resource-rich developing countries up the manufacturing ladder and away from pure 'extractivism,' which benefits Western countries. There needs to be equitable development trajectories for these countries. This is about shared prosperity.

Is global collaboration happening?

The private sector understands that they cannot hide or be disconnected from this issue. We need to foster cooperation among a broader range of stakeholders. At COP, we have seen many governments starting to see the value of doing this, with more nonstate actors attending and engaging in the multilateral process, making deals in the context of climate solutions. While I think this is great, there need to be some safeguards. We need accountability and governance to ensure there's no corporate capture[179] and misdemeanours. This is why the executive secretary of the UNFCCC is keen that more efforts are being made to strengthen the accountability of nonstate actors.

For example, while we are seeing more Indigenous people attending COP, we need to avoid tokenism and ensure that they are influencing its outcomes and that once they leave COP, they are protected back home. There's a vicious trend where some of these environmental activists and climate defenders, often the real heroes standing up against polluting fossil fuel companies, are being threatened, and many are even being killed.

What do you think is the key role of the private sector in climate action?

The private sector must be part of the solution and has a role to play in reducing its own carbon footprint and being transparent. While the UNFCCC has thorough measurement and reporting processes, requiring every country to report on the progress it has made to fulfil its commitments, the same systemic process does not exist for the private sector. But efforts are emerging to make the private sector accountable for its commitments.

We have had enough of greenwashing! Polluters need to be held accountable to the societies they have impacted and take more proactive measures to compensate them. This is why there's conversation about global taxation and what type of levy will be issued for the fossil fuel industry, or the maritime or aviation sectors. It is important to support the financial mobilization that is needed, especially for those who don't have the means of implementation, who haven't been responsible for the problems created and yet are disproportionately affected by climate change.

We need new approaches to foster more investments. There are a lot of discussions going on about blended architecture to bring together different types of investors, from philanthropy to pension funds and commercial banks. This means that we need to tap into investments that are not only commercial but also have a social dividend. As mentioned, we need accountability to avoid greenwashing and techwashing. We need to align technology with Indigenous knowledge to have the revolution that we want to create.

Finally, the private sector needs to invest more in adaptation – even if it is not as profitable in the short term as mitigation actions. This is still a neglected area.

'The revolution that we want to create' is a powerful line, which leads me to ask: do you think the private sector recognizes the importance of integrating climate risk into its business models?

I think there's more recognition in the private sector of the need to integrate climate risk and risk management into its business models, through the use of tools like ESG[180] or financial disclosures. Again, it's always important to ensure that we are considering vulnerable nations and striving to minimize unintended consequences for small island states, for instance, which are systematically exposed to hurricanes – if the application of such measures means that businesses will invest less in these small and vulnerable nations, then that's a problem. It's not just about the importance of integrating the risk – it's about managing and mitigating those risks, while still figuring out ways to maximize economic support for big and small markets.

Again, for me it is about ensuring justice for those countries and communities that need it, and this is why the international financial architecture needs to be revamped to create better accessibility and more effective incentives. This includes taxing the polluters more through the 'polluter pays' principle,[181] especially the developed countries and the fossil fuel industry, maritime and aviation sectors, which have been responsible for the effects of climate change for longer or are among the highest emitters.

Staying with climate risks, should insurance companies review their business models and how can they contribute to tackling losses and damages?

In many countries, including in the North, more companies are refusing to insure homeowners in climate-risk areas. This is not going to resolve the problem and is a symptom of the crisis the insurance sector is facing. There's a lot of discussions happening about how to create a trigger-based mechanism that enables countries and communities to be compensated based on scenario analysis, ahead of a climate event and/or shortly after, with an emphasis on how to get them better prepared ahead of time.

In continental France, in January 2024, there have been unprecedented floods. Because of the frequency, intensity and length of the floods, many people kept trying to rebuild their homes, only to be hit by another flood. They're mentally overwhelmed and desperate, scared to face a freezing winter without working heat pumps. Many are thinking of leaving their places for good. I cannot but think of the unprecedented hurricane that have crossed many southern African countries when most of them had not managed to recover from the one that had hit them a year or so before. I cannot help but think of the Caribbean and Pacific islanders constantly hit by hurricanes, having to rebuild at a higher cost – since their credit rates are higher than those of Western countries – which forces them into debt. Can this create more solidarity or justice?! What is needed is innovative and effective approaches to city planning, timely cash transfers, and better preparedness to reduce incurred losses and damages, or at least the means to implement coping measures more quickly, reducing the residual effects and cost.

My last question: what do you want your legacy to be with regard to this climate conversation?

Look, I am from a small island, and I bring the perspective of vulnerable countries and communities whose voices are not heard enough and suffer disproportionately from the impacts of climate change they have not caused. These communities do not position themselves as victims and are incubators, often pioneering some amazing solutions. While small island states may be tiny lands, together they add up to a big ocean state. So, the way you approach prosperity and challenge existing power dynamics may be more a question of perspective and mindset. Being underrated could be a badge of honour, and the power of the underestimated can be enough to challenge the status quo. This is the spirit I am promoting.

In addition, as a chemical engineer by training, I am committed to finding transformative solutions. And as an islander with ancestors from Africa and who comes from the French West Indies, a vibrant culture that emerged from the melting pot of migrants from all continents, I see myself as a bridge-builder. The combination makes me a firm believer in the power of consortiums, coalitions and partnerships to shape solutions and reimagine a more sustainable future. I strongly believe that "if you want to go fast, go alone, and if you want to go far, go together."[182] To be legitimate, to create the required action at the needed scale, you need to bring people together – and while this is harder to do, it is more credible and the rewards are so much greater.

So, my legacy is the ability to connect, build bridges, bring key stakeholders together, including the less than usual suspects – and create the right synergy, minimize adverse effects, maximize effectiveness, and pioneer impactful and transformative solutions. In doing so, I want to empower the most marginalized and amplify the voices of women and youth, while confronting racial inequities.

JIM N. R. DALE

FOUNDER AND SENIOR METEOROLOGICAL CONSULTANT AT BRITISH WEATHER SERVICES

In September 2023, I spoke with Jim N. R. Dale, founder and Senior Meteorological Consultant at British Weather Services. Jim has over 40 years' experience of working on global weather impact. His work includes stints with the British Royal Navy, Formula and Ford World Rally. He qualified as a meteorological observer at the Royal Naval School of Meteorology and Oceanography. He offers knowledge and vast international experience to weather-sensitive companies. Jim is the author of *Weather or Not?*[183] and *Surviving Extreme Weather* (coauthored with US survivalist Mykel Hawke),[184] in both of which he shares his experiences and advice with businesses and far beyond regarding how to become weather safe and weather savvy.

I'm sure you feel at times that you're similar to Nostradamus as you spoke about wildfires 40 years ago, and they are now happening. Have we reached a tipping point on global climate?

The first thing to say is that there are various tipping points – there is not just one. Different ecosystems have their own tipping points because they will be at different stages where detrimental impact can occur. But each ecosystem will eventually reach a point of no return where it has a domino effect on another ecosystem, which sadly we are beginning to experience of late.

We have seen a range of record temperatures in the oceans and on land, in every continent, and at different times of the year. When I say 'record temperatures,' I am not going back to prehistoric times, or even Roman times, but to modern times, when accurate measurements became possible. However, experts who look at other historical actors, such as tree rings, ice cores and so on, will have their own view and, of course, the world has changed in terms of its dynamics, its geography and topography. This is one of the arguments that climate change deniers use, saying, "The Earth has been here before, and it has been hotter." But I'm a big believer in joining the relevant dots, and each day there seems to be another weather impact story happening somewhere or other. You don't see records like we've seen of late, obliterating all previous records, without an overriding single causation.

By joining the dots with temperature records, you see the bigger picture, but you could equally do this with extreme events, such as flooding and wildfires.

Sometimes here in the UK, as we live on our relatively small island, we can be divorced from reality, particularly regarding the developing world. As small kids, we used to join the dots to make a picture – well, that's what I do and have done for some time. I'm seeing a clear picture of things materializing that were previously unrecognizable, even by the best climate scientists. Forty years ago, I could see background threats ahead of us, from insect invasions to different types of diseases, which is why joining the many erroneous dots is very important to see what might lie ahead.

I believe we've reached a pivotal time – I really do! There are too many records being broken and too many weather-related occurrences, but everything won't collapse all at once like it does in blockbuster Hollywood films. It doesn't happen that way with the climate – you don't get a massive explosion and the world dies tomorrow. Instead, it happens in bits and pieces, something here, something there, other things elsewhere.

What advice would you give to businesses wanting to be prepared for climate change and how can they be weather safe and weather savvy?

Let's go back to my book *Weather or Not?* Weather and climate are different beasts, but they are also like siblings – brother and sister, if you will. The first thing I always say to businesses is "feel the pulse" – understand what the weather is all about and how it impacts you as a business. It's also about common sense and not doing the opposite of what might be required. The weather is the most important external factor in our lives, simply because it controls us. We need to understand it, including the many nuances within it, as we've then got a chance to comprehend the next bit, which is climate and indeed the bigger picture of where we are heading.

"Feeling the pulse" can be done long term or short term – in terms of weather, this means day to day, week to week or sometimes month to month. If, for example, you see that the month of October is set to be very warm, maybe record-breaking, and you are a wet and cold weather merchant, then you should start to plan to perhaps cut your losses, even diversify. Businesses need to be flexible and adapt to future changes – the idea of the survival of the fittest is apt here.

Businesses also need to educate themselves in terms of what the weather might mean for them, especially as approximately 75% of businesses are acutely weather sensitive. Even those that think they're not, they are – because, for example, weather can lead to absenteeism from the workplace or productivity lapses, even in the most weather-safe vocations. I want to stress that education is a big part of the equation, and that we do need to prepare the next generation.

We need to invest in schools to ensure that children are being taught the latest thinking about the world's climate and cascading weather impacts because everything has already moved on. Children and our youth need to be wise about where we are now, what's happening, and challenges and opportunities that lie ahead.

Do you think business leaders have a better understanding about climate change than some politicians?

That's a good question and I'm not sure if there's a direct 'yes' or 'no' answer. For sure, some politicians do have an understanding, and some do not. We have just talked about education and feeling the pulse, and many businesses just do not do that – it will be the last thing they think of. But some businesses are sharper, such as most supermarket companies, which do take weather feeds and monitor their sales against certain weather types. However, I often walk into those very same stores and see the barbecue products being displayed when I know the next two weeks are going to have dreadful weather and they're not going to be selling those items. They failed to capture the moment.

There should be more awareness among all of our politicians. Recently, I was invited onto a number of national TV shows to talk about the climate with politicians, many of whom are not climate aware. Some are also climate change deniers and what I would call 'career politicians,' who are governed by the party line. A good example of politics meddling in climate and net zero retraction comes from Rishi Sunak, prime minister of the UK.[185] He made a U-turn on the government's green initiatives for his party's own political short-term gain in September 2023, because he believed edging backwards would give him and his party a political advantage. But the reality was that this wasn't going to be a win. The Sunak government travelled in reverse gear in a way that was detrimental to planet Earth, and people by and large are not stupid.

That's the difference between a politician at work and a reputable forward-thinking business at work, because an authentic, successful business runs to effectively make money and to serve the public in the way that best serves everyone. I do, of course, appreciate the unique difficulties as far as politicians are concerned, but nonetheless, I think caring for the environment has become a vote winner, not a vote loser. It means more jobs, more innovation and more inward investment in the UK.

How can employers and employees protect themselves during a heatwave?

Most people will say let's put the fan on or turn the air conditioning higher, but it all comes down to the basics, and the first basic is hydration. Then it's the right attire and learning from other countries to understand why they wear what they do – for example, wearing loose cotton clothing in light rather than dark colours, and staying out of the sun. If you touch a white surface on a hot day, it will normally be cooler than the surrounding surfaces. So, there are lessons to be learned and again a lot of them come down to education and common sense. If a heatwave is about to strike and it is going to detrimentally affect your work, then make sure you plan for it – maybe shift your hours of work to suit. Another thing is that there is no need to travel where it is practical not to. Working from home is now possible for many and shows that we have become far more flexible.

Also, it is vital to understand the seasons and the weather they may bring, remembering that when it comes to heat, in the northern hemisphere we are talking about six months of the year – April, May, June, July, August and September. While in the southern hemisphere, the hot months are in November, December and January. Again, there is common sense involved as the weather within those months will ebb and flow. Again, we also need to be guided by what other countries do in overheated weather – how they operate, even down to what they might eat and drink. I think we have to copy some of that, and there's no problem in copying something that works well!

All businesses need to have a plan of action, not just for the heat but also for the other aspects of extreme weather, including extreme cold. This comes back to feeling the pulse – making sure you know what is coming and when. It also relates to education, so people know what to do when there's a blizzard or flood, when it's freezing cold, when the heat hits the fan, when it's stormy or when the skies are full of thunder.

For example, take the lightning incident we experienced in the UK in October 2023 and the subsequent fire that happened in Oxford at the biogas plant. People should know the perils that can ensue within a thunderstorm. For instance, I have seen children coming out of school and walking across an open field in the middle of a thunderstorm; they made themselves an instant target and should have waited for the storm to pass. Again, it's very simple things that are the difference between success and failure, life and potential death.

My last question: what legacy do you want to leave in this climate change space?

The first thing to say is that for too many years I was a hypocrite, doing things I shouldn't have been doing, even though I knew I should be leading by example. So, I'm the first to admit that I was foolish. But now I am doing things to make a difference, from changing my car to a more sustainable choice to changing what I eat and walking more than driving. So, being able to recognize my former foolishness is important because I saw where I went wrong and addressed it. That in itself is a huge positive step to take.

I feel part of my legacy was knowing I was aligned with other experts who saw the same thing as me with regard to the changing climate. While I wasn't the first by a long way, I did see a few of those 'dots' ahead of many. When you recognize something is pertinent to our future wellbeing, whether it's an illness or anything else of importance, that's a major key to providing the solutions.

I'm certainly not the most brilliant scientist in the world, but the most brilliant scientists aren't necessarily the best people for getting the message across. Sometimes scientific speak is a bit quiet or too complex and I often think, "Jeez, you're losing me, and if you're losing me, you're likely losing your audience." I'm not knocking these people – they are very intelligent and way beyond my IQ level – but there's a way of getting the message across. Being able to deliver the message and raise awareness is one of my strengths, and I believe part of my ongoing legacy.

In terms of what I can do best, whether it's being on TV or the radio or writing books, these are things that people can pick up and run with. I'd call it 'passing the baton.' That's what I've effectively done and I'm continuing to do. Where there is a battle to be fought, such as with the climate change deniers, I'm prepared to take up my sword and shield. Having said that, we learn nothing if we don't try to educate even the most vociferous opponent, so we must strive to get the various messages across in a way that can be easily consumed. It is a passion within me that burns brightly, no matter how I do it.

Every one of us can always do at least one thing very well. I am not a technologist. I can't make the rocket that goes up and captures carbon dioxide to save the planet – I will leave that to the people who can. But I'll write the word and talk the good talk. If I have a room of 20 people and one person walks away with a positive and/or constructive message to take to the next person they meet, then that is a worthwhile legacy.

NICHOLAS JANNI

AWARD-WINNING AUTHOR AND LEADERSHIP PRACTITIONER

In February 2024, I spoke to Nicholas Janni, who is regarded as one of the key leadership practitioners and thought leaders of our times. Nicholas teaches at world-class business schools, including the International Institute for Management Development (IMD). He is an international speaker and media commentator. In 2023, Nicholas's seminal book, *Leader as Healer*, won Business Book of the Year at the UK's Business Book Awards.[186]

In your book, *Leader as Healer*, you talk about peak performance leadership and the culture that ensues. With this in mind, do we need a new type of business leader to face the scope and threats of global challenges, particularly the climate crisis? And what qualities do you think are needed?

I was just writing a new piece about this subject earlier this morning. We do need a new type of leader in every domain. We need to face the fact that whether it's in government or in any other type of organization, there are almost none of what I would call 'advanced or evolved souls.' So, we are in the hands of people who do not have the capacity to be in these positions. When I speak of an advanced or evolved soul, I mean someone who has a lifelong commitment to inner development. In my work, this is based on two pillars – the pillars of awakening and the pillars of healing.

The awakening is the deep meditative practice and body work, which means that consciousness can gradually open to the deeper level of pure consciousness, which every wisdom tradition has spoken about and which new science confirms as the fundamental nature of reality. The healing pillar is where we work with our personal ancestral and collective layers of constriction in our system.

I recognize that 'advanced or evolved soul' is a strange term for some. Essentially, it is someone who is in the stream of development. I believe anyone in any kind of leadership position should be required to develop themselves. It's outrageous that people can be responsible for and affect thousands of people and yet be monstrously undeveloped! That's why we're in such crisis.

A radically new type of leadership is urgently required. We're heading toward extinction; it's very real and climate change has become a joke. Ages ago, we lost the opportunity to reverse things and now we act as though it's okay. We are pretending that we're doing something about it with regard to the 2030 commitments, such as net zero. It's pathetic, just like COP28 was, being hosted by an oil magnate, Sultan Al Jaber, head of the United Arab Emirates's state oil company, the Abu Dhabi National Oil Company. It is the world's 12th largest oil company by production.

We are not looking at the problem because it's too big. Instead, people are looking the other way and carrying on as if we're doing something about the climate. We're nowhere near what's needed.

Do you have hope?

Hope is dangerous because we are functioning by hoping that somehow everything is going to be okay and it's not. We're on a fast downward track right now. Hope is not what's needed. Let me read to you one of my favourite quotes by Václav Havel – it's a very important quote: "Hope … is not the conviction that something will turn out well, but the certainty that something makes sense, regardless of how it turns out."[187]

I believe we cannot live with the hope that things are going to get better, because we don't know! There's no wellbeing in hope and if our wellbeing depends on a version of hope, we're truly lost. Instead, I live knowing what is the right thing to do. I love doing it – I'm gifted to do it. In 2023, I was given a whole new platform through my book winning the Business Book of the Year Award, and all the subsequent international media interviews have opened up these conversations. I'm following what makes absolute sense for me, not in the hope that it's going to reverse the direction we're in; hope is not going to make the changes.

What do you feel has gone wrong?

I do think a lot about the overall arc of human development. We were first in a matriarchy, which was followed by patriarchy and then came the development of the intellectual mind, which brings many gifts, but also creates chronic separation.

I'm a great fan of psychiatrist, neuroscience researcher, philosopher and literary scholar Iain McGilchrist, who is committed to the idea that the mind and brain can be understood only by seeing them in the broadest possible context: that of the whole of our physical and spiritual existence, and of the wider human culture in which they arise – the culture that helps to mould, and in turn is moulded by, our minds and brains. I think the left brain has totally taken over. There's an old proverb: "Is your mind your master or your servant?" And certainly in all organizational life, the mind is the master and it's disastrous. We operate in a very tiny part of who we really are and we're trying to manage the world with tools that are not fit for purpose, where we create what would generally be called 'trauma,' which we don't deal with. We're altogether functioning in a way that is very limited.

Then within that, we've become addicted to the materialistic version of the world, the scientific materialism, which new science obviously shows us is the wrong version of reality. But the mainstream is not ready to address that yet.

People call it the 'meaning crisis,' the 'mental crisis,' and that's what we're in, because without heart, soul and spirit, there is no meaning. These are not things you buy and are not part of the materialist world. I think humanity is profoundly lost, and I know that many old traditions saw this period of darkness coming. At the moment, we're in the dark.

Do business management courses need to change?

Yes, totally! I work at two of the top business schools, including IMD, which is the number one business school, and there's nothing that addresses what I'm speaking about.

What do we need to do ourselves in society to make room for this next generation of businesses?

We should be committing totally to our own awakening and healing forever, making that an absolute priority in our life, so that little by little we show up with coherence and the capacity to really serve and the capacity to really relate.

What legacy do you want to leave?

I know that my work has been life-changing for some people and has brought people into deeper coherence. My work engages deep awakening practices, it is deeply healing, where people journey with it to the extent that they're ready to change. Where they experience different phases and I awaken leaders to feel free and at home with themselves. I have the absolute conviction that what I'm bringing, along with others, is what's needed.

I believe that deep down everyone knows the truth of who we are, but they don't have a space to face it. They're in environments that don't want them to face it and it's not even on their radar. So, if you provide a safe enough – a clear enough, coherent enough and credible enough space – the majority of people will go on the journey. Not everyone, but that's okay.

My legacy would be to scale my work as much as possible and serve the awakening of humanity, which is deeply asleep.

MALIN CUNNINGHAM

FOUNDER AND OWNER OF HATTRICK

In April 2024, I spoke with Malin Cunningham, founder and owner of Hattrick, a communications agency that uses Scandi thinking, which is a balanced approach to life in order to do things you enjoy, and is applied at Hattrick to redefine the future for businesses. Hattrick is a certified B Corp, a business-to-business consultancy that works with organizations in the built environment and industrial sectors to help them tell their stories to make an impact. Malin is passionate about carbon literacy – the awareness of climate change and the opportunities in the green economy. She is a certified trainer, helping to educate others and drive awareness.

What is the role of business in a more sustainable future?

When we think of a 'sustainable future,' it's easy to get stuck in a negative narrative around what we have to lose – rather than what we have to gain! The truth is, we all have a choice here. We can either be part of the action and lead the way, or be dragged along, which will be a much harder and more expensive transition.

In fact, from a business perspective, 'sustainability' presents a huge opportunity – as most challenges do. They drive innovation and new ways of doing things, which is what has always been propelling us forward.

The reality is that we have become too accustomed to not paying the true cost of the resources we use, from raw materials to labour. The future of business lies in finding the right balance between people, planet and profit. This kind of thinking is aligned with the Swedish concept of *lagom* – not too much, not too little – and with the B Corp movement, which is a system of verification for organizations that meet high social and environmental performance, transparency and accountability standards.

Going forward, businesses will continue to create jobs – providing the goods and services that we need, of course. They will generate profits but without depleting the natural world and ultimately threatening lives and livelihoods by doing so.

How important is business leadership for protecting the environment?

Absolutely essential! We're in the middle of a huge transition – a paradigm shift – that is changing how we live and work, and it can be very unsettling.

When we deliver our carbon literacy, we come across a lot of people who feel afraid, disempowered and lost. It's not just about climate change, but all the macro and global issues that are playing out, including AI, wars, misinformation and divisive politics.

These call for strong leadership. We need leaders who are transparent about the challenges we're facing and open about what it will take to tackle them as well as the opportunities they present – both in business and in politics.

Are there any business leaders that you admire?

There are a lot of businesses and leaders that are pushing boundaries. In the building sector, perhaps surprisingly, there are a couple of roofing companies that stand out: Axter and Bauder. They are both training their entire workforce in carbon literacy and Axter is also striving to become a B Corp, which is unusual in this sector.

Another admirable leader is Ankita Dwivedi, who founded Firstplanit, a platform that democratizes decision-making in the built environment. It helps all users, regardless of technical knowledge, to make better decisions to rapidly improve the impact buildings are having on people and the planet. It allows designers, builders, developers, property owners and manufacturers to find products based on social value and location with a simple scoring system, making it easier for nontechnical users to make informed choices.

How would you like to see businesses communicate with their employees and customers regarding the climate crisis?

The most important aspect is transparency, which I think makes many businesses uncomfortable. Traditionally, businesses play their cards close to their chest. However, to maintain credibility and bring employees and customers with them, organizations need to be more open about the challenges we're collectively facing – and what they are doing to address them.

What's more, we need to include other organizations in our sector too – including the competition. That might sound counterintuitive, but in reality, we don't need lots of businesses trying to solve the same problems over and over again. Instead, if we can communicate and collaborate, we can solve things quicker.

By being transparent, it will also be easier for people to understand what can be solved quickly – and what can't. It will give them more licence to experiment, try things out, and recognize that this is a journey.

What types of businesses do you believe are actively solving the climate crisis? What sectors do you think could be doing more?

We primarily work in traditional sectors such as the built environment, which are always likely to lag behind others such as tech. That said, there are many entrepreneurs and start-ups – like Firstplanit; Low Carbon Materials, which is decarbonizing concrete; and Aira, a heat pump company – that are tackling big challenges with more sustainable solutions.

Low Carbon Materials was shortlisted for the Earthshot Prize and has found a way to decarbonize cement, which represents 8% of global emissions. Aira, on the other hand, is helping households in the UK and beyond move away from traditional gas heating systems in favour of electric heat pumps. These types of organizations can innovate and pivot significantly faster than large, traditional businesses stuck in existing systems.

While traditional sectors show willingness to change, they operate in risk-averse ecosystems and find it hard to understand how new solutions will work. They often seek more regulation and incentives but are not born innovators. Many prefer to follow rather than lead.

What legacy do you want to leave?

To help businesses focus on what they can do, rather than what they can't – yet. I want to help them understand where their responsibilities lie and that they need to act rather than point fingers at everybody else, saying "there's not enough legislation," "there's not enough incentives" or "there are countries that are emitting a lot more than the UK." All of that is just a distraction.

If we – the Hattrick team – can empower the leaders and businesses that we work with to take ownership and drive action, that would be incredibly powerful and a job well done.

CHAPTER 15

THE OCEAN

The ocean, the seas, rivers, lakes and ponds bring so much calm and tranquilly – we love to sit beside a river or pond, or sun ourselves on a sandy beach. Yet, when we talk about climate change, we seem to concentrate more on what's happening on land, and forget about the ocean and the vital role it plays. Take note here, it is ocean – not oceans. That is because in the environmental world it is regarded as one entity, irrespective of whether it's the Pacific, the Atlantic, the Indian or any other. It is one ocean. In truth, we typically only think about the ocean in relation to holidays and thoughts about dipping our toes in aqua-green water, swimming and diving to see exotic fish. But imagine if we were not able to do that anymore. That there were no fish to see, that the vast ocean was no longer vast. Sadly, we are in danger of all this happening.

The ocean is where life on Earth began and makes up 71% of the Earth's surface. It contains sodium chloride and other minerals necessary for our survival, while marine phytoplankton provide half of all the oxygen we breathe. And because, as a species, we do like to monetize everything, the ocean is also known as the blue economy, and estimated to be worth over $1.5 trillion per year globally.[188] It provides over 30 million jobs and supplies protein to over three billion people. Now, with new large-scale industrial activities, such as offshore renewable energy, as well as the growing interest in ocean mining and marine biotechnology, the ocean has moved to the top of the political and economic agendas.

This ecosystem, almost like a giant organism, controls the climate, the weather and the water cycle. It's the planet's largest ecosystem – and, guess what, the largest carbon sink – absorbing excess heat and energy released from rising greenhouse gas emissions trapped in the Earth's system. It is estimated that the ocean has absorbed 90% of the heat generated by rising emissions created from fossil fuels and over a quarter of human-made carbon dioxide emissions annually. It has shielded us from the most extreme impacts of climate change, absorbing most of the excess heat.[189] It is our lungs. However, while immense and still largely unexplored, the ocean is also finite, fragile and fast approaching irreversible tipping points. There are big risks to the health of our ocean, mainly because we don't have a lot of research or knowledge about ocean life.

As excess heat and energy warm the ocean, the change in temperature will lead to unparalleled cascading effects, including melting ice, a rising sea level and ocean acidification. These changes will ultimately have a lasting impact on marine biodiversity and on the lives and livelihoods of coastal communities and beyond. This includes around 680 million people living in low-lying coastal areas – and almost two billion who live in half of the world's megacities that are located on the coast.[190]

RISING SEA LEVELS

The world's ocean is now heating faster than ever, and temperatures are the highest ever recorded. Warming waters have a domino effect, forcing marine mammals, fish, shellfish and crustaceans to search for colder water as their natural homes become uninhabitable. Melting sea ice is killing land animals like polar bears and penguins that rely on it for hunting. Sea warming causes oxygen loss, which sends species in search of oxygenated waters. As waters warm, they expand. According to NASA, this effect is thought to have contributed one third to one half of the global sea-level rise we have seen since around the year 2000, and this effect has hastened in recent decades.[191]

Plus, believe it or not, there is something called a 'marine heatwave.' These have doubled in frequency and have become longer lasting, more intense and more extensive. The Intergovernmental Panel on Climate Change says that human influence has been their primary cause since the 1970s.[192] So far, the majority of marine heatwaves took place between 2006 and 2015, causing widespread coral bleaching and reef degradation. In 2021, nearly 60% of our ocean experienced at least one spell of marine heatwaves.[193]

The UN Environment Programme says that all the world's coral reefs could bleach by the end of the century if the water continues to warm.[194] Coral bleaching occurs as reefs lose their life-sustaining microscopic algae when under stress. Because of the diversity of life found in the habitats created by corals, reefs are called the 'rainforests of the sea.' It is estimated that 25% of the ocean's fish depend on healthy coral reefs. Fish and other organisms shelter, find food, reproduce and rear their young in the many nooks and crannies formed by corals – reef corals build homes for millions of species of marine life. They support healthy ocean food chains and they protect our coastlines.

Ocean habitats, such as seagrass meadows and mangroves, are highly valuable in the fight against climate change. Mangroves are some of the most carbon-rich ecosystems on the planet, storing on average 1,000 tonnes of carbon per hectare in their biomass and underlying soils.[195] They also support healthy fisheries, improve water quality, and provide coastal protection against floods and storms. The trees within mangrove forests absorb carbon dioxide and reduce the planet's exposure to dangerous gases, while many fisheries rely on mangroves as breeding grounds.

SMALL ISLAND DEVELOPING STATES

Small island developing states (SIDS) are uniquely threatened by climate change and rising sea levels. Two Pacific islands, one of which is Tuvalu, are at risk of disappearing by the end of this century, and some communities are already having to relocate.[196] Communities in low-lying atoll countries such as Kiribati and the Maldives may be forced to move if the sea level rises above a metre.[197] All SIDS benefit in different ways from an intimate relationship with the ocean. Singapore, for instance, makes use of its strategic geographic position within the global trading system. Other countries, like the Marshall Islands, depend on their fish resources. For many SIDS, sea-related tourism has become a mainstay of the economy. The loss of land along coastlines due to rising sea levels, especially on atolls and low limestone islands, is likely to disrupt all the economic and social sectors in these countries. Coastal erosion will have profoundly adverse impacts on the tourism industry and on infrastructure.

These small islands have long been recognized by the international community as a special case whose needs and concerns have to be addressed. These countries are among the least responsible for climate change, yet they are likely to suffer the most from its adverse effects. This is what makes them a special case requiring the help and attention of the international community.

At COP26, Prime Minister Narendra Modi launched the Infrastructure for Resilient Island States (IRIS). IRIS aims to develop the infrastructure of small island nations and has received financial contributions from Australia, the UK and other countries. The idea behind IRIS is to give new hope, confidence and satisfaction at doing something for the most vulnerable countries. At the launch event, Prime Minister Modi said, "The last few decades have proved that no one is untouched by the wrath of climate change. Whether they are developed countries or countries rich in natural resources, this is a big threat to everyone. … It is the collective responsibility of all of us toward mankind. It is, in a way, a common atonement for our sins."[198]

Climate change is likely to have far-reaching effects on the environment and economic prospects of SIDS, as well as on the health of the people living in these areas. The availability of freshwater is a major limiting factor for economic and social development in SIDS. Many of these countries rely entirely on a single source of water supply, making them highly vulnerable to climatic and other environmental changes. In SIDS, where rainwater is the primary source of supply, water availability is sensitive to rainfall patterns and changes in storm tracks. A reduction in rainfall coupled with sea-level rises, changes in the intensity and frequency of the El Niño[199] weather pattern, and changes in rainfall seasonality would decrease the volume of drinking water.

There is a lack of information about the complex interplay between and within natural and human systems in SIDS. There is also a gap in the provision of information on likely changes in climate and human systems at the small island scale. As a result, most SIDS have not yet been able to undertake an in-depth, nationwide climate change impact and vulnerability assessment in an integrated manner. Without these assessments, planning adaptation policies, strategies and programmes will be difficult to do.

LOSS OF MARINE LIFE

The ocean is home to a rich diversity of marine life – animals, plants and microorganisms. Some places have such a large variety of species that they are called biological 'hotspots.' These areas of high biodiversity generally support important biological processes such as spawning, nurseries or feeding areas. Some also have species not found anywhere else in the world.

The loss of marine biodiversity is weakening the ocean ecosystem and its ability to withstand disturbances, adapt to climate change, and play its role as a global ecological and climate regulator. Life in the ocean is an essential component of climate regulation. Climate change due to human activity has a direct impact on marine species. It alters their abundance, diversity, distribution, feeding, breeding and development, as well as the relationships between species. Another factor in the loss of marine life is plastic pollution. It is estimated that by 2050 there could be more plastic in the sea than fish.[200] As the plastic piles up, fish disappear. Since industrialized fishing began in the mid-20th century, the ocean has been transformed.

OVERFISHING

Overfishing is severely impacting marine biodiversity: around 34% of the world's fish stock are overfished.[201] If this continues, there will be less fish in the ocean for future generations as well as less biodiversity. Overfishing not only impacts the fish that are targeted for harvesting but also other marine species that interact with fishing vessels. Oceanic shark and ray species have declined by 71% since the 1970s as a result of overfishing. Part of this is bycatch, which consists of species that are caught but cannot be used or are not wanted. Bycatch is one of the other leading threats, and it is estimated that around 10% of annual catches are discarded by marine commercial fisheries each year.[202] Estimates show that if overfishing continues at the current rate, fish populations could collapse by 2048.[203]

In 2003, scientists claimed that 90% of large predatory fish, such as tuna, cod and groupers, had already disappeared since 1950,[204] while in 2017, the UN's Food and Agricultural Organization said 90% of global marine fish stocks had been fully exploited, overexploited or depleted.[205] The alarming decline is a result of overfishing – populations cannot reproduce fast enough to keep up with the global appetite for fish.

Added to this is bottom trawling, the practice of dragging heavy nets along the seabed, which releases as much carbon into the atmosphere each year as the entire aviation industry.[206] An average of 1.47 gigatons of carbon is produced by boats trawling the ocean floor looking for shrimp, increasing ocean acidification and affecting biodiversity. Additionally, some shrimp trawling catches 90% nonshrimp species (another example of bycatch), meaning that many animals are caught and then discarded.[207]

CONCLUSION

The ocean is the lungs of the planet, generating 50% of the oxygen we need, absorbing 25% of all carbon dioxide emissions and capturing 90% of the excess heat generated by these emissions.[208] It sustains us and provides oxygen, food and medicine. It is a source of recreation, discovery, identity and culture, and more than three billion people rely on food from the ocean as a significant source of protein and nutrition.[209] If we safeguard the ocean's health and biodiversity, it will in turn protect human health and wellbeing, and help ensure our survival.

There was a time when we thought the ocean was endless and we treated it that way. Entanglements with fishing gear, ocean noise pollution, overfishing, marine plastics and human actions have all been negatively impacting the ocean for decades at a rate that it cannot keep up with. If we don't change our ways, there will be more plastic than fish, because as the plastic piles up, the fish disappear.

Warm water holds less oxygen, which is a big problem for marine animals. As anyone who owns a fish tank knows, you need air bubbling through it because the fish inside will use up the oxygen. When the oxygen levels go down, dead zones will expand. These are areas of the ocean where the water quality is too poor to sustain life. Pollution is adding to the devastation.

But all is not lost, as there are sustainable fisheries using innovative technology and creative fishing practices to protect biodiversity. Scientists, fishers, students and nonprofits are working together worldwide to develop sustainable techniques to transform marine environments. Again, we need to act quickly for future generations.

TAKEAWAY

The fish that we eat impact the health of our ocean and marine life. We know that certain fish are severely endangered, yet they are still finding their way onto our plates. So, buy sustainably sourced fish and remember that 'local' does not automatically mean 'sustainable.' When we, as consumers, choose sustainable seafood, it encourages supermarkets and restaurants to demand it from their suppliers, and this demand can reward fishers and fish farmers who adopt sustainable practices. It also encourages governments to improve management, which then supports the social and economic prosperity of many coastal communities and countries.

Another little thing that makes a difference is if you visit the beach, always take your rubbish home – don't leave it on the beach.

CHAPTER 16

IN CONVERSATION WITH OCEAN EXPERTS

I spoke to some wonderful voices for this chapter: someone who is working to protect our ocean, someone who understands the power of mangroves, someone who works with humpback whales and someone from an organization making a real global impact on sustainable fishing. The four voices are Antoinette Vermilye, co-founder of the Gallifrey Foundation and SHE Changes Climate; Pradeep Tripathi, co-founder of the award-winning non-profit organization Green Yatra; Rachel Cartwright, naturalist and humpback whale researcher; and Jim Cannon, CEO and founder of Sustainable Fisheries Partnership.

ANTOINETTE VERMILYE

COFOUNDER OF THE GALLIFREY FOUNDATION AND SHE CHANGES CLIMATE

In early October 2023, I spoke with Antoinette Vermilye, cofounder of the Gallifrey Foundation and SHE Changes Climate. The Gallifrey Foundation is focused on the protection of our ocean and marine life, while SHE Changes Climate is a campaigning organization aiming to get more women into top-level negotiating positions at the Conference of the Parties (COP), a major annual climate conference between almost all countries. Antoinette is a passionate expert with knowledge about the complex interrelationships between the ocean, plastics, gender and overfishing and how they affect social injustice, human health and the environment.

Tell me about the work of the Gallifrey Foundation and why you set it up.

The ocean covers 70% of the planet, yet gets the least attention. It has the biggest impact on our future and is key to getting us out of this mess, but this lack of awareness could lead to our destruction. Importantly, it is also underfunded. SDG[210] 14, which relates to life below water, is by far the least funded, representing 0.01% of all SDG funding from development finance up to 2019. The ocean plays a huge part in atmospheric conditions and the climate, and its degradation is causing biodiversity loss, impacting not just human health, but also social justice, gender equality, Indigenous and coastal people, intersectional environmentalism – I could go on! The effects of single-use – plastic – food packaging, overfishing, sharks, deep seabed mining are all having a negative impact. It's like taking a juggernaut, driving it down a hill and not applying the brakes. We need to apply the brakes.

When I cofounded the Gallifrey Foundation with my husband, we wanted to identify collaborative opportunities to tackle ocean conservation issues, which are at the heart of our modus operandi. We did not want to reinvent the wheel and are focused on finding the actions that can specifically move the needle in the shortest amount of time, with the most outcomes, because we don't have time. We pinpoint and fill the gaps where we find little or no action is taking place or collaborate with other groups for greater impact. As a result, we've got various projects in different areas, which means our work is truly representative of the natural world, where everything is connected.

It is going to take time to get us back to a liveable planet – that's the big picture we are looking at right now. There is very worrying information coming out about deep seabed mining, which again is not getting the global attention or action that it should. It's one of the few frontiers we have not yet officially crossed. Let's try not to cross it.

How do we start to recognize the ocean as one of the most important resources?

I am going to start by saying we need to use the word 'ocean' in the singular because we tend to silo it into different names, such as the Pacific Ocean, the Atlantic, etc., when in fact it's one body of water – it is all connected. It's very important to acknowledge this and it's something that we in the marine world are trying raise awareness about.

We, as a species, have come from the ocean: technically it's our mother, and it's where we have evolved from – we spend the first nine months of our existence in water! Both our planet and our own bodies comprise 60 to 70% water. We are literally the embodiment of planet Earth in our physiology, and we need to not only recognize the ocean as a resource, but appreciate that it gives us 50% of the air we breathe, along with impacting our weather.

I'm going to give you an incredible fact that few people are aware of. We know that 2023 has been the year when the ocean surface temperature has warmed the most, due to increased fossil fuel burning. The ocean has been absorbing 90% of human-generated heat from greenhouse gas emissions. That is the equivalent of the energy of seven Hiroshima bombs exploding per second! That's how much it's absorbing. It's been doing this for the last 30 or 40 years, and scientists have calculated the full total, which is a bit over a billion Hiroshima bombs. How much longer can it keep doing what it is doing?!

So, the ocean plays a vital role in maintaining an average surface temperature of 15°C. Without it, we would be at 50°C, which means we would have been to the end of the line much faster.

We take the ocean for granted. It's a service that helps us live, and we don't even value it. Instead, we see it as something to either extract from or dump stuff into. Usually we take out up to half the weight of the world's population in fish annually, and then discard up to 40% of it as bycatch before we even get the fish haul to land. It's cavalier – there's no respect. It's abuse.

Consequently, 90% of all the fish in our ocean have gone. We've so overfished, we are trawling for fish right down to the bottom of the proverbial barrel. We have also renamed and rebranded fish to make them more marketable for consumer demands, which has consequences. For example, the famous Chilean sea bass is in fact called the Patagonian toothfish and is an ocean bottom dweller, but we have cleared it out of Chile and now go to Antarctica to fish for it. It has been exploited to such an extent that it's now vulnerable. Then there's the orange roughy, which is the rebrand of the slimehead fish.

Not only that, but we dump our chemical waste and our plastic pollution, and approximately 80% of the world's wastewater enters the ocean untreated. These are all reasons we need to act and why we need to care. We've lost compassion, care and connection. I am passionate about getting us all learning to connect the dots, to make that circular connection.

What are some of the simple things we can do to make a difference?

My dream would be for everyone to look at their lives and think about how their actions can make a difference. It could be simple things such as eating less meat and dairy. Just by doing that, we stop our dependence on petrochemicals for fertilizer and will help reduce methane, which is 80 times more potent than carbon dioxide. We need to get rid of cruel mass production, where creatures who are sentient beings are treated as walking meat. It is about using less fossil fuel transport, as fossil fuels go into the atmosphere. I often use this analogy – if you put yourself in a small room and start filling it with balloons, then keep filling it with balloons, you soon won't be able to move around. It's going to get uncomfortable. Keep filling it with balloons and soon you're not going to be able to breathe. We're basically at that point now.

People always raise aviation as a key culprit for greenhouse gas emissions. I agree aviation is definitely a contributor. However, do you know that bottom trawling emits the same quantity of greenhouse gas? So, eat less fish, cut plastic out of your life – it's derived from oil, gas and coal) and create games by thinking of pro-planet challenges when you go around the shops to see what you can find that's not wrapped in plastic. This is about everything we can do. Walk or cycle, use public transport or shared transport – all of those are better than your individual car. This includes where you place your financial investments, your pension. These are little things, but they add up to a lot.

Use your voice and use your purse. And the most important idea is leveraging the six degrees of separation.[211] We all know someone in our circle who's influential: they may be on a board, or head of a company or even a politician – they have more power to make change. We need to remember that systemic change is going to be driven by a demand from the bottom up. Voting is probably the most important thing we can do. We've seen this with climate strike walkouts by the youth who have been protesting. All of these things are showing us the will of the people and that we want something to happen. The frustration is that's it's not and I think that is the biggest worry.

We also need gender inclusion, and my work with SHE Changes Climate focuses on women who are the most impacted by the climate on our coasts and within Indigenous communities. Women are usually the ones who are portrayed as the victims. Well, it's not actually that they're victims – it's that they've been put on the front line. Women are normally the carers at home, looking after the children, the elderly and other family members. So, when floods happen, they're usually the first to drown. Ironically, many of these women living in vulnerable climate change regions have the solutions, but those solutions are not being heard. Women will keep striving for more equality, but I want men to be our allies – where they walk into a meeting and ask, "Where are the women?" Or I want men to say, "I want to hear what you've got to say" and actively seek out the women in the room.

We need to understand intersectional environmentalism and research the painful truth of our roles in climate colonialism – the impact that it has had. The best book to read is *The Nutmeg's Curse* by Amitav Ghosh, which is brilliant.[212] Colonialism is the key driver of everything that has led to the position we are in now, but that doesn't mean we need to beat ourselves up. It's important to understand and appreciate the past – to make sure that those voices that have not been allowed to be part of the solutions become part of the conversation. We all have a role that we can play at any point.

Education is important at the Gallifrey Foundation. Tell me about the scholarships.

About 10–15 years ago, my husband and I identified the need for education. We did not have the time to implement any educational strategies but we wanted to act. We were looking for upstream long- and short-term solutions, and if we were going to effect systemic change, we needed to start with the institutions that were part of the problem. I hate to say it, but business schools are basically about how to make more money: go off, grow a business, ignore the externalities and the fact that your business might be polluting water, polluting air, damaging Nature, starving people and/or depriving them of resources.

At the moment, shareholder value trumps all environmental and social goals. At the foundation, we wanted to change that thinking. While we are a small organization, we wanted to create big change and realized that we could target business schools. We started with the London Business School. Full disclosure: my husband went there and loved it because it has a large body of international students, which meant a lot of perspectives from around the world. This was a criterion for us.

We came up with the idea to award a scholarship for people from NGOs, to maximize the social and environmental impact. We selected NGOs because they have a lot of passionate experts, but they don't necessarily have the skills to really scale up change. Plus, if you own an NGO, you are fully aware of the environment, of social responsibility and social entrepreneurship. The idea was to combine those two elements together: to be able to scale up for good. We want to incorporate more social and environmental entrepreneurship. The aim is to widen the lens of doing business for good and bring in those different perspectives.

We don't have a say in who is selected, but our scholarship stipulates that it is people from the Global South, preferably women and from NGOs. It is important to ensure that mix. After ten years of doing this, the school has grown exponentially, too, in terms of its own sustainability. We're facing a planetary crisis, and we need businesses to think very carefully about their externalities and how they have to mitigate them right now.

What legacy do you want to leave?

I've struggled over this question and, in reality, my legacy is a drop in the ocean. What I believe we need is for everyone to be doing something, so there is a wave that can change the world. My pragmatic view of life on this planet is that it's very fleeting and illusory.

What I care about is my responsibility to the future generations that are going to live with the effects of what we've done. I was in New York last week for Global Climate Change Week NYC 2023 and a video of Sir David Attenborough was screened as part of a panel that I was on. He talked about his life on this planet, what he's seen and everything we could do to put things right. Significantly, Attenborough said that if we applied everything we need to do today, we could be back to where we were in 80 years. Now, that sounds very hopeful. But I'm going to be a grandmother at the end of this year, and that 80 years will be the lifetime of my new grandson, who will be facing and dealing with the more severe consequences of our actions. It should not be something that his generation has to deal with. This crisis is my fault. It happened on my watch, in my lifetime.

My responsibility is to help the youth, and it's just not about giving them a platform, but to be their active supporter. In Switzerland, an Intergovernmental Panel on Climate Change climate scientist gave university lectures three or four years ago and engaged all the young students, who were inspired to create change. But when she returned this year to talk to the students again, they were completely apathetic. She found that the huge conversation about the youth and how they had submitted their demands to governments had led to nothing, and they had felt gamed for photoshoots and to further political agendas. And that's the problem. How do we deal with growing eco-anxiety of the young and adults? How do we deal with a system that is geared to promoting business as usual and even growing it?!

I want to mention something about our greater responsibility that goes beyond our local communities. Last week in the UK, a teenager went and felled the famous Sycamore Gap tree at Hadrian's Wall, which is absolutely tragic.[213] But I have to sit back and look at the bigger picture and think about the football-pitch-sized fields of the Amazon forests that have been cut down *daily*. There has been no huge international outrage over the last 10–15 years. Let's put that in perspective. We can take action to stop further deforestation. We can protect areas and support those groups that are fighting to protect them. We need to support the Indigenous communities that make up 3% of the world's population but are protecting 80% of the biodiversity we have left. We can ensure our governments and our own consumer choices move in the right direction.

There are some incredible groups working together on the climate front that have galvanized people – We Don't Have Time; Just Stop Oil; Extinction Rebellion; climate champions like Jane Fonda, whom I met at Global Climate Change Week NYC. She was amazing and said, "There is nothing more liberating than being handcuffed for your beliefs!"

The financial power that the oil and gas companies have is crushing us, and they are paying the media and politicians. It is overwhelming. If you watch the Chris Packham documentary, it shows how the Just Stop Oil protesters are being portrayed by the mainstream UK media and government as terrorists.[214] Nearly every mainstream editorial piece positions them as ecoterrorists who are disrupting normal life. All of these things are deliberate tactics and relate to the agenda of the oil and gas sector. How do you think they've expanded oil and gas here in the UK or in the US?!

The conversation we are having about migration is a troubling one. We are being told by politicians and the media that these are economic migrants, but many of these people are moving because of climate change in their country, where there is a drought mainly driven by Western greenhouse gas emissions, which means there is no work – no farming, no fishing. If we're going to do things, we need to understand the context to effect and influence change.

We have to be the mosquito – we're not going to be the elephant. We've got to find ways to do things strategically. We need to be wily like a fox to help push change forward. We're on a ticking time bomb, and my legacy would be to help us wake up and connect the dots to see the bigger picture.

PRADEEP TRIPATHI

COFOUNDER OF GREEN YATRA

In September 2023, I spoke to Pradeep Tripathi, cofounder of the award-winning nonprofit organization Green Yatra, based in India. The organization's focus is to fight the climate crisis, with a mission to reduce pollution, rejuvenate the ecosystem, plant trees and support the need for Nature in big urban cities. This work also extends to restoring mangrove ecosystems in coastal regions.

Tell me about the work of Green Yatra and what inspired you to set it up.

The story of how Green Yatra began is an interesting one, as I never thought while I was at school or college that I was going to run a nonprofit organization. My parents wanted me to go into the medical field, but I realized that medicine was not my thing. I also had this strong idea that I should follow my dream, which was inspired by Swami Vivekananda, who said we have one life, and we must make the best use of it, and do what we want to do in our lives.[215] I grew up in a very small village, in the foothills, surrounded by Nature in the state of Madhya Pradesh in a district called Satna. I moved here to Mumbai years ago when I was studying and I still do not feel like a city guy. At that time when I moved here, I realized people were coming to the city for a better life. But instead, what I saw were the high levels of pollution.

Before I set up Green Yatra, there was nothing much happening in Mumbai with a green focus or awareness of the environment, even though there were global initiatives like the UN's Conference of the Parties and the Sustainable Development Goals. That's when I thought, "This is what I would love to do." I decided to set up the organization in 2008 with my friend Durgesh Gupta.

Durgesh is a practising lawyer in the Bombay High Court and the Supreme Court of India, and we never thought we would reach the level we have now.

Green Yatra has a Nature-centric approach to finding solutions. People talk about the government not doing enough or not finding the answers to local eco-challenges, but actually the responsibility lies with each of us to contribute and be part of society. We all need to be accountable. At the early stages of Green Yatra, we ran two projects. One was Go GREEN Ganesha, to promote an eco-friendly celebration of India's ancestral festival Ganesh Chaturthi, and the other was Go GREEN Kids, where children taught their parents how to adopt a green lifestyle. We realized that people had lots of daily pressures at work and home, and if you told them about the environment, they were not that interested. But if their children learned something new and shared it with the whole family, it had a domino effect. We found that by teaching children, we had an impact, and today we are associated with more than 10,000 schools across India.

All of our projects have always been absolutely free. We don't charge government bodies, such as local governments, government schools or officials, because we believe that these government workers are service providers who clean our streets, collect our rubbish, and maintain a regular supply of water and an electricity supply.

One of the things we are committed to at Green Yatra, and this is very important to us, is to ensure that the trees we plant survive to become mature trees. As a result, we invest a lot of time nurturing these trees. We want to be accountable for the projects we are doing. We track all our work on social media, continuously sharing it. You can see the before, the inbetween and the after images of the trees, and we use drones to shoot from all angles and locations.

What have been the challenges?

We have had a lot of learning along the way and have learned from the mistakes we made in the beginning. In the early days of our work, we found that while we were raising awareness, the awareness was not translating to action and the environment needs action. That's when we decided to do more work on the ground, along with awareness-raising. We started doing small planting projects with schools, colleges and housing societies. But a lot has happened since we began, as now globally there is considerable awareness about climate change, where being carbon neutral is understood and high on the corporate agenda. People are focusing on all these things.

We wanted to make environmental literacy key, because of the pollution everywhere. Our focus is mostly on urban spaces, especially since some of the most polluted cities in the world are Indian cities. The development of cities and construction work here means that we have lost our tree coverage and, with that, biodiversity. People living in cities are being deprived and restricted in their access to fresh air and natural spaces. In cities like Mumbai and Delhi, we have beautiful houses, multistorey buildings, air-conditioned cars, electricity 24/7, but when it comes to oxygen and natural open spaces, we don't have enough of that. Plus, India has a water problem. The country used to have an ecosystem with water bodies such as wells, but they have become polluted, and big cities such as Delhi, Bengaluru, Chennai and Mumbai don't have their own water.

This is how our tree plantation, water body restoration, climate education and school awareness programmes started.

Have you noticed people and corporates becoming interested in helping and supporting the work?

When we started in early 2008, people were only interested in getting involved on World Environment Day. Now, over a decade later, people are involved throughout the year. We receive thousands of calls and emails from people, schools and corporates that want to participate in doing something good for the planet.

People want to celebrate their birthday by planting a tree, including at children's birthday parties. People want workshops on topics from how to adopt a green lifestyle to how to reduce plastic use. Corporates too are keen to be involved because of the corporate social responsibility mandate here in India, and many want to be carbon neutral. Now that is a change! However, there is still lots of work to be done. Though we have already crossed the line with climate change where we can't fix things, we can definitely control things.

Tell me about the mangrove plantation work you do and why mangroves are so important for the climate.

At Green Yatra, we like to call mangroves the 'unsung warrior.' We know and understand a lot about terrestrial plants and trees, which are all on land, because we can see the benefits, yet mangroves also do a lot of work for the planet. People don't venture into the mangrove areas because they're in marshy land. Yet they are the biggest carbon sink – mangroves can produce up to eight times more oxygen than other types of forests and store up to four times more carbon than tropical forests. India's main mangrove regions are in West Bengal, Gujarat, Maharashtra, and the Andaman and Nicobar Islands.

The other thing about mangroves is that they have a dual purpose, as apart from being great carbon sinks, they also provide livelihood to fishing communities. They nurture small fish and are wonderful breeding grounds, especially as the big fish can't enter the network of branches that surrounds the marsh areas. Plus, now these mangrove regions are producing products such as grapes, honey and even alcohol. I would like to share a quick insight into mangrove honey, which smells completely different than other honey. It has its own fragrance and tastes different too. It is a special honey that is organic and of high quality. In fact, it was showcased at the G20 when India hosted the summit in September 2023. The Indian government gifted every head of state and all those who attended in an official capacity with a jar of mangrove honey called Bonphool, which is produced in Sundarbans, West Bengal, by local women's self-help groups.

At Green Yatra, we have implemented an innovative mangrove plantation technique called the 'fishbone channel method,' which has restored a degraded urban coastal area in Mumbai under our Blue Yatra initiative. The fishbone channel uses biomimicry to restore and rejuvenate spoiled mangrove forests by supplying them with water. It artificially waters areas that have dried up because they do not receive regular tidal water. The shape of the fishbone allows the water to reach every corner of the field channels and allows areas to be flooded so they turn back into wetlands, where new mangroves can be reforested. The method converts barren land with a high saline content into fertile land to support the survival of mangrove plant species.

From the restoration work we have been doing with mangroves, we have seen how rich their biodiversity is, from butterflies to bees and the new birds they attract, even to species such as the golden jackal, snakes and eagles. Another reason mangroves are unsung warriors is that, apart from supporting livelihoods and fishing, they are the first line of defence in a tsunami or any kind of ocean water calamity. They support the blue economy. If we don't restore mangroves, the oceans will start to reclaim the land, and there will be more natural disasters such as flooding and costal erosion.

What legacy do you want to leave?

My dream is to leave this world better than how I found it, where breathing fresh oxygen shouldn't be a privilege. I am trying to create a better future for ourselves and the next generation. I'm following my dream and today at Green Yatra we are doing good work. The organization is one of the big four environmental implementation NGOs in India, where we are recognized for credible work.

Even when we are pushed to capacity, we will still adopt a whole city to help make it green. A good example of our work is at Navi Mumbai Municipal Corporation, which is a satellite city that's part of Mumbai. We planted over 300,000 trees there, and we have now extended our work in most of the metro cities across India, which include Delhi National Capital Region, Hyderabad, Jaipur, Pune, Nagpur and Bengaluru.

As mentioned, we have a clear policy to never take a single penny from any government body. We do million-dollar projects absolutely free for the government, and for that we are thankful to our corporate partners. They are investing financially through their corporate social responsibility initiatives.

Right now, I am on a mission to change corporate office behaviours. This is because through the rise of office developments, I am seeing more air purifiers and air conditioners being installed in new builds, which is not sustainable, as they use lots of energy. These huge office buildings that are being built have no windows and no natural daylight, and have large air conditioners where you find hundreds of people in summer working with their sweaters on! Apart from being energy exhaustive, it's not healthy, as the air is polluted and making people sick. I want to get offices to put in windows to allow natural air circulation. This will save energy and is a simple practice; it's not anything new.

I want to help inspire people with simple daily green practices. At Green Yatra, we ask people to dedicate 10% of their daily screen time to researching something about the planet and how they can participate. I want to encourage people to go out with their children to experience Nature; we can all make changes – it starts with us. It could be a simple thing such as creating a kitchen garden. These days, many children do not know where their food comes from. We are losing our vegetable markets here in India. They have been replaced by grocery stores and shopping malls, or food is being delivered to the doorstep. Children have forgotten how things are sourced.

I believe we need to prepare our next generation so they can deal with the climate problems that they will have to face. They need to be ready for the mistakes we have made. At school, they are not being taught about what they should do for the climate conditions ahead – the climate situations arising from disasters that will happen in their future from increased flooding and rises in pollution and heat. They don't know how to protect themselves. That is one of our visions at Green Yatra.

On a more personal note, I have a daughter who is two and a half years old and, for her birthday, I started a tiny urban forest in Mumbai. It is my gift to her and for every birthday that we celebrate, I will keep planting trees. We will ensure that she continues to see this forest and is connected to it too.

It is so important for me to practise what I preach. As a family, we have started to grow our own vegetables, and we want to be self-sufficient. Life is not all about having a better car, or a big house, or what you're studying, or being at a nice school or college. It is about having fresh air to breathe, and a healthy and happy life. Money is not a motivation for me. While we need money to survive, it's not my purpose.

I hope by creating these forests that in 200 years' time, people can experience them and say there was some crazy man who converted many dumping and debris yards into urban forests. This is not only for humans, but for the birds, the animals and the insects, such as fireflies, which are in decline. We are destroying so much, at least I can give back to society. We get so much from Nature – oxygen, life, food – and everything we get from Nature is for free. Mother Nature is not asking to be paid or charging us. This is my service to Mother Nature. Everything I am doing is for my happiness.

RACHEL CARTWRIGHT

NATURALIST AND HUMPBACK WHALE RESEARCHER

In February 2024, I spoke to naturalist and researcher Rachel Cartwright, who is focused on the behavioural ecology of humpback whales, mostly in Hawaiian waters. Rachel holds a PhD in conservation biology, and her research programmes are focused on advancing knowledge and creating nurseries to protect the whales and enable them to safely raise their young. Rachel leads the research team at the Keiki Kohola Project, which promotes the protection of humpback whale mother and calf pairs during their time in Hawaiian waters.[216]

> What made you start researching the dynamics of the mother and calf humpback whales in the North Pacific region?

I come from Manchester in the north of England, which is very industrial, and sometimes when I look at what I'm doing now, I'm as surprised as anybody! I originally trained as a biologist, graduating in the 1980s, but there were no jobs at that time, so I trained as a teacher and was sent to the Bahamas, as a Commonwealth ambassador, teaching science. From the Bahamas, I travelled to Alaska. Alaska is a very emotive place and when I arrived, I was struck by the scenery, the grandeur and the wildness. I can remember my first whale sighting, which was at four o'clock in the morning. In that moment, I couldn't believe what I was seeing, especially as it was so far removed from my background. Importantly, at that time in the 1990s, whale numbers were still very low.

Whales were resurging from the days of commercial whaling, but their recovery at this time was still slow. It was very evocative to see them for the first time, even at a distance.

As the weather turned cooler as the summer waned in Alaska, the whales – and lots of the locals – headed to Hawaii for the winter. I followed along. Fast forward to early December in Hawaii. I was out in a boat with friends when a group of three whales came right over to our little boat, literally playing around by the side of us. I'd never seen anything like it before and that's when I decided I wanted to work as a naturalist on the boats in Hawaii. I was interested in the relationship between the mothers and their calves – whales give birth to only one calf. It's really a beautifully close relationship. It was this connection with Nature, which I hadn't had before, which drew me in, and I knew I wanted to stay and contribute by doing research. I worked out of Lahaina Harbor, which opened out onto a wide channel, the 'Au'Au Channel, which lies between the islands of Maui and Lanai. I didn't realize then, but this is literally one of the best places in the world to encounter humpback whale mother and calf pairs.

So, when people ask, "Why research whales?" my first thought is, "Why not whales?" The closer you get to them, the more remarkable they become. This is an animal that we took to the brink of extinction in our lifetimes. Seeing something so large, yet so gentle, at first it can seem an intimidating creature to get to know, but soon you discover that this is such a responsive animal. Honestly, I do believe that they look at us with the same interest that we have for them.

Have you ever swum with them?

As part of the research, we are in the water with them, but only when the research really justifies it. Around mothers and calves, we're especially careful, but if you have patience, on some occasions you can gain a degree of trust and they allow you to be with them in the water. There's a certain way of doing it, and you have mentors when you first start going in the water to help you understand how to approach them, because they get easily spooked and disappear in no time. As soon as you get off the back of the boat and the second you touch the water, they know you're there. So, then it's all about whether or not they're going to tolerate you. If you can approach them in a way that doesn't intimidate them, then they will allow you to be in the water with them. If not, then they're just gone in the blink of an eye.

What have you learned about these mammals that has surprised you?

When I started to do my research, I approached my questions in a quantitative way. My work was statistically based, looking at the behavioural development of the calves to determine how fast they went through different behavioural phases, and then to determine how this would impact their survival rates. I'm part of a research team, the Keiki Kohola Project. I feel we have made a worthwhile contribution, but it's our latest research on empathy that is perhaps the most surprising.

We had an incident that became part of a documentary that we filmed recently with National Geographic, involving a young female whale that had become tangled up in nets. To give you the background, in many areas of the world, marine debris, including things like large, discarded fishing nets, is the single biggest cause of mortality for large whales right now. She was first sighted in Hawaiian waters in February 2021, already tangled up in nets. This was the second sighting of her, and when we found her, around five o'clock one day in early March, she wasn't looking good. She was extremely emaciated, covered in whale lice and only moving with difficulty. The entanglement team came out and moved as many lines as they could, but there was one right through her mouth that couldn't be removed. The next day, we were out on the water again, doing research, and we came across this whale again. This time, we had the documentary team with us, so we had drones in the air and experienced photographers onboard. So, we had a few different ways of keeping track of this little whale as she floated along, without adding to her distress. From the air, we could see tiger sharks trailing behind, trying to bite her tail. But as we were giving up hope for this young female whale, along comes another whale. This second whale then stayed with her for the next six hours. Checking our records later, we were able to determine that this was a male, at least 25 years old, and one that would normally travel to Japanese waters in the winter, so unlikely to be related in any way to the young female. As the day progressed and the young female became weaker still, the second whale lifted her up to the surface of the water so she could breathe. He would leave her side to circle her and bat away the sharks with his tail and then, each time, he would come back beside her.

I delved into this behaviour and found detailed accounts from whaling days describing whales coming to help other whales when they're caught in whalers' lines. The behaviours described were remarkably similar. And this happened even though there was no benefit for the whale that was providing the help, and whaling crews would often catch the second whale too. These examples show how whales have developed and refined a novel behaviour in response to a problem that humans have created. The real irony of it is the last time that these types of behaviours were recorded was at the height of the whaling days, and today the same behaviour is resurging to address yet another problem of our creation.

It's likely that this trait of compassion and empathetic response, called epimeletic behaviour, would have been weeded out of the whale population quickly because nice whales would have been taken, and these behaviours would have disappeared. But through a process known as behavioural plasticity, it seems to be reemerging in response to the high risks of entanglement.

Are all whales so empathetic?

Well, studies have identified cells associated with empathy. These have been identified in humans through the study of stroke victims, autistic individuals and neurodivergent people. These specific cells occur at the front of the brain and are exactly the same in whales, gorillas and elephants, who all have the same innate empathetic responses. Further evidence shows that this trait is heritable and varies between individuals. This means that it is may be driven by evolution, and the idea that whales are figuring out how to deal with this massive challenge that we've placed in the water is interesting. Recent studies show that up to 80% of large whales in areas of high productivity – where whales feed and fishing activities are also prevalent – have been entangled, and as many as 25% may be entangled year by year. Based on these numbers, we know that some whales are able to disentangle themselves from the debris, perhaps by throwing their tails around and potentially watching out for each other, which would certainly help keep the sharks away during such a vulnerable time.

In my 25 years of working with whales, this occasion on Maui was the first time I'd seen this behaviour, where one whale came in to help another in distress. There are accounts of this type of behaviour in other animals. For instance, when a well-known matriarch elephant passed away, other elephants came from up to six kilometres away to the very spot where she passed. There are also reports of gorillas adopting juveniles, and myriad other stories where animals, including whales and dolphins, come to the aid of others at times of distress.

What is a marine heatwave and how does it impact whales and the ocean?

Marine heatwaves are events that occur in specific locations, where the water in that location becomes hotter than usual for a sustained period of time. Essentially, it's similar to a heatwave on land. It can be caused for various reasons – such as disruptions in currents, or unusual amounts of heat from the sun

– creating hot areas in the ocean. Other factors could be a reduction in the flow of the water, or the flow of water from a warm area to what would otherwise be a cooler area. This changes the ocean temperature from its original baseline in a specific area, where you could have a marine heatwave in a cooler area, raising the baseline temperature in that region.

Usually, the ocean stays really constant in temperature and constant in pH, which is basically a measure of the acidity of the ocean. When these things move and alter, they can have catastrophic effects on the system. Both the change and the rate of change may cause problems. Wherever they occur, marine heatwaves are a consequence of a hotter atmosphere. Many of these systems are large scale too, such as El Niño, which happens in one place but impacts things elsewhere.

One of the most severe marine heatwaves in recent years occurred from 2014 to 2016 in the North Pacific. Eventually, it became known as the 'blob.'[217] Essentially, heat flowed in from the tropics to a nontropical area. The water continuously warmed up and did not dissipate. The warming effect then moved north, throughout the waters of the eastern North Pacific. In cooler, temperate areas, such as along the coastline of Alaska, the entire food chain was impacted. There are several reasons behind this, but primarily, the inflow of warm water capped upwellings[218] in this region that essentially support a food chain that permeates through the entire system. At the very base of this food chain are phytoplankton and zooplankton. Nutrients that are drawn up from deep water by upwellings support massive blooms of plankton, but with the upwellings capped, growth rates slowed. In addition, those plankton that usually feed in the area prefer cooler water, so those plankton headed north, in search of waters within their normal temperature range. Warmer-water species replaced them, but these warm-water plankton had a far lower nutritive value. Whales and other marine fauna such as seabirds fed on this new type of plankton, and it was like eating popcorn. The low-calorie content just wasn't enough to support the region's marine life.

By 2015, we saw this playing out in the Alaska area, where we started to see skinny whales. In 2016, the numbers of whales that came to Hawaii dropped. However, it was only later that we saw associated drops in the reproductive rate. Potentially, skinny females just didn't have the resources to support reproduction. Just as in humans, the hormones required to trigger ovulation are produced within fat cells. Skinny females did not even begin the process. The following two seasons we saw only very low numbers of calves in Hawaii, and following those years, there are some indications that the calves we did see in Hawaii might not have made it to Alaska, to their feeding areas. And it wasn't just the humpback whales that were impacted. We may have lost close to a million tufted puffins and crested auklets because they too couldn't find the food they needed. There were also unusual mortality events due to harmful algal blooms in fin whales. The whole system was negatively altered.

Perhaps the most concerning aspect of this is the trend we see as we look ahead. As the baseline ocean temperature becomes warmer and we get more disruptive weather patterns, marine heatwaves will become more frequent, and these warm-water events may only become more frequent.

What are some of the ways humpback whales and other large whales can offset climate change?

A paper from the International Monetary Fund's finance journal looked at the cost or the value of a whale in terms of its carbon sequestration potential.[219] I believe that as scientists, we've got to somehow showcase this larger economic value – the ecosystem capital – that the natural world offers. To put it simply, the sheer size of the whale means that everything it consumes becomes part of a vast living pool of carbon that then may remain in the marine cycle. You could literally think of whales as floating forests, with carbon from the atmosphere locked into their body tissues.

When whales eventually die and fall to the deep ocean floor, this is one of the few ways that nutrients enter the deep ocean to become a food source. Equally importantly, though, what remains of this once living tissue becomes fixed into marine sediments, and that ensures the carbon the tissue contains is taken out of the system for millions of years, which is positive.

But there is another even more fascinating side to this story. In feeding areas, whales become the gardeners of their own food resources. As we discussed, the gases and light needed for photosynthesis flood the top few metres of the water, but in deep marine systems, nutrients sink to the bottom, into the deep, dark depths. As whales move up and down through the water column, they mix these layers, Plus, they poop, producing large quantities of faeces, which puts iron, a key nutrient, into the surface waters. It's like fertilizer for the garden! It's literally like they're spraying lots of Miracle-Gro across the sunlit surface waters. This increases the rate of photosynthesis, which means more plankton, more fish and more food flowing through this system, and more carbon fixed into this living portion of the marine system.

Just as you would grow a forest to fix carbon on land, you can grow a marine system and fix carbon within it.

What final thoughts do you want to leave us with about whales?

I would just say healthy whales mean healthy oceans. When you see a whale, you're seeing a world that is wild enough for that whale to survive. You know by the whale's very presence that it will enrich the world around it, and in return that system can meet the needs of that great whale.

My last question: what would you like your legacy to be?

We need to support the next generation coming into this field. We need to make the world of conservation science accessible. We need to support young scientists and young people who want to go into conservation. And we need to provide them with meaningful experiences, so they can connect with the natural world.

Looking beyond this, as scientists, we've got to step out of the science bubble. It's our responsibility to connect with the general public in ways that make people see the value of the places and the systems that we're trying to protect. Being stuck in our echo chambers means we haven't passed on what we really know. The challenge for any scientist, to make sure our work matters, means we have to make every effort to tell our stories.

JIM CANNON

CEO AND FOUNDER OF SUSTAINABLE FISHERIES PARTNERSHIP

In late February 2024, I spoke to Jim Cannon, CEO and founder of Sustainable Fisheries Partnership (SFP). Jim founded SFP in 2006 to scale up the impact of fisheries' improvement efforts. At the time, there was no organization like SFP working with the seafood industry to drive change through its supply chains. The model for fisheries conservation that Jim and the SFP team created is now the standard approach to seafood sustainability in seafood companies around the world. Before starting SFP, Jim jointly edited the UN Food and Agriculture Organization's *Review of the State of World Marine Fishery Resources*[220] and worked at Conservation International, first as head of the conservation economics programme and then as cofounder of the Centre for Conservation and Government Affairs. In 2019, he joined the board of directors of Verra to help scale up financing of projects that tackle climate change and plastics pollution via voluntary offsets markets.

It's known that 30% of the world's fish stocks are already overfished.[221] What solution is SFP providing to help combat this?

We started work just over 20 years ago, sitting down with retailers and restaurant chains that were concerned about the fish supply. The concern was: "We are running out of fish and we need to figure out what we do about it." The solution I proposed was to talk to the supply chain to understand who could get meetings with the fishery ministers, who were the ones setting and implementing the rules. This pre-dated brand and environmental concerns, and my reason for this approach was that for about ten years I had been trying to have the same conversations from a nonprofit environmental perspective with little success. So, I thought, let's see if there is an industry voice in favour of conservation and long-term management, and the answer was "Yes!" The next question was, are they influential? Again, the answer was "Yes!" The case the supply chain made to ministers was completely different from the one that environmental NGOs make about why we need to protect the oceans. The industry talks about protecting the oceans because you need to protect jobs – a lot of those jobs are in remote coastal communities with little alternative opportunities. The industry is able to make the link from the health of the fish stock to long-term employment of lots of people within the fishing industry. This is important for politicians. We achieved great results early on, working primarily in Europe, Canada, the US and Russia.

The very first company we worked with was McDonald's, who use white fish such as cod, haddock, hake and pollock. This comes from countries with cooler waters such as Argentina, Canada, Chile, New Zealand, Norway, Russia and the US, which are the natural habitats of this type of fish. These countries tend to already have quite good governance with management systems in place, but they weren't all good at making decisions, and this is where SFP added value. We were able to change the decision-making environment quite quickly by having the CEOs of these large fishing and processing companies speak in favour of more cautious management, rebuilding of the fish stocks and so on.

To put it into context: McDonald's, a well-known brand, had a problem when its Filet-O-Fish sandwich was under threat. Almost all the North Atlantic cod was in crisis with the cod collapses in Canada, which is a famous example of overfishing. People still think about it and are working hard to recover the stock. It is now coming back, but it has taken a long time to fix. By the end of the 1990s, because of overfishing and bad management decisions, McDonald's, which had in the 1980s been able to look at 30 different abundant fish stocks, was now down to only five stable sources left when I spoke to them in 2002. The challenge wasn't that they couldn't fix the problem by only buying from those remaining supply sources. No, what they had to do was figure out how to reverse the overfishing and the depletion in the other stocks. That's what took me on this journey to figure out how to get political leverage and build constituencies for positive change – and to do that through the supply chain.

The supply chain is influential and gives you the means to communicate throughout it to drive change. That's what we started to do at SFP systematically. We reached out to Walmart, who made a big, bold commitment in 2006 based on what they saw as the early successes of the work with McDonald's: they would begin to source only certified sustainable fish within a certain timeframe, and they would do this by engaging their supply chain and improving fishery partnerships. From the perspective of a white fish buyer like McDonald's today, the sector is now in rude health – there are over 20 stocks that they can responsibly buy from that are in good condition and well managed.

When we think about the 30% that's overfished, that was true 25 years ago and is still true today. But it masks that fisheries in many regions have stopped overfishing and rebuilt stocks. Instead, what we are seeing is that other stocks, particularly in the developing world and in middle-income countries, are being overfished and depleted. There's been a shift in that 30%. Our biggest challenge is moving forward. It is not about Europe or North America or New Zealand anymore. Instead, we are seeing continued deterioration in Southeast Asia, throughout South Asia, around Africa, throughout Central America and in some parts of South America. This situation is going to continue to get worse for the foreseeable future.

The nature of the work shifts, because you're now talking about helping build fishery management systems that rely on institutions and governance that were built over 100 years, and these countries are not going to do that overnight. Therefore, we are looking at what we call a partnership model, where the industry works with government to do the monitoring and helps set the regulations. I'm talking about helping a government to enforce its existing domestic fishery regulations.

What is bycatch? And why should retailers care?

You could have a well-managed fishery from the perspective of the target stock, which means that the fish they intend to catch could be very well controlled, with no illegal fishing at all. But what may happen is that the equipment that they're using to catch the fish is inadvertently having an impact on other marine life. This happens in different ways, such as when you put a hook in the water, where there's bait on the hook and the birds will flock to your boat to take the bait off the hook. Some of the birds will get caught by the hook, where the line sinks and they drown. This, for example, can be an issue for the albatross[222] in the southern oceans. They live by flying around, hardly coming onto land to breed.

They have been impacted by the long-liners in the southern ocean. The question then becomes what do we need to do? The answer is to find a technical solution that is viable and that we know works because there are some fishers already using it.

However, it's not only birds that are impacted. You've also got whale interactions with what we call 'vertical gear,' which is currently a big issue along the East Coast of the US and Canada with whales getting tangled in lines. When you've got a highly endangered species, you only need a few entanglements to jeopardize the entire species over time. There are simple solutions, such as keeping those lines out of the water during the migratory season for these whales and moving the fishing season. Or it could be a technical measure, in what's called 'on-demand fishing,' which is a system where you pull a rope, which inflates a bag that rises to the surface to pull a trap up. This means there's no vertical line until you press a button on the boat that sends a signal down to the trap to inflate the bag to bring it up to the surface. Those fisheries are very successful, dramatically reducing the risk of entanglement, and there are lots of examples of them now.

The retailers care because of the reputational issue and brand risk, and they are also aware of endangered species protection measures that could shut the fishery down if they don't solve the problem. Or at least place very onerous restrictions. If you can work with the fishers to find a solution for the endangered species, you can see the impact. This is the smart way forward, and a lot of fishers would agree with me.

But it is not cost-free. Sometimes people are told to put these new practices in place overnight, and fishers don't often have the resources to do that, in which case they can be put out of business. This is where SFP's Bycatch Solutions Hub come in, because as the fishers' gear wears out, it will need to be replaced, and instead of them replacing it with dated equipment that has the bycatch problem, we help them replace it with the latest apparatus. We also see if retailers can help with the costs. The bycatch hub creates a marketplace where retailers can help to finance fisheries trying to adopt better practices and pilot-test innovative equipment. We support people from the invention stage to those pilot-testing to the people needing support to take a solution to mass market in a big fishery.

How is your organization addressing the challenges of illegal, unreported and unregulated fishing?

It's important to break this down carefully, as these are different things. The number one problem is illegal fishing. Fishing is highly regulated, and everything is reported on, but there are people still trying to break the rules and cheat the system. For example, people might land in the middle of the night with their fish and put it onto a truck with no inspections. A lot of times the regulations are poorly written, and this form of illegal fishing can quickly be fixed by better enforcement. Countless times we have seen situations where there's a lot of illegal fishing going on because one person didn't get caught, so everyone else thought, "Right, I'll just go for it." What you need to do is to stop the people who are driving that behaviour and make an example of them. As soon as you can show that there's a reasonable level of enforcement, the industry as a whole will support it.

To give you an example: we worked in Mexico with shrimp fisheries, and they had the rule that you could not fish close to the mouth of a river, which is where the shrimp develop. This regulation was intended to help the shrimp grow, and then catch them at a bigger size, when they are worth more. The fishers all lined up at the boundary, going back and forth on what is called the zipper line, catching the shrimp as they moved out when they were bigger. But then one person crossed the line, going into the prohibited area, where there's no competition because there are no other fishers. This fisherman caught lots of shrimp, even though they were smaller, but was making a lot more money because his catch rates had gone up because he had no competition. This bad behaviour encouraged everyone else to cross the line. Then they were all competing again and the catch rates dropped, and the shrimp were smaller, and everyone was losing.

The solution was to push everybody back out and show that you're going after the people who are behaving badly. That's the key to any of these regulatory approaches – you have to ensure that you are not targeting the responsible producers, and only go after the ones who are actively trying to break the rules. In the Mexican situation, we used satellite imagery and showed the industry that we could detect the vessels that were fishing illegally. We were then able to get agreements from the retailers and food service companies to buy only from the boats that had not crossed the line. Those that had were excluded.

Then you have the unreported and unregulated categories, which are two distinct and different things again. This is where you're talking about fisheries in lower- or middle-income countries that don't have registration requirements, vessel lists or vessel-monitoring systems of whatever description. And even if the vessels are formally registered, they're not actively reporting. It's hard to know what's going on, and that's the unreported problem. Many of these fisheries, particularly smaller fisheries, or even big fisheries in very poor countries where the government has very little capacity, have very little regulation and are underregulated.

There's another specific problem. Small-scale fisheries are often ignored by their governments, because the government has limited resources and limited capacity and is focused on the big industrial fisheries that generate a lot of export earnings. These small fisheries find it hard to get legal rights and other support. At SFP, we're working very hard to turn this round – clearly, no one's at fault and it's not illegal fishing. We're working to change national policies, making it easier for fishers to exert their rights not just to fish but to comanage the fishery.

You've mentioned small-scale fisheries. What are they and why are they important?

Every country defines small-scale fisheries a little differently, but the main differentiator is that the owner of the vessel is typically on the boat – even if they own multiple boats, they are still actively fishing. This is key, as these are typically family-owned operations. It's also about the size of the vessel, as you don't typically see very large boats that are family owned, though it does happen in some countries. Most of the time, you're talking about relatively small vessels making short fishing trips, or they might be out for a couple of nights, but they're not going out for weeks at a time.

The defining character of small fisheries for me is that they represent around 40 to 50% of the landings globally, but near 90% of the employment. So, when you're in a lower-middle-income country where there's a lot of young people and jobs are hard to find, a lot of people end up working in the seafood sector. The goal for a lot of these governments is to ensure that they are keeping people employed and making sure people are able to eat.

If you have a big boat, you need big infrastructure to land the fish. Along with a port, a big concrete dock has to exist and there needs to be a factory where you can offload the huge volume. This is how Western fisheries – the big ones – typically run. This is important in how central government fisheries-management systems work because you have fish inspectors at the dock and in the processing plant. Plus, there are only 50 big boats out there and the coast guard can intercept a few of them every day, and that makes a difference.

Now go to a small-scale fishery of thousands of small boats landing on beaches and villages all up and down the coastline, where they are processing their catch on the beach and putting it into a small truck, and you have lots of trucks going to many local wet fish markets. It is not easy to manage, and the only way you can do so is to give the fishers some incentive, rights and power to manage the fishery themselves and be part of the solution. For example, fishers can help collect data and share it with scientists – we've seen lots of programmes do that. They can also help devise the regulations and in some countries that do this, they have something called community comanaged fisheries with comanagement rules. The country authorities will typically say, "Here is the outcome we want, and we will delegate how to do it." There are some restrictions, but for the most part, they'll delegate the decision-making to fishers' cooperatives or associations for particular fisheries, or particular geographies. They make their own rules and police themselves.

The state will help a bit, depending on the rules. However, a lot still needs to happen, and none of these situations are perfect. Probably the best examples that I've seen firsthand are in Galicia, where the Spanish government puts a lot of resources into building out capacity among the traditional fishing guilds so leaders can manage the resource and work together.

What legacy do you want to leave with the work you are doing?

We have been successful in bringing fishers from around the world together, particularly when they come to the annual seafood show in North America, or the one in Europe. The fishers attend to sell their seafood and learn what the market wants, and if we get people organized in time, we take them to see good management system examples like the one in Galicia. This is a very specialized industry that is vertically segmented by the type of species, because of the transaction costs in trading. A lot of expertise is involved. We organize the supply chain into roundtables by sector, where we have about 150 companies, and only a few are members of more than one roundtable. Overall, about 80% are members of a single supply chain roundtable, because that's all they do.

We've been able to get a lot of small-scale fishing boats – several thousand – registered in Peru for the first time. They have formed associations where they are negotiating with the government over management rights, and we help organize and empower them. This is our highest level of intervention. We work directly with associations and local NGOs and go into the field to sit down with the fishers to try to form associations, where we can then engage the government around regulations and vessel registration and things like that. We really want to drive the registration of small-scale fishers in six or seven countries and we're about to double this work. We'd love to be able to receive more funding. Community rights tend to get ignored. If a community is being excluded from their traditional fishing grounds, the impact is awful. We're very proud of the work we do to help communities keep their marine tenure rights.

I'd also like to demonstrate improvements in the health of entire marine ecosystems. This will require new marine protected areas, new endangered species protection measures, and measures to ensure that all fisheries in an ecosystem are being managed sustainably. We need to recognize that fish move, and we need to have good fishery management systems to maintain the fish stocks. Marine-protected areas cannot do this on their own. It's simply not possible, given how these creatures live – where the fish go. It's important to have a stable food web, in addition to marine-protected areas. It is absolutely critical for biodiversity. Without a stable food system, you will start to see a loss of biodiversity and all sorts of weird things happening, such as an explosion of algae blooms. This large marine ecosystem is interconnected, and we're starting to put our data from individual fisheries together to help understand the marine ecosystem.

The good thing is that our retail partners are now buying 90% or more of their product from certified sources. The farms, the fishing boats, the fisheries – everything is certified. When you look around, this supply certification doesn't just apply to seafood. It includes coffee, cocoa oil, palm, palm oil, bananas – these are farms that are certified, sustainable or responsible. However, crucially, the ecosystems around these good-practice farms are continuing to decline. So clearly, while the farm-level approach is absolutely essential, it's not sufficient. We need to do more, and I think this is where SFP can step in, because from day one we have had a jurisdictional approach, talking to government about how to regulate the area as a whole. We've been doing that for 20-plus years. You have to build constituencies – while this is not easy, it's not impossible. It is very difficult when you're dealing with very large ecosystems. What I'm trying to do next in terms of impact is come up with solutions that will drive improvements at the ecosystem level.

CHAPTER 17

COMMUNITIES

We all are part of something, whether it's a village, a neighbourhood, a community, or now in modern-day life a Facebook community group or a family or school WhatsApp group. They help us feel supported, give us strength, keep us informed about local news and events, and can even keep us safe. We all belong somewhere; engaged communities give us a sense of belonging. They enable us to share personal stories and support the growth of each other, ourselves and our environment.

THARAKA, KENYA

Before I continue with this chapter, I want to share with you a perfect story about community action.[223] This story takes us to Tharaka, in Kenya, the 'Land of the Bees,' which are everything to this region and have been central to the cultural, spiritual and ecological fabric for generations. The community would look at these pollinators to tell them about the weather, particularly if rain was coming. The honey was used to brew beer for ceremonies at sacred sites – rituals that would bring clans together.

Simon Mitambo, a member of this local Tharaka community, started to see the bees decline. His observations have been supported by various pieces of research showing that bee extinction is speeding up because of us – humans – due to insecticides created in the 1980s and currently used in 120 countries, called neonicotinoids.[224] Cheap and toxic, these insecticides impair bees' central nervous system to such an extent that they cannot even fly home. Every single African country is using neonicotinoids, and back in Kenya, Simon discovered that industrial farms are spraying them on a vast scale.

Despite scientific evidence of neonicotinoids' impact, companies from the Global North are still supplying them to the Global South in huge quantities. Restrictions in the Global South are weak and allow for the devastation of biodiversity hotspots like Tharaka. This is contributing to climate change.

But Simon has been supporting the Tharakan people to work together to repair the damage, by encouraging everyone to abandon insecticides and use organic farming methods instead. Today the local community is farming agroecologically, using Indigenous seeds, harvesting rainwater and eliminating chemicals like neonicotinoids. Tharakans are replanting and protecting the trees where bees nest, reviving their bee-keeping traditions and brewing honey beer again. This is bringing people and place together once more, through ecological governance of their territory and ceremonies that celebrate it.

COMMUNITIES IN THE UK AND BEYOND

Over the last ten years, I have seen the strength of local groups grow, becoming the backbone of many neighbourhoods. Where I live, we have one such powerful community group that came out of the London riots in 2011, called Love Your Doorstep (LYDS), set up by Emma Rigby. The purpose of LYDS is to connect local people to local businesses, so we all shop where we live to help boost the local economy. It also raises awareness about threats to safety on the high street and to local greenbelt areas. It plays an important role, and it has been recognized nationally numerous times for its work and won many awards. Sometimes, I wonder how we all managed without it. LYDS has ignited the spirit of community within us all.

Now with frequent unprecedented weather events caused by climate change, we are experiencing how just how the climate crisis impacts our societies irrespective of where we live in the world. It is disrupting food supplies, supply chains and financial markets, damaging homes and cities, and harming health.

Here in the UK, we began 2024 with Storm Henk, which caused terrible flooding across the country.[225] This was followed by Storm Isha[226] and then by Storm Jocelyn.[227] This is just one example of what's happening, as there are many more locations in other parts of the world that have been hit by flooding.

My heart goes out to those people and businesses that have been impacted by these disasters. Unfortunately, we need to recognize that these abnormal weather patterns are going to become more frequent and challenging to manage in the UK and elsewhere in the coming years because of rising sea levels and changes in rainfall patterns, both driven by the climate crisis; land use changes, including house building due to population growth and urban encroachment into flood-prone areas; the ongoing decline in natural habitats that act as a buffer to flooding; and ageing assets that were built years ago as defence systems.

Climate change will force communities to act together to find solutions to improve the way we manage these natural disasters here in the UK and elsewhere around the world. We are facing a perfect storm (pun intended), and we need to act now together. Climate change is deeply intertwined with global patterns of inequality, where the poorest and most vulnerable bear the impacts of this crisis, yet have contributed the least to it. As the burden of climate change mounts, millions of vulnerable people will face disproportionate challenges in terms of extreme events; health effects; food, water and livelihood security issues; migration and forced displacement; loss of cultural identity; and other risks.

Certain social groups are particularly vulnerable to the crises – women at home, children, Indigenous communities, people with disabilities, ethnic minorities, migrant workers, displaced persons, older people and other socially marginalized groups. Their vulnerability lies in a combination of their geographical locations; their financial, socioeconomic, cultural and gender status; and their access to resources, services, decision-making power and justice. This is more than an environmental crisis. We need to address issues of inequality on various levels – between wealthy and poor countries, between the rich and poor within countries, between men and women, and between generations.

INDIGENOUS COMMUNITIES

Our community lives started thousands of years ago with Indigenous communities, who have been protectors of the natural world. Not to sound too Marvel Comics, but they have been the guardians of our planet since the beginning. They have lived in synergy with their local biospheres, looking after their lands, respecting wildlife and using traditional knowledge passed down through generations. These are communities spread across the world from the Arctic to the South Pacific, and according to a common definition that says those who lived in a country or a geographical region at the time when other people of different cultures or ethnic origins arrived. They are the holders of unique languages, wisdom and beliefs, possessing invaluable knowledge of practices aimed at the sustainable management of natural resources, with a special relationship to their traditional land.

Their ancestral land has a fundamental importance for their collective physical and cultural survival as peoples. They hold their own diverse concepts of development, based on their traditional values, visions, needs and priorities, and they have an intimate relationship with their lands and the natural world. Among the Indigenous peoples are those of the Americas, such as the Lakota in the US, the Maya in Guatemala, the Aymara in Bolivia, the Aleut and Inuit of the circumpolar region, the Sámi of Northern Europe, the Aborigines and Torres Strait Islanders of Australia, and the Māori of New Zealand.

However, despite representing less than 5% of the world's population, Indigenous peoples steward more than a quarter of Earth's land and seas and protect 80% of global biodiversity.[228]

THE KOGI

But there is one Indigenous community that I would like to introduce you to, the Kogi (or Cogui or Kágaba), which means 'jaguar' in the Kogi language. They possess an extraordinary prescience. They live in the Sierra Nevada de Santa Marta mountains in northern Colombia, where their culture has existed since before the Columbian era. The Kogi have historically tried to resist contact with the outside world, and for more than 500 years have lived in isolation. But just over 30 years ago, they sent a message to the world. In 1990, in a celebrated BBC documentary, the Kogi told us the environment was being compromised and warned that we faced the destruction of society if we failed to embrace Nature.[229] The Kogi had watched, waited and listened to Nature. They had witnessed landslides, floods, deforestation, the drying up of lakes and rivers, the stripping bare of mountaintops, and the dying of trees – as, eerily, the Sierra Nevada, because of its unique ecological structure, mirrors the rest of the planet.

Needless to say, we didn't listen to their warning, and they tried again, calling back the filmmaker they had worked with the first time. This time the leaders, the Kogi Mama, which means 'enlightened ones,' set out to show in a factual way the delicate and critical interconnections that exist within the natural world. The film was called *Aluna*, and it takes us into the world of the Kogi.[230] At the heart of their belief system is that 'Aluna' is a cosmic consciousness that is the source of all life and intelligence. In fact, all Indigenous people have this belief.[231] Many Kogi Mama are raised in darkness during their formative years so they can learn to connect with this cosmic consciousness. This enables them to respond to its needs to keep the world in balance.

The Kogi people believe that when time began, Mother Earth laid an invisible black thread linking special sites along the coast to locations in the mountains. What happens in one specific site is echoed in others miles away. Keen to illustrate this, in their film *Aluna*, they devised a plan to lay a golden colour thread showing the connections that exist between special sites. They wanted to show the damage caused by logging, mining, the building of power stations and roads, and the construction of ports along the coast and at the mouths of rivers. These activities were destroying the natural resources and impacting what happened at the tops of the mountains, where the once pristine white-capped peaks were now brown and bare. In addition, lakes were parched and the trees and vegetation vital to them were dying.

But it's not all despair, as *Aluna* ends with a message of hope from the Kogi: "Don't abandon your lives … just protect the rivers."

THE MESSAGE

The story of the Kogi shows why these often-marginalized groups are vital stewards of our environment and its fast-depleting resources. Their traditions and belief systems mean that they regard Nature with deep respect and have a strong sense of place and belonging. This sustains knowledge and ways of life that are in sync with modern notions of Nature conservation and the sustainable use of natural resources. Indigenous communities have been strong opponents of development imposed from outside, and have defended their lands against illegal encroachments and destructive exploitation, from dams across their rivers to logging and mining in their forests.

Their contributions are essential in designing and implementing solutions for ecosystems. Traditional knowledge and heritage can contribute to environmental assessments and sustainable ecosystem management. For example, Indigenous people's sustainable production of their traditional food has invaluable benefits for natural resources and ecosystems, contributing to a healthier diet and helping mitigate climate change.

This makes Indigenous peoples the best custodians of the landscapes and ecosystems that are central to efforts to limit climate change and adapt to its effects. Indigenous peoples and local communities cannot imagine their life divorced from Nature. But sadly, this also makes them targets, as communities that stand up against powerful economic and political interests remain under intense pressure in many parts of the world. Yamide Dagnet eloquently makes this point in Chapter 14.

The rights of Indigenous communities are now protected by the UN's Declaration on the Rights of Indigenous Peoples (2007) and are reflected in the policies of governments and the strategies of conservation organizations. Indigenous communities want more say in how to address the environmental challenges that we all face, and their empowerment, combined with their knowledge and long-term planning skills, are essential to the survival of future generations of both humans and wildlife. This is backed up by a growing body of scientific research showing the vital role Indigenous communities play in environmental conservation.[232] Dr Kimberley Miner's interview in Chapter 2 talks about some of her research and the idea that we can't protect the planet without the traditional knowledge and sustainable agricultural practices of Indigenous communities.

CONCLUSION

People are acting, and we're seeing results. Communities bring unique perspectives and skills and a wealth of knowledge to the challenge of strengthening resilience and addressing climate change challenges. Research and experience have shown that community leaders can set priorities, influence ownership, and design and implement investment programmes that are responsive to their community's own needs.

By empowering community leaders to act, we can create a culture of innovation and experimentation that can lead to breakthroughs in the fight against climate change and environmental injustice. These developments can then be shared and scaled up to benefit communities worldwide. Local-level actions will only make a difference when many local and national governments, households and industries act together.

TAKEAWAY

Communities thrive through their people. I know that many of us are time poor, but equally there are more of us working from home, spending less time travelling to work. Because we are more home-based, our neighbourhoods have become more important to us. There are simple things you can do, from volunteering at community action projects to planting trees or doing a litter pick-up once a month. Just be involved. It is that simple.

My other tip is to encourage you to create a communal salad garden. They are a great way of bringing people together, feeding people and making local areas green. Communal salad gardens can be cultivated anywhere – disused public buildings, parks, schools, the flat roofs of offices. They bring a lot of joy and nourishment, are good for the pollinators, and enrich local areas, making them greener. However, there are a few things to consider before you get started on your community spot - contact the local authority to find out who the landowner is to then seek permission for your project; do a risk assessment of the plot and survey the site; and look into insurance to safeguard from any unforeseen issues.

CHAPTER 18

IN CONVERSATION WITH CHANGE-MAKERS

To help show the power of communities, I had the privilege to speak with various change-makers around the globe whose work has been transformative, making a real impact. As in the butterfly effect, where tiny changes add up to a bigger effect, their work is helping us all to wake up, join the dots and start making that difference too. These four powerful voices are Nemonte Nenquimo, an Indigenous Waorani leader; Julian Lennon, founder of the White Feather Foundation; Marimuthu Yoganathan, famous South Indian environmental activist; and Ingmar Rentzhog, cofounder and CEO at We Don't Have Time.

NEMONTE NENQUIMO

INDIGENOUS WAORANI LEADER

This is a conversation that took place in September 2023 with Nemonte Nenquimo, an Indigenous Waorani leader and the first female president of the Waorani of Pastaza, with the help of interpreters. Nemonte is an Indigenous activist from the Amazonian region of Ecuador and is cofounder of the Indigenous-led nonprofit organization Ceibo Alliance. In 2020, she was named by *Time* magazine as one of the most influential people in the world.[233] She is a winner of both the 2020 UN Environment Programme's Champions of the Earth award for Inspiration and Action and the Goldman Environmental Prize.

Nemonte led an Indigenous campaign and legal action that resulted in a court ruling protecting 500,000 acres of Amazonian rainforest and Waorani territory from oil extraction. It was a historic moment, where Ecuadorians voted to halt the development of all new oil wells in the Yasuní national park in the Amazon.[234]

Congratulations on the victory this August! How have things changed for you personally and for the Waorani since this vote?

So far, nothing has changed, but as an Indigenous community, we are clear that we have decided that there will be no more oil extraction on our ancestral territory, which is a sacred place for us, the Waorani people. However, despite this win, we are still deeply concerned because the oil companies continue to exploit and operate as usual, which means they are still infringing upon our rights, violating our right to life and the rights of Nature.

We need people to listen to our voices, the voices of the Indigenous people, and respect the collective decision that was made with both the non-Indigenous Ecuadorian community and the Indigenous people. We need the rest of the world to wake up to stop continuing to disrespect Mother Earth! We, the Indigenous people, have always respected Mother Earth, and we are living and protecting her from climate change. We need the international community to listen to us, respect us and support us with the resources needed to be able to continue living in our territory, where we will continue to seek front-line solutions to climate change and the extinction crisis.

Do you feel that you were destined to do the work you do and be the voice of Mother Nature?

I am not the voice of Mother Nature; this is a collective struggle of all Indigenous people, and this call comes from our ancestors. I am here to convey a message about the values of respect and knowledge of Indigenous people and to tell the world, the people, that we are all 'children of the Earth.' We are listening to the rest of the world and what it has to say and, in return, we want the world to respect us and listen to us, so that we can come together to address and halt climate change, and the global warming that we are all experiencing today. If people do not listen and do not respect Indigenous people, then we will all be engulfed by Mother Nature.

Now, with the threat of the climate crisis becoming even more apparent, does the world need more examples of meaningful political action that empower people of all ages and communities?

Indigenous communities have a collective struggle, and it is not just our problem. I have travelled all over the world and have observed people working in their workspaces alone, working in silos. When you are alone, there is no strength, no support to catch you when you fall. In Indigenous communities, we face our struggles together – we are a collective and this is our strength. I would like to ask the world, especially the young people and students, to give space to the voices of women, and to those female leaders who are fighting on our behalf. Also, we need to be included in decision-making spaces to allow for joint decision-making between Indigenous and non-Indigenous people.

We also need to provide the resources required in our territory, to help us continue defending and protecting our natural resources. For example, in the recent case of Yasuní, all the Indigenous people came together to share their knowledge and convey a message to the rest of Ecuadorian civil society.

This allowed us all to connect, which was powerful and helped us face a great challenge together. This is a good example of not only having hope but also having collective power. It shows other countries what is possible by working together and uniting. It is possible for us all to live in harmony, to have respect and love for Mother Nature, who is protecting us all. This will give us life for the future.

What can the Cowori, which I understand is your word for 'outsiders,' learn from Indigenous communities, to be more like them with regard to their relationship with Mother Nature?

My message to the Cowori is to respect all Indigenous people and value our culture because we possess ancient knowledge and wisdom that can help them too. They need to spiritually connect to Mother Nature, to understand the meaning of respect, culture and the value of Indigenous knowledge.

What can people in industrialized nations do to support Indigenous peoples to protect their land and help ensure that biological and cultural diversity can flourish?

I would say to the people living in cities that they should become self-aware of what they are consuming. Gasoline and the entire capitalist consumption in cities are a significant threat to our territory because beneath our land there is oil, and its extraction threatens many of our natural resources.

We need the youth to awaken and say, "We will no longer consume fuel that destroys Nature, our homes and our lives." Fossil fuels harm the natural world, causing cultural impacts on our territory. I would really like to encourage the youth to start working, raise their voices and put pressure on the companies that invest in fossil fuels, so they don't come to our territory and destroy Nature, pollute the rivers and the land. It's vital for the youth to come together to launch a campaign alongside Indigenous communities to prevent this and protect our planet, where we all live. I would also like to tell the youth that they should not just go into Nature to reconnect with the land but also reconnect with the mindset of living in harmony with Nature.

My other message is to all, especially to the next generation, and that is to stop overconsuming – it's harmful. People should also stop creating plastic waste. Please do not throw away more plastics – it is harmful too.

We need support and the resources that directly assist the grassroots communities in their struggle. Often, resources are given to large organizations, but these large organizations are not connected to the local communities. This, too, has been a significant failing on the part of environmentalists, who need to see who we are at the grassroots level and understand what we are fighting for. It would be beneficial for them, as well, to provide us with the resources we need to continue protecting and caring for our territory.

What legacy do you want to leave?

I want to leave behind a healthy Earth and clean water, so that our children and grandchildren can live with dignity, free from pollution, and be able to preserve their own culture and knowledge.

The struggle of communities and the fight of women who raise their voices must also be respected and heard, to ensure that we can continue living on this planet with good health and wellbeing. It's important for everyone to know that our struggle is not just for Indigenous people but for the entire globe, so that we can all live with clean air and water.

JULIAN LENNON

FOUNDER OF THE WHITE FEATHER FOUNDATION

In October 2023, I spoke with Julian Lennon via email. Julian founded the White Feather Foundation in 2007 to help give a voice to the Mirning people, an Aboriginal tribe in Australia. This nonprofit supports projects worldwide to promote the betterment of all life in the areas of Indigenous cultures, the environment, clean water, education and health. Julian has been recognized by Prince Albert II of Monaco, who honoured him with the Better World Environmental Award in 2008 for his work through the foundation. In addition, Julian was recognized with the World Literacy Award in 2021 and the CC Forum Philanthropy Award in 2020. Also in 2020, he was named a UNESCO Center for Peace Cross-Cultural and Peace Crafter laureate.

Sir David Attenborough has said that the climate crisis is a communication challenge and now we hear of climate crisis fatigue. Yet, the White Feather Foundation has been successful in raising awareness on so many issues related to the environment. Is this because the foundation understands the power of storytelling through different mediums, such as film and photography? Is this a more effective way to communicate our current environmental crisis?

Indeed. We all want to feel an emotional connection to the causes we support. How can we truly empathize with an issue if we haven't been touched by a cause through any number of mediums? The more ways are used to get the message out there, the better chance we all have of coming together to help on those issues.

The White Feather Foundation, incidentally, started with storytelling. We made the documentary, *Whaledreamers*,[235] to amplify the voices of the Mirning people in Australia. As the foundation grew, and I was able to spend time with our charity partners in places such as Ethiopia and Colombia, my photographs became the lens through which our supporters saw the people we helped.

As an artist, the most natural way for me to express myself is through creative projects, such as music, photography, film, writing and so on, so we have continued to build our charity community through those outlets as well. The Netflix film *Kiss the Ground*,[236] which I was an executive producer on and which the foundation sponsored, is a good example of how to tell a climate change story that has a sense of real urgency, without being preachy. Which neither I nor the foundation want to be.

The only way forward with the climate crisis is to tell the truth about what will happen to humans, and really drive home the specifics about how our lives will significantly change for the worse if we don't intervene.

How does investing in education for underprivileged girls help save the planet?

It's simple, really. The more educated girls are, the less likely they are to suffer abuse and the more likely they are to gain meaningful employment and invest back into their communities. When girls are educated, they share their knowledge with those around them. Knowledge is power and power fuels progress.

Why is defending Indigenous people's rights important in fighting climate change?

Indigenous peoples are the original caretakers of our planet and their lands contain 80% of the world's remaining biodiversity. Listening to their ancient wisdom is crucial if we're serious about restoring the health of this planet and ourselves.

In the forests, Indigenous people can make lands less vulnerable to wildfires; in the ocean, they are able to use their knowledge to protect essential marine life and ultimately help preserve our largest source of oxygen. If we don't defend and protect these sacred people and the land they steward, planet Earth will be in a dismal state in a matter of decades.

Has working with Indigenous communities inspired your own creative work? If so, how?

Absolutely. I often refer to the brief time I spent with the Kogi tribe in Colombia as one of the happiest, most peaceful times of my life. From their community, I learned that to disconnect from the daily grind and reconnect with Nature – to simply breathe – is vital both for mental and physical health. A good recharge is the best medicine for productivity in the creative space.

To take a power walk in Nature or properly rest invites an abundance of ideas and dreams to come to life.

What would you want your legacy to be?

I'd like to be remembered as an artist who has made a difference for the better, but above all else as a man who lived a life of kindness that reflected the sincere love I have for my family, friends, kindred spirits and planet Earth.

MARIMUTHU YOGANATHAN

SOUTH INDIAN ENVIRONMENTAL ACTIVIST

In June 2023, I spoke to Marimuthu Yoganathan, a famous South Indian environmental activist who is also lovingly known as Tree Man. He lives in Tamil Nadu, India. Yoganathan is a bus conductor and family man. For more than 35 years, he has been dedicated to planting more than 600,000 tree saplings around the state of Tamil Nadu. He visits schools, colleges, universities and various industries, all with the mission to raise awareness about the environment.

When I spoke to Yoganathan, he was recovering from a major operation to have a lung removed in response to cancer and was still going through his cancer treatment. His daughter Sathya helped with this conversation as an interpreter, and also gave me a wonderful personal perspective on her father.

Yoganathan's work has won him numerous awards and accolades, including the Eco Warrior award from Indian Vice-President Hamid Ansari in 2008 and the Real Heroes Award from CNN-IBN in 2011. In March 2022, Prime Minister Narendra Modi acknowledged Yoganathan in his monthly national radio address, *Mann Ki Baat*. In 2022, he was named a Climate Warrior by the Ministry of Jal Shakti (Department of Water Resources, River Development and Ganga Rejuvenation in India).

What inspired you to start planting trees?

It all started when I was growing up, which was in the beautiful settings of the tea plantation regions of the Nilgiris, a stunning mountain range that borders Tamil Nadu, Karnataka and Kerala. My mother worked in Nilgiris as a leaf picker.

Around the age of 16, living in this special place, full of lush forests and wildlife, I became aware of how these forests were being destroyed by the 'Timber Mafia,' who were illegally cutting down the trees. I decided to protest and blocked the road by lying in front of a truck loaded with the illegal timber, which created a scene where people came to see what was happening. This is how my awareness work began. I seized the moment to inform the local people about what was happening to the forests.

My environmental work evolved and expanded, and while still in my teens, I started to do street plays to educate local communities. My plays were about the importance of trees, what impact they had on the local biodiversity and what action was needed to protect the forests. From my street plays, I went on to do slide presentations for the villages using wildlife photography that highlighted the importance of the elephant corridors, which are narrow, natural habitat throughways that allow elephants to move between secure habitats without being disturbed by humans.

As I got older and then got married, I had responsibilities and I needed to find work, which I did, as a bus conductor. But I was not going to give up on my environmental work. I asked my employer to give me Mondays off to allow me to continue my work about the importance of saving trees and planting samplings. And while my salary as a bus conductor is modest, and it's not easy to juggle my job and environmental work, I have always been determined for more people to understand the importance of saving our Nature. I have visited many, many schools, colleges, universities and industries to drive awareness.

What difference to the planet will you make by planting trees?

While I have been doing this awareness work from such a young age, it is only in the last 30 years that I have started to be heard. It has been a long struggle to help people understand the values of trees and get them to plant and care for trees. Planting trees and looking after the forests will, in turn, look after the birds that migrate here; birds are vital to the natural biodiversity.

When the numbers of these migratory birds plummeted, we saw the impact through climate change and the climate changed without these birds. It had a domino effect on the weather and the tea plantations, which are the main livelihood for many.

I wanted to help the birds, the forest and tea plantations, and the solution was to plant more trees to create a bird sanctuary, which I have successfully been able to do in the area of Mopperipalayam. It has been a three-year project, with 36 acres dedicated to this bird sanctuary, where now migratory birds arrive.

How important is it for us as individuals to make positive change for the planet? And can we, as individuals, make a difference?

There's a Tamil saying, "UyirVaza Oru Mararn," which means "If you want to live, plant a single tree." I have lived by this proverb, which has been my motto from the very start of my work. I have used it throughout to raise awareness and encourage people to plant trees.

I believe it is vital to work with children to create a legacy. Over the years, I have worked closely with a government elementary school in Coimbatore, where the schoolchildren have planted a tree sapling on their birthday. And now, as these children have become older, going to college and working, they are helping to spread my environmental message.

These children have also been taught about how CFCs[237] are damaging the ozone layer and the climate. As a result, the children don't use perfumes, aerosols, or even nail polish or fireworks. They are also aware of plastic pollution and will not use plastic cups or bottles.

They are making sure they are creating a positive green living space and are creating awareness with the people where they now live. They are having a domino effect and will be raising awareness all over Tamil Nadu and India, and who knows, maybe even the world.

What advice would you give to anyone wanting to make a positive impact in their community?

You live your life on this planet, your children live here, your grandchildren will live here. Our parents left the planet to us in a good state. It is, therefore, our responsibility to ensure that the planet is left in a good shape for our children.

(Sathya adds) As a young man, my father saw a lot of sparrows growing up, and I see the sparrows too, but I don't know whether my children, his grandchildren, will see the sparrows. My father used to write poems while in the forests and I would like to recite this poem of his:

My father saw water in a river,
I saw water in a pond,
My children saw water in a pump,
My grandchildren saw water in a Bisleri waterbottle
I don't know how my daughter's grandchildren will see water.

(Yoganathan continues) It is your responsibility to do these things. Be aware of what is good for the planet. Recycle and don't use plastic bags, bottles or fireworks. Be conscious. If you keep your surroundings clean, it will influence others, then society itself will be conscious. It has a ripple effect.

Who inspires you?

There has been no one person, but I am thankful to all the different guides who have supported me and my work along the way. I would like to add that seeing the forests being destroyed and green spaces becoming empty deeply impacted me. Really it is Mother Nature who inspired me and always inspires me.

What would you like to be remembered for? What footprint do you want to leave behind?

The trees are what I live for and all I wanted to live for, and when I take my last breath, it will be for trees. I wanted to plant trees, I wanted to make a difference and create awareness among people.

(Sathya adds) He's known as Tree Man and wants to die as Tree Man.

(The interview took a different turn here and I started to have a conversation with Sathya.)

Sathya, does your dad inspire you?

Absolutely, and we, his family, will carry on his legacy. We have grown up with his work, accompanying him to do the planting of trees and supporting him with the environmental awareness campaigns. We were the first people to help him on his clean-up initiatives.

Our father has had a deep influence on our lives. We have been brought up to never use plastic bags in our home – we use only use cloth bags. I have never used fireworks for festivals, so in this family's next generation, which is now my nephew, who is five years old – he does not know what fireworks are!

My parents worked well together, and our mother supported my father, which allowed him to do this important work. Everything has been for Mother Nature.

He works tirelessly and with purpose. He does his tree work on Mondays for a reason, because after the weekend people are fresh and ready to learn about the trees and the environment. It's the best day to create awareness with people because on Fridays people are tired after the long week, and not interested in learning about the planet.

My father then starts his bus work again on Tuesday mornings, going to work, and when he returns home on Wednesday afternoon after work, he refreshes himself and starts again his tree work. The only time he is not working is when he is sleeping!

What would you like to say about your father's legacy?

My father has been like a soldier looking after the trees. I have never seen him stay at home. Recently, after he was diagnosed with lung cancer, he was forced to stay at home, because of the treatment and the physical exhaustion. After the surgery for his vocal cords, he wasn't able to talk for so long and his left lung was removed. He was not supposed to go outside and had to rest for the next three to four months. But he still went when he could to look after the trees. It's just not about planting them, but watering and caring for them, and he still found the strength to be productive as much as possible.

We didn't let people know about his cancer, but when people found out that he'd had surgery and had his left lung removed, we had so much support. This period has been so horrible for us. We are also not very wealthy people, but when people found out, they helped us financially.

(Laughing and full of love, Sathya adds) My father used to spend 40% of his salary on buying saplings. He never saved anything for us! When he got sick, we found ourselves on very hard times without any financial sources. But people came and helped us – some anonymously - including people we did not know.

This is the legacy of our father. He has not just created forests but an ecosystem of unconditional love within our local community. People have given their love and when he returned from hospital, people were praying for his recovery. These days we are busy keeping his diary, because so many people want to make appointments to visit. But because his immune system is vulnerable due to the treatment, he is not allowed visitors. So, people come and wave, standing outside the house, just to see him. Our father has earned this love and respect from the last 36 years of his service to the planet.

A doctor who we do not know called the hospital where my dad was going to have his operation and told the hospital doctors that he would be paying for all my father's medical expenses, and he should have the best treatment.

We are not even sure how this doctor found out that my father was ill, but he called my father's medical team directly to take care of everything.

A single person's responsibility is to look after the planet. It is every person's responsibility to create awareness among people about the impact and importance of forests. It's every individual's responsibility to know – why we need to plant trees, why we should not damage the ozone layer with CFC products. And if you create awareness, for example, among ten people, then you could be reaching another ten people and then another ten and another ten. That's how change happens. It will multiply.

This is what my father has done – created a ripple effect. This is his legacy.

INGMAR RENTZHOG

FOUNDER AND CEO OF WE DON'T HAVE TIME

In September 2023, I spoke to Ingmar Rentzhog, a Swedish entrepreneur and climate champion. Ingmar is the cofounder and CEO of We Don't Have Time, a social network for fighting the climate crisis. He discovered and gave visibility to Greta Thunberg, from her lonely protest in front of the Swedish Parliament to her first speech at the UN. He has been called Mark ZuckerVert by France TV2.

What inspired you to set up We Don't Have Time?

I was inspired by two things. The birth of my first child, my daughter, was when I began to think about the future. I became interested in Nature and the planet, and from there the climate. I started to read extensively but I didn't really do anything further than educate myself. At the time, I was running a successful financial communication consulting firm, where I was helping rich people become richer. While we did a lot of positive things, like helping companies with renewables initiatives and other things like that, the main focus of the firm was to drive business.

The second thing that really inspired me to go from boardroom to action was Donald Trump when he won the US election. It was a pivotal moment for me and it was when many things came together. It was November, I was living in Stockholm and we were experiencing crazy weather. The whole city was shut down – we had a metre and a half of snow in just 24 hours, which is not common at all. Everything from the transport to schools and businesses was shut down. The city was at a standstill and enveloped in silence. I was at home with my daughter, and I was also at a standstill, away from the stresses of work, which allowed me to think.

When I woke up that morning, Donald Trump was all over the news. He was now president of the US, and it hit me hard, because I realized that Trump was the only global leader telling the truth. Trump told everyone that "he didn't care about the future, or anything," whereas other world leaders were pretending they were doing things, but they were not really doing anything. But here was Trump, as the new president, telling us "I don't give a shit." That made me realize that I wanted to do something. I wanted to use my communication skills to build networks, to gather people who were actually doing things and leading. That's when I came up with We Don't Have Time, with the purpose of connecting everyone, to show each other leadership, because we can't really rely on the top leaders that we have today.

Your daughter is 11 now, so you've been on this journey for the last 11 years?

My daughter was five years old when Donald Trump won the election, so it's been six years. It's been a journey. After the moment when Trump became president, I made it my mission to really understand the climate issue – not just read, but really learn – and I signed up for everything. I joined websites, newsletters, all the webpages that were related to anything to do with the climate. One month later, I got an invitation from Al Gore to attend his training. That was the last time I was in the US, and it was to be trained by him. I gained a lot of learning from attending that training.

Sorry to interrupt you, but that's wild! I have never heard of anyone signing up to lots of climate-focused newsletters and then being invited by Al Gore to come and learn with him. It seems your destiny was calling.

Yes, I remember vividly that I was sitting on the bus and up pops this invitation and I applied immediately. When I think back now it was strange, because I've never heard of anyone else receiving an invitation this way to do his training. Normally people need to apply. But I knew it was important for me to attend because I wasn't an expert in the climate. When I returned home, I suddenly had something to say.

In fact, the very first presentation I did was about two days after I came home from training. It was one of the hardest lectures I've ever done, and I did it at my daughter's day care, for a group of five- to six-year-olds. Now that was a challenge. It was crazy, because I was talking for an hour and there were lots of breaks with children saying, "We need to go to toilet, please."

So, from Al Gore to your presentation at the day care centre, you set up We Don't Have Time.

Yes, though I wasn't clear about how the platform would work – it was more a vision. I wanted to use my communication skills and networks. But the real execution happened three days later when I had dinner with my now cofounder, David Olsson. We were sitting at a fancy restaurant and I thought he would say, "You're crazy" when I told him my idea, but he actually said, "Let's do it!" Without him, I don't think I would be standing here.

You are making an impact. I joined We Don't Have Time and thought it was such a cool and empowering platform. There's nothing like it out there. What's its mission?

While we can't weaken the oil industry right now, what we can do is to scale the climate movement and support those who are implementing solutions. The platform aims to inspire people about those solutions. We see the purpose of We Don't Have Time as being a catalyst for change that will have an impact. Our focus is to get people together. For example, local efforts happening in Sweden can encourage people in Australia to do the same, and so on.

The other secret sauce is that we must also have those wider conversations with people in this field – those who are working on solutions – and we need to get them out from their bubble. Otherwise, it's just the same people talking about the same problem with each other and that will not change anything. We Don't Have Time is a platform, which is something that not many others are doing – well, at least they weren't when we started.

Our mission is to get the leaders to meet and learn from each other and be inspired by each other. We want to get this awareness out to millions.

As you were talking, it occurred to me, why hasn't any other tech entrepreneur, like Mark Zuckerberg or now Elon Musk thought about creating something like this?

I'm asking that question myself! My theory is that if you have too much money, you become a slave to the money and lose your freedom. I think people believe in the myth that money means freedom. But the absurdity is that when you acquire a ludicrous amount of wealth, there's no freedom anymore. It's the other way around – the money controls you. You will start to do a lot of things that do not give you freedom. You will move to a country because you want to pay low taxes, but you don't like it there. Or you need to have security, as you can't live normally, and suddenly you are in a race competing with the other super-rich, building rockets to prove something strange. You're so afraid of losing your wealth that you become chained to the system, and it's the system that's wrong. We need to break free from this system.

Has We Don't Have Time ever reached out to Musk or Zuckerberg to collaborate?

Actually, we have a good relationship with Twitter, as it was before Elon Musk took over, but the reality is we don't have a close relationship. I do dream that someone will eventually reach out and ask, "How can we help?" But that's not happened yet. But I think the reality is it will never happen, because those people are caught in the system.

Egos play a big role, too, where wealthy entrepreneurs want to have their names on everything, and they want it to be their initiative. If you go against the big power structure, you will feel the force of the resistance, which is why you need a lot of strength.

Building a platform is very different from building and running a consulting firm, and there was a lot of learning. When you run a business, people applaud you for creating jobs, etc., so when I started We Don't Have Time, I thought that if I built a company doing something good for the planet, people would support us. But it's when you try to disrupt the way the world operates that you discover that the support is not there, and instead you will be met by a powerful force from the powers that control the lobbyists. They will put a lot of challenges in your path. I experienced many strange things in the beginning when we were building the platform. It is exhausting and worrying – who is tapping your phone, reading your emails and listening to everything you do? They find ways to try to stop what you are doing. They don't want you to find the solutions.

Do you think people worldwide are starting to care about the climate and their own impact on it? Or is it only the people who are being impacted by the devastation of climate change who care?

I think many people today are really bothered. But what people need is leadership. At the beginning of my own climate journey, I thought that everyone would do what I do, if they just understood the problem. However, I don't think that anymore and I realize that most people are programmed to follow and not to lead. If you think about it, that's okay, because our societies will not work if everyone wants to be a leader. The way that we as humans operate is to come together and follow our leaders. The problem here is that we have the wrong leaders.

We have seen this throughout history, where sometimes the leaders go in the wrong direction, and you have people mobilizing to create new leadership, like in the French Revolution, which was one of those pivotal moments. But those moments have the potential to lead to a lot of hate and chaos, where you don't know how the situation will finally end. Instead, what we need is a peaceful revolution, which shows other kinds of leadership. We need to really promote a different of leadership – that's what people need and want. We have much to do here.

Can everyone make a difference? Can one person make change?

Everyone thinks that they are small – they can't create change in the world. Yet, they have the power if they want to have the power. Everyone can start change in their local communities. Everyone can make change by saying something instead of being quiet.

People should speak up and find the positives. So, instead of saying, "Why are you flying on your vacation?" look for the positive, and if someone says, "I took the train," applaud them. Make people feel comfortable – don't create negative feelings. I believe we need positive power, and I would like to see a climate movement embracing positive feelings. People are worried about the climate, yet now when someone says, "Join me," people are reluctant, because they don't want all the negativity that goes with it. We need to use the power of positivity to mobilize people.

In order to really make things happen, we need leadership for sure, but we also need people power. I am focusing on igniting a positive movement out there, because that is what the climate movement is missing. We Don't Have Time is creating this positive catalyst for change.

How do you deal with the climate deniers?

I don't care about those who don't care. There's no debate about believing in climate change or not – there's a debate about doing or not acting, and the climate deniers are not important. They are fooled by those powers who want people to live in denial because they have self-interest.

What is relevant is the people doing wrong things, and that's more frustrating. Let's take the UK, which like the rest of the world saw the extreme weather that happened this summer, where in July we went over the 1.5°C threshold. We have now witnessed excellent examples of the climate crisis, where you can't deny it anymore. But what is the UK doing? The government decides it is going to ignore the signs and opens 100 new oil rigs. It tries to justify what it is going to do, by saying it is necessary to be more energy secure and to drive net zero. That's not denial – that's delusional and it's a dangerous thing.

The problem is when people know what they're doing but they don't care. They just want to have the power and the money, and they think, "We don't care because we will not personally be affected." That's what we're up against.

But I also think this is like the final battle, because what we see now is those who are representing this old power structure. They know they're going to lose, so they are trying to grab all the power and money before their time is up. They are desperate and know that they will lose.

Is there any leader in the world who inspires you? Any political leader in any region, any country, any community right now?

I will say Al Gore, though he's no longer working politically anymore, unfortunately. But what he has done for the climate movement is incredible. If you look at political leadership, it's hard to name someone. Take António Guterres, secretary-general of the UN, who is saying all the right things about the climate and making bold statements, yet it's hard for me to look up to someone like that because they are powerless.

It very sad, as the secretary-general is saying everything that needs to be done, that we need to stop collaborating with oil, we need to phase out fossil fuels, etc. – and yet his very own organization is hosting our climate meeting, COP28, in Dubai, United Arab Emirates, where Sultan Al Jaber, the CEO of the Abu Dhabi National Oil Company, is presiding. It shows that the secretary-general of the UN has no clout. It's the same way with the US president, Joe Biden, who is doing a lot of good things for the climate. Yet, the Biden administration has approved more drilling for oil and gas in the last two years than in Trump's first two years.

Is Biden on the wrong side? No, he's not! While he might not have the power to combat the oil industry head on, he has certainly made progress in other areas. Though he hasn't been able to end the global fossil fuel subsidies, which currently stand at a staggering $7 trillion according to the International Monetary Fund, he has made strides in other directions. What Joe Biden has succeeded in doing is providing subsidies to green solutions, thanks to the US Inflation Reduction Act, amounting to over $1 trillion. For this, he deserves immense credit. He is pushing for positive change! However, there is still much more work to be done to level the playing field.

But still, it's hard to have a role model in political leadership today, because the leaders are not really the ones in control.

Will you consider going into politics?

I don't think so, because politicians are powerless. We need a lot of good people in politics, in conservative parties, in left parties. It's not about the side. I believe I can do more outside politics, because the current political systems don't have enough power to fight. What we really need is to mobilize enough people in society, and that's where I think I can contribute. I also really do believe that we need love and not hate to fix this.

Do you think that it's still possible to have a future?

Absolutely! Otherwise, I would do something else. Of course, there are doubts, but if we look throughout history, we have been in very dark times, many, many times. Just look at the UK – without Churchill, a great leader during the Second World War, saying, "We can make it, we can win," the world would have been different. I believe we can turn things around, and the good side will win. It's just a matter of how many losses were are willing to take beforehand.

What do you want your legacy to be?

I want to contribute to a society where we have the climate crisis under control. I'm not doing this to be remembered or anything. I'm doing this because I want to have a future myself.

CHAPTER 19

EPILOGUE

A conclusion to this book didn't seem right, as there is still so much to play for. The future is still unfolding and is yet to be written. Therefore, I am going to call this an epilogue – or perhaps you might think of it as a footnote.

I hope that after reading this book, you feel more informed and inspired. You have heard from the experts and been given the facts, and you have take-aways to help you make changes. I hope you will now decide to connect or reconnect with Nature, realizing that every choice you make today will have an impact on tomorrow. Not only for future generations, but all other species and ecosystems. We are all interlinked – we have learned that through the global COVID-19 pandemic. Doing one positive thing is not insignificant – it has a ripple effect that will lead on to other positive changes, and you will also inspire yourself to keep on going.

The reality is that the real power lies with you. What happens next is everyone's personal responsibility, whether in business or politics, or as employees, students, parents, carers, guardians or citizens. It is down to you and me, wherever we live in the world.

So, what will your legacy be?

ENDNOTES

1. Leo Hickman, "How the Burning of Fossil Fuels Was Linked to a Warming World in 1938" (*The Guardian*), last modified 22 April 2013, https://www.theguardian.com/environment/blog/2013/apr/22/guy-callendar-climate-fossil-fuels.
2. John H. Mercer, "Antarctic Ice and Sangamon Sea Level," *International Association of Scientific Hydrology, Commission of Snow and Ice, General Assembly of Bern*, pub. no. 79 (1968): 217–225, accessed 3 July 2024, https://iahs.info/uploads/dms/079020.pdf.
3. *Climate Change: The IPCC 1990 and 1992 Assessments* (Intergovernmental Panel on Climate Change, 1992), accessed 3 July 2024, https://www.ipcc.ch/site/assets/uploads/2018/05/ipcc_90_92_assessments_far_full_report.pdf.
4. *IPCC Second Assessment: Climate Change 1995* (Intergovernmental Panel on Climate Change, 1995), accessed 3 July 2024, https://archive.ipcc.ch/pdf/climate-changes-1995/ipcc-2nd-assessment/2nd-assessment-en.pdf; *Kyoto Protocol to the United Nations Framework Convention on Climate Change* (United Nations, 1998), accessed 3 July 2024, https://unfccc.int/resource/docs/convkp/kpeng.pdf.
5. *AR5 Synthesis Report: Climate Change 2014* (Intergovernmental Panel on Climate Change, 2014), accessed 3 July 2024, https://www.ipcc.ch/report/ar5/syr; *Paris Agreement* (United Nations, 2015), accessed 3 July 2024, https://unfccc.int/sites/default/files/english_paris_agreement.pdf.
6. S. V. Smith and R. W. Buddemeier, "Global Change and Coral Reef Ecosystems," *Annual Review of Ecology, Evolution, and Systematics* 23 (1992): 89–118.
7. Alice McCarthy, "Exxon Disputed Climate Findings for Years. Its Scientists Knew Better" (*Harvard Gazette*), last modified 12 January 2023, https://news.harvard.edu/gazette/story/2023/01/harvard-led-analysis-finds-exxonmobil-internal-research-accurately-predicted-climate-change.
8. António Guterres, "Secretary-General's Opening Remarks at Press Conference on Climate" (United Nations Secretary-General), last modified 27 July 2023, https://www.un.org/sg/en/content/sg/speeches/2023-07-27/secretary-generals-opening-remarks-press-conference-climate.
9. *Climate Change 2022: Impacts, Adaptation and Vulnerability – Summary for Policymakers* (Intergovernmental Panel on Climate Change, 2021), accessed 3 July 2024, https://www.ipcc.ch/report/ar6/wg2/downloads/report/IPCC_AR6_WGII_SummaryForPolicymakers.pdf.
10. "Global Hating: How Online Abuse of Climate Scientists Harms Climate Action" (Global Witness), last modified 4 April 2023, https://www.globalwitness.org/en/campaigns/digital-threats/global-hating.
11. Valerie Volcovici, "Scientists Target PR and Ad Firms They Accuse of Spreading Disinformation" (Reuters), last modified 19 January 2022, https://www.reuters.com/business/cop/scientists-target-pr-ad-firms-they-accuse-spreading-disinformation-2022-01-19.
12. *Denial, Disinformation, and Doublespeak: Big Oil's Evolving Efforts to Avoid Accountability for Climate Change* (House Committee on Oversight and Accountability, 2024), accessed 3 July 2024, https://www.budget.senate.gov/imo/media/doc/fossil_fuel_report1.pdf.
13. "Harvard Investigation Reveals Social Media as the New Frontier of Climate Deception and Delay" (Greenpeace), last modified 21 September 2022, https://www.greenpeace.org/international/press-release/55714/harvard-investigation-reveals-social-media-as-the-new-frontier-of-climate-deception-and-delay.
14. Nathaniel Geiger, Karen Gasper, Janet K. Swim and John Fraser, "Untangling the Components of Hope: Increasing Pathways (not Agency) Explains the Success of an Intervention that Increases Educators' Climate Change Discussions," *Journal of Environmental Psychology* 66 (2019): 101366, accessed 3 July 2024, https://www.researchgate.net/publication/336833312.
15. Intergovernmental Panel on Climate Change.
16. Al Gore, "What the Fossil Fuel Industry Doesn't Want You to Know" (TED), last modified July 2023, https://www.ted.com/talks/al_gore_what_the_fossil_fuel_industry_doesn_t_want_you_to_know.
17. Energy nexus in science means the link between energy, food and water.
18. The Artic and Antarctic are covered in ice and snow, which keeps the world cool, as they reflect heat back into the atmosphere. The loss of ice and snow in the Artic and Antarctic means less heat is reflected back, resulting in more intense heatwaves globally.
19. Robert Putnam, *Bowling Alone: The Collapse and Revival of American Community* (New York: Simon & Schuster, 2021).

20. *AR5 Synthesis Report: Climate Change 2014* (Intergovernmental Panel on Climate Change, 2014), accessed 3 July 2024, https://www.ipcc.ch/report/ar5/syr.
21. "World Bank Group Climate Change Action Plan" (World Bank Group), accessed 3 July 2024, https://www.worldbank.org/en/programs/cities-and-climate-change-platform/overview.
22. The World Bank report *Reality Check* highlights 25 successful climate policies from countries as disparate as China, Egypt, Niger and Peru. See *Reality Check: Lessons from 25 Policies Advancing a Low-Carbon Future* (World Bank Group, 2023), https://openknowledge.worldbank.org/server/api/core/bitstreams/b98ee473-12bb-4ff7-bb46-9fcdcb7d72c6/content.
23. Daniel Gerszon Mahler, Philip Randolph Wollburg and Stéphane Hallegatte, "The Climate Implications of Ending Global Poverty" (Data Blog, World Bank), last modified 29 June 2023, https://elibrary.worldbank.org/doi/abs/10.1596/1813-9450-10318.
24. Margaret Thatcher was UK prime minister between 1979 and 1990.
25. The parts of the Earth covered by ice.
26. Wind crossing the equator.
27. Ryan Heath, "The World Is on Fire and Our Leaders Are Failing, Poll Finds" (Politico), last modified 2 August 2022, https://www.politico.com/news/2022/02/08/citizens-politicians-combat-climate-change-00004590.
28. Sangeeta Waldron, *Corporate Social Responsibility Is Not Public Relations: How to Put CSR at the Heart of Your Company and Maximize the Business Benefits* (Madrid: LID Publishing).
29. United Nations Framework Convention on Climate Change (United Nations, 1992), accessed 3 July 2024, https://unfccc.int/resource/docs/convkp/conveng.pdf.
30. "Standing Firm: The Land and Environmental Defenders on the Frontlines of the Climate Crisis" (Global Witness), last modified 15 September 2023, https://www.globalwitness.org/en/campaigns/environmental-activists/standing-firm.
31. Bob Yirka, "Anger Found to Be the Primary Driver of Climate Activism" (Phys.org), last modified 25 August 2023, https://phys.org/news/2023-08-anger-primary-driver-climate.html.
32. *Planet Earth II* (BBC, 2016).
33. "President Biden's Historic Climate Agenda" (White House), last modified 27 January 2021, https://www.whitehouse.gov/climate.
34. POLITICO Morning Consult Global Sustainability Poll. August 2022, https://www.politico.com/news/2022/02/08/citizens-politicians-combat-climate-change-00004590
35. Aubrey Allegretti, "'I Realize How Serious It Is': Voters in England Support Action on Climate Crisis" (*The Guardian*), last modified 29 July 2023, https://www.theguardian.com/environment/2023/jul/29/i-realise-how-serious-it-is-voters-in-england-support-action-on-climate-crisis.
36. IEA Global EV Outlook 2024, https://www.iea.org/reports/global-ev-outlook-2024/trends-in-electric-cars
37. One Trillion Trees, World Economic Forum 2022, https://www.weforum.org/impact/investing-in-trees/#:~:text=And%20at%20the%20World%20Economic,70%20billion%20trees%20by%202030.
38. Quoted at "Nobel Prize Summit: Al Gore" (The Nobel Prize), accessed 3 July 2024, https://www.nobelprize.org/events/nobel-prize-summit/2021/panellists/al-gore.
39. "Speech by the Honourable Mia Amor Mottley, Prime Minister of Barbados on Climate Change, COP26" (Ministry of Foreign Affairs and Foreign Trade), accessed 3 July 2024, https://www.foreign.gov.bb/public-diplomacy/speech-by-the-honourable-mia-amor-mottley-prime-minister-of-barbados-on-climate-change-cop26.
40. Recent drying over the Amazon could be the "first warning signal" that the rainforest is approaching a tipping point, new research says. CarbonBrief, October 2023, https://www.carbonbrief.org/drying-of-amazon-could-be-early-warning-of-tipping-point-for-the-rainforest/#:~:text=Deforestation%20in%20the%20Brazilian%20Amazon,Silva%20took%20power%20in%20Brazil
41. Philip Oltermann, "The Trials of Robert Habeck: Is the World's Most Powerful Green Politician Doomed to Fail?" (*The Guardian*), last modified 26 September 2023, https://www.theguardian.com/environment/2023/sep/26/robert-habeck-vice-chancellor-germany-greens-climate-policy-backlash.
42. "The World's 50 Greatest Leaders: Tri Rismaharini" (*Fortune*), accessed 3 July 2024, https://fortune.com/ranking/worlds-greatest-leaders/2015/tri-rismaharini.
43. International Criminal Court.
44. A chemical herbicide extensively used by the US military during the Vietnam War. It has had long-lasting detrimental effects on the environment and human health.
45. Richard A. Falk, *Environmental Warfare and Ecocide—Facts, Appraisal and Proposals*, 9(1) Revue Belge de Droit International [RBDI/Belg. Rev. Int'l L.] 1 annex at 21–24 (1973) (Belg.) (A Proposed International Convention on the Crime of Ecocide). https://ecocidelaw.com/portfolio/richard-a-falk-2/
46. "Convention on the Prohibition of Military or Any Other Hostile Use of Environmental Modification Techniques (ENMOD)" (UN Office for Disarmament Affairs, 1978), accessed 3 July 2024, https://disarmament.unoda.org/enmod.

47. The Kunming–Montreal Global Biodiversity Framework, a global agreement on biodiversity, was adopted in 2022.
48. A US political action organization around climate change.
49. A global environmental movement founded in the UK that focuses on using nonviolent civil disobedience to combat the climate crisis.
50. A chemical accident that occurred on 2–3 December 1984 at the Union Carbide India pesticide plant in Bhopal, Madhya Pradesh, India.
51. An oil spill in the Gulf of Mexico on 20 April 2010 widely thought to be the largest marine oil spill in the petroleum industry's history.
52. A serious nuclear accident at the Fukushima Daiichi Nuclear Power Plant in Ōkuma, Fukushima, Japan, in 2011.
53. A legal case brought against Texaco (later bought by Chevron) in 1993 relating to contamination resulting from crude oil production in Ecuador.
54. Enron was a large American energy, commodities and services company, which used deceptive accounting tactics to cover its fraudulent practices. The scandal and its collapse shook Wall Street.
55. *The Pivot Point* (High Level Climate Champions, 2022), accessed 3 July 2024, https://climatechampions.unfccc.int/wp-content/uploads/2022/09/R2Z-Pivot-Point-Report.pdf.
56. Jacob Dahl, *In Search of Time: Understanding the Nature and Experience of Time for a Better Life* (London: LID Publishing, 2022).
57. Joanna Barsh and Lareina Yee, *Unlocking the Full Potential of Women at Work* (McKinsey & Company, 2012), accessed 3 July 2024, https://www.mckinsey.com/~/media/mckinsey/dotcom/client_service/organization/2012_may_women_matter/unlocking_full_potential_of_women_at_work_v2.ashx.
58. Langley Sharp, *The Habit of Excellence: Why British Army Leadership Works* (London: Penguin, 2021).
59. Francis Fukuyama is an American political scientist, political economist, scholar and writer.
60. The Ultra Low Emission Zone is an area in London that drivers must pay to enter unless their vehicle meets certain standards.
61. Jim Collins, *Good to Great* (London: Random House Business, 2001).
62. Jim Collins, "Level 5 Leadership: The Triumph of Humility and Fierce Resolve" (*Harvard Business Review*), last modified 1 January 2001, https://hbr.org/2001/01/level-5-leadership-the-triumph-of-humility-and-fierce-resolve-2.
63. Grand strategy also known as high strategy is a country's plan of how its military and nonmilitary are used to advance and achieve its national interests.
64. Stephen Scott, "Coercive Competition: A New Paradigm for Culture and Conduct Risk Management," *Seattle University Law Review* 43 (2020), accessed 3 July 2024, https://digitalcommons.law.seattleu.edu/cgi/viewcontent.cgi?article=2653&context=sulr.
65. Ira Chaleff, *Intelligent Disobedience: Doing Right When What You're Told to Do Is Wrong* (San Francisco: Berrett-Koehler, 2015). See also Ira Chaleff, "Intelligent Disobedience by Ira Chaleff at the Centre for Army Leadership" (Army Leader), last modified 4 October 2017, https://thearmyleader.co.uk/intelligent-disobedience-ira-chaleff.
66. W. Richard Scott, *Institutions and Organizations: Ideas, Interests, and Identities* (Los Angeles: SAGE, 2013).
67. Sandra Laville, "MoD Must Act to Tackle Impact of Climate Crisis on UK Forces, MPs Say" (*The Guardian*), last modified 18 August 2023, https://www.theguardian.com/uk-news/2023/aug/18/mod-must-act-to-tackle-impact-of-climate-crisis-on-uk-forces-mps-say.
68. Craig T. Robertson, "How People Access and Think about Climate Change News" (Reuters), last modified 15 June 2023, https://reutersinstitute.politics.ox.ac.uk/digital-news-report/2022/how-people-access-and-think-about-climate-change-news.
69. Aliya Uteuova, "Nearly 15% of Americans Don't Believe Climate Change Is Real, Study Finds" (*The Guardian*), last modified 14 February 2024, https://www.theguardian.com/us-news/2024/feb/14/americans-believe-climate-change-study.
70. See https://enfielddispatch.co.uk.
71. See https://www.socialspidercommunitynews.co.uk.
72. The longest river in Britain.
73. John Steinbeck, *The Log from the Sea of Cortez* (New York: Viking Press, 1951).
74. In December 1971, the US Congress passed the Alaska Native Claims Settlement Act, which created Alaska Native Corporations as a way of distributing land and monetary benefits to Alaska Natives.
75. See https://news.mongabay.com.
76. SEAL Environmental Journalism Awards https://sealawards.com/twelve-journalists-recognized-as-2022-seal-environmental-journalism-award-winners/

77. Karla Mendes, "Victims of Brazil's Biggest Environmental Disaster Still Fighting for Compensation" (Reuters), last modified 7 November 2017, https://www.reuters.com/article/idUSKBN1D7202. https://www.reuters.com/article/idUSKBN1D7202/

78. "Edward Snowden: The Whistleblower Behind the NSA Surveillance Revelations," *The Guardian*, June 2013, https://www.theguardian.com/world/2013/jun/09/edward-snowden-nsa-whistleblower-surveillance

79. Karla Mendes, "'Guardian of the Forest' Ambushed and Murdered in Brazilian Amazon" (Mongabay), last modified 2 November 2019, https://news.mongabay.com/2019/11/guardian-of-the-forest-ambushed-and-murdered-in-brazilian-amazon.

80. "What Is Happening to Agrobiodiversity?" (Food and Agriculture Organization), accessed 3 July 2024, https://www.fao.org/3/y5609e/y5609e02.htm.

81. *Future 50 Foods* (Knorr and WFF, 2019), accessed 3 July 2024, https://www.wwf.org.uk/sites/default/files/2019-02/Knorr_Future_50_Report_FINAL_Online.pdf.

82. *The Global Risks Report 2023* (World Economic Forum, 2023), accessed 3 July 2024, https://www3.weforum.org/docs/WEF_Global_Risks_Report_2023.pdf.

83. José Graziano Da Silva, "Feeding the World Sustainably" (United Nations), last modified June 2012, https://www.un.org/en/chronicle/article/feeding-world-sustainably.

84. Margaret Bartlett, "Why Is There a Tomato and Vegetable Shortage on UK Shelves?" (Countryfile), last modified 24 February 2023, https://www.countryfile.com/news/why-is-there-a-tomato-and-vegetable-shortage-on-uk-shelves.

85. Food and Agriculture Organization of the United Nations, https://www.fao.org/fsnforum/resources/reports-and-briefs/healthy-soils-are-basis-healthy-food-production#:~:text=In%20fact%2C%20it%20is%20estimated,need%20to%20grow%20and%20flourish.

86. "Politico, Mud and Guts: Europe's Forgotten Environmental Crisis," April 2019, accessed 18 July 2024, https://www.politico.eu/article/europe-forgotten-environmental-crisis-soil/#:~:text=The%20European%20Commission%20estimates%20Europe,of%20topsoil%20can%20take%20centuries.

87. "Healthy Soils, a Necessity for the EU" (European Commission Joint Research Centre), last modified 1 June 2022, https://joint-research-centre.ec.europa.eu/jrc-news-and-updates/healthy-soils-necessity-eu-2022-06-09_en.

88. Quota, Soil degradation costs the UK £1.2 billion each year, January 2022, https://quota.media/soil-degradation-costs-the-uk-1-2-billion-each-year/

89. "Chronic Land Degradation: UN offers stark warning and practical remedies in Global Land Outlook 2," April 2022, https://www.unccd.int/news-stories/press-releases/chronic-land-degradation-un-offers-stark-warnings-and-practical

90. Hannah Ritchie, "Do We Only Have 60 Harvests Left?" (Our World in Data), last modified 14 January 2021, https://ourworldindata.org/soil-lifespans.

91. Save soil, https://consciousplanet.org/en/save-soil/community-events

92. "A Beginner's Guide to Sustainable Farming" (UN Environment Programme), last modified 17 June 2021, https://www.unep.org/news-and-stories/story/beginners-guide-sustainable-farming.

93. S. L. Bridle, *Food and Climate Change without the Hot Air* (Cambridge: UIT Cambridge, 2020).

94. Breadbasket is a country or region that produces large quantities of wheat or other grain because of fertile soil and good climate.

95. *2021 Global Nutrition Report: The State of Global Nutrition* (Development Initiatives, 2021), accessed 3 July 2024, https://www.un.org/nutrition/sites/www.un.org.nutrition/files/global_nutrition_report_2021.pdf.

96. Chimimba David Phiri, Sara Mbago-Bhunu and Menghestab Haile, "Effective and Sustainable Financing, Key to Improving Africa's Nutrition Status" (ReliefWeb), last modified 20 July 2023, https://reliefweb.int/report/world/effective-and-sustainable-financing-key-improving-africas-nutrition-status.

97. See https://www.hospitalitymavericks.com.

98. See https://pulse.kitchen.

99. Regions where people's lives seem to be longer and healthier. Examples include California, Costa Rica, Greece, Italy and Japan.

100. The Enhanced Lima Work Programme on Gender, United Nations, Climate Change, https://unfccc.int/topics/gender/workstreams/the-enhanced-lima-work-programme-on-gender

101. *Energy Times*, "India Fastest in Renewal Energy Capacity Addition Among Major Economies," March 2023, https://energy.economictimes.indiatimes.com/news/renewable/india-fastest-in-renewal-energy-capacity-addition-among-major-economies/98530834

102. *Energy Times*, "India Fastest in Renewal Energy Capacity Addition Among Major Economies," March 2023, https://energy.economictimes.indiatimes.com/news/renewable/india-fastest-in-renewal-energy-capacity-addition-among-major-economies/98530834

103. Invest India, Creating a Sustainable World, https://www.investindia.gov.in/sector/renewable-energy

104. India's Green Hydrogen Revolution, "An Ambitious Approach," May 2024, https://static.pib.gov.in/WriteReadData/specificdocs/documents/2024/may/doc2024510336301.pdf
105. "Indian Economy Continues to Show Resilience Amid Global Uncertainties" (World Bank Group), last modified 4 April 2023, https://www.worldbank.org/en/news/press-release/2023/04/04/indian-economy-continues-to-show-resilience-amid-global-uncertainties.
106. "India Holds the Key to Hotting Global Climate Change Targets," World Economic Forum, January 2023, https://www.weforum.org/agenda/2023/01/india-holds-the-key-to-hitting-global-climate-change-targets-here-s-why/#:~:text=Coal%20is%20its%20primary%20source,low%20per%20capita%20CO2%20emissions.
107. "A Greener Cooling Pathway Can Create a $1.6 Trillion Investment Opportunity in India, Says World Bank Report" (World Bank Group), last modified 30 November 2022, https://www.worldbank.org/en/news/press-release/2022/11/30/a-greener-cooling-pathway-can-create-a-1-6-trillion-investment-opportunity-in-india-says-world-bank-report.
108. *2021 World Air Quality Report* (IQ Air, 2022), accessed 3 July 2024, https://www.iqair.com/newsroom/waqr_2021_pr.
109. "Commitments Made under CoP 26" (Ministry of Environment, Forest and Climate Change), last modified 12 December 2022, https://pib.gov.in/PressReleaseIframePage.aspx?PRID=1882840.
110. The United Nations Population Fund – India, https://india.unfpa.org/en/topics/adolescents-and-youth-8#:~:text=India%20has%20its%20largest%20ever,that%20will%20last%20till%202025.
111. *India's Youth Dividend: High Hopes for Today and Tomorrow*, Gallup, September 2023, https://news.gallup.com/poll/509756/india-youth-dividend-high-hopes-today-tomorrow.aspx#:~:text=One%2Dhalf%20(50%25)%20of,opinions%20about%20%2D%2D%20the%20world.
112. *Rising to the Challenge: Youth Perspectives on Climate Change and Education in India* (UNICEF, 2021), accessed 3 July 2024, https://www.unicef.org/rosa/media/12646/file/Rising%20to%20the%20Challenge%20-%20Youth%20Perspectives%20on%20Climate%20Change%20and%20Education%20in%20India.pdf.
113. "India to Become Third Largest Economy with GDP of $5 Trillion in Three Years: Finance Ministry," *The Hindu*, January 2024, https://www.thehindu.com/business/Economy/india-to-become-third-largest-economy-with-gdp-of-5-trillion-in-three-years-finance-ministry/article67788662.ece
114. "India's Clean Energy Transition is Rapidly Underway, Benefiting the Entire World," The International Energy Agency, January 2022, https://www.iea.org/commentaries/india-s-clean-energy-transition-is-rapidly-underway-benefiting-the-entire-world
115. International Solar Alliance, https://www.ccacoalition.org/partners/international-solar-alliance-isa#:~:text=The%20International%20Solar%20Alliance%20(ISA,President%20Fran%C3%A7ois%20Hollande%20of%20France
116. "Gandhi Jayanti: 40 Timeless Quotes by Mahatma Gandhi That Are Relevant Even Today," *The Times of India*, October 2023, http://timesofindia.indiatimes.com/articleshow/104051842.cms?utm_source=contentofinterest&utm_medium=text&utm_campaign=cppst
117. Amitav Ghosh, "Sunita Narain" (*Time*), last modified 21 April 2016, https://time.com/collection-post/4299642/sunita-narain-2016-time-100.
118. The United Progressive Alliance was formed in India in 2004 from a group of centre-left political parties.
119. "Climate India 2023: An Assessment of Extreme Weather Events" (Centre for Science and Environment), last modified 28 November 2023, https://www.cseindia.org/india-2023-extreme-weather-events-11973.
120. An ancient Indian collection of animal fables.
121. Amitav Ghosh is an Indian writer and a recipient of the Jnanpith Award, India's highest literary honour.
122. Tarun Tejpal is an Indian journalist, publisher, novelist and magazine editor.
123. Gopal Krishna Gokhale CIE was a political leader during the Indian independence movement and a mentor to Mahatma Gandhi.
124. Rajmohan Gandhi is a grandson of Mahatma Gandhi and an Indian biographer, historian and research professor in the US.
125. Anosh Irani is an Indo-Canadian novelist and playwright.
126. Anosh Irani, *The Parcel* (Melbourne: Scribe, 2017).
127. Manoranjan Byapari is an Indian Bengali writer, sociopolitical activist and politician.
128. A group of far-left radical communists who support Maoist ideology and politics.
129. Mahasweta Devi was an Indian writer in Bengali and an activist.
130. Sustainable Development Goal.
131. One Sun One World One Mission is an initiative by Prime Minister Modi of India, which aims to connect the energy supply across borders.
132. Lifestyle for Environment (LiFE) aims to engage individuals in mitigating the adverse effects of climate change by encouraging a lifestyle that focuses on mindful use of resources.

133. Sustainable Development Goals.
134. nari shakti is a Sanskrit term, where nari means woman and shakti means power. Today in India, this term means women's empowerment and is also an Indian government initiative working toward gender parity.
135. "India Vital for Sustainable Development Goals' Success, Fighting Climate Crisis, Debt Relief Reform, Secretary-General Says at Country's Anniversary Celebration," United Nation's Press Release, October 2022, https://press.un.org/en/2022/sgsm21543.doc.htm
136. Nationally determined contributions are climate commitments countries make under the UN Framework Convention on Climate Change.
137. Lifestyle for Environment (LiFE) aims to engage individuals in mitigating the adverse effects of climate change by encouraging a lifestyle that focuses on mindful use of resources.
138. At COP 15 in 2009, developed countries committed to giving US$100 billion annually in climate finance by 2020 to developing nations, to help them respond to and mitigate the effects of climate change.
139. G20 Independent Experts Group, *The Triple Agenda* (G20, 2023), accessed 3 July 2024, https://www.cgdev.org/sites/default/files/The_Triple_Agenda_G20-IEG_Report_Volume1_2023.pdf.
140. A system that allows people to access multiple bank accounts from one app.
141. UN Environment Programme.
142. SEWA, which is the SELF EMPLOYED WOMEN'S ASSOCIATION works with the poor, self-employed women workers from the informal economy across 18 Indian states, https://sewabharat.org/?gad_source=1&gclid=Cj0KCQjwwO20BhCJARIsAAnTIVQ8DlIPLM8wOy1iJx1Ro8f7AySmQ15FL16wNYZmiWcCTC8jk8zMHWEaAgl3EALw_wcB
143. An Indian actor and film producer.
144. Red Chillies Entertainment, 2007.
145. The Tlingit People, https://thetlingitpeople.weebly.com/history.html
146. "Research finds nature sounds 'benefit mental health,'" BBC News, March 2022, https://www.bbc.co.uk/news/uk-england-devon-60840759
147. See https://www.musicdeclares.net.
148. "Music Consumption Has Unintended Economic and Environmental Costs" (University of Glasgow), last modified 8 April 2019, https://www.gla.ac.uk/news/archiveofnews/2019/april/headline_643297_en.html.
149. DIMPACT, https://dimpact.org/about
150. "Green Stages, Global Changes: The Sustainable Shift in Music Events", Party Headphones.com, https://partyheadphones.com/green-stages-global-changes-the-sustainable-shift-music-events/#:~:text=Events%20like%20Coachella%2C%20Stagecoach%2C%20and,pounds%20of%20waste%20per%20day.
151. Øya Festival, https://www.oyafestivalen.no/
152. Terraforma, https://www.terraformafestival.com/
153. Glastonbury's Energy Policy, https://www.glastonburyfestivals.co.uk/information/sustainability/our-green-policies/energy-policy/
154. "Music Fans Care More about Climate Change and Want the Music Industry to Do Extra on the Issue" (University of Glasgow), last modified 9 May 2022, https://www.gla.ac.uk/news/archiveofnews/2022/may/headline_849057_en.html.
155. United Nation's Act Now Campaign, https://www.un.org/en/actnow#:~:text=ActNow%20is%20the%20United%20Nations,Safer%20cities
156. "Race to Zero" (Climate Champions), accessed 3 July 2024, https://climatechampions.unfccc.int/system/race-to-zero.
157. "The Evidence is Clear: The Time for Action is Now. We Can Halve Emissions by 2030," Intergovernmental Panel on Climate Change Press Release, April 2022, https://www.ipcc.ch/2022/04/04/ipcc-ar6-wgiii-pressrelease/
158. See https://yourope.org/know-how/green-roadmap.
159. See https://www.musicdeclares.net.
160. See https://www.earthpercent.org.
161. See https://www.headcount.org.
162. *Oxford Principles for Net Zero Aligned Carbon Offsetting* (University of Oxford, 2024), accessed 3 July 2024, https://www.smithschool.ox.ac.uk/sites/default/files/2024-02/Oxford-Principles-for-Net-Zero-Aligned-Carbon-Offsetting-revised-2024.pdf
163. The process of capturing and storing atmospheric carbon dioxide.
164. "Global Green Skills Report 2022," LinkedIn, https://economicgraph.linkedin.com/content/dam/me/economicgraph/en-us/global-green-skills-report/global-green-skills-report-pdf/li-green-economy-report-2022-annex.pdf

165. "COP-27 – Why embracing diversity is critical in the fight against climate change," The Association of Commonwealth Universities, December 2022, https://www.acu.ac.uk/news/cop27-guest-article-diversity-and-climate-change/
166. "United Nations Global Compact – Accenture CEO Study," January 2023, https://www.accenture.com/content/dam/accenture/final/accenture-com/document/Accenture-CEO-Study-United-Nations-Global-Compact.pdf
167. "Business Is a Key Driver of Global Climate Action," United Nations press release, June 2016, https://unfccc.int/news/business-is-key-driver-of-global-climate-action#:~:text=%E2%80%9CThis%20report%20makes%20it%20clear,business%20action%20on%20climate%20change.
168. "Purpose: Shifting From Why to How," McKinsey & Company, April 2022, https://www.mckinsey.com/capabilities/people-and-organizational-performance/our-insights/purpose-shifting-from-why-to-how
169. "Linking Corporate Social Responsibility to Organizational Commitment: The Role of Employee Job Satisfaction," *Journal of Global Responsibility*, May 2024, https://www.emerald.com/insight/content/doi/10.1108/JGR-01-2023-0012/full/html
170. Sangeeta Waldron, *Corporate Social Responsibility Is Not Public Relations: How to Put CSR at the Heart of Your Company and Maximize the Business Benefits* (Madrid: LID Publishing).
171. "We Are Campaigns" (Lush), last modified 28 October 2022, https://weare.lush.com/lush-life/our-campaigns/we-are-campaigns.
172. Jillian Ambrose, "Europe's Banks Helped Fossil Fuel Firms Raise More Than €1tn from Global Bond Markets" (*The Guardian*), last modified 26 September 2023, https://www.theguardian.com/business/2023/sep/26/europes-banks-helped-fossil-fuel-firms-raise-more-than-1tn-from-global-bond-markets.
173. "How War Impacts Climate Change," Fight Climate Change, October 2022, https://fightclimatechange.earth/2022/10/13/how-war-impacts-climate-change-and-the-environment/#:~:text=Bombings%20and%20other%20methods%20of,unsafe%20for%20people%20to%20inhabit.
174. Khondoker Abdul Mottaleb et al., "Potential impacts of Ukraine-Russia armed conflict on global wheat food security: A quantitative exploration," Science Direct (December 2022), https://www.sciencedirect.com/science/article/pii/S2211912422000499#:~:text=In%20particular%2C%2050%20countries%20in,exports%20from%20Russia%20and%20Ukraine
175. "US Military Consumes More Hydrocarbons Than Most Countries – With a Massive Hidden Impact on the Climate," Lancaster University, June 2019, https://www.lancaster.ac.uk/news/us-military-consumes-more-hydrocarbons-than-most-countries-with-a-massive-hidden-impact-on-the-climate#:~:text=The%20research%20provides%20an%20independent,the%20emission%20from%20fuel%20usage.
176. Lennard de Klerk et al., "Climate Damage Caused by Russia's War in Ukraine" (Initiative on GHG Accounting of War, 2024), accessed 3 July 2024, https://en.ecoaction.org.ua/wp-content/uploads/2024/06/Climate-Damage-Caused-by-War-24-months-EN.pdf.
177. Arthur Wyns, "25 Female Climate Leaders Shaping 2019" (*The Ecologist*), last modified 8 March 2019, https://theecologist.org/2019/mar/08/25-female-climate-leaders-shaping-2019.
178. 'Techwashing' is when countries or organizations use technology to misrepresent their climate credentials.
179. Corporate capture is when a company uses its political influence to try to control the decision-making process of a government.
180. Environmental, social and governance standards.
181. The idea that the producers of pollution should bear the costs of managing it.
182. African proverb.
183. Jim N. R. Dale, *Weather or Not? The Personal and Commercial Impacts of Weather and Climate* (London: LID Publishing, 2020).
184. Mykel Hawke and Jim N. R. Dale, *Surviving Extreme Weather: The Complete Climate Change Preparedness Manual* (New York: Skyhorse, 2024).
185. Rishi Sunak was prime minister of the UK until July 2024.
186. Nicholas Janni, *Leader as Healer* (Madrid: LID Publishing, 2022).
187. Václav Havel was a Czech statesman, author, poet and playwright. Quoted in *Oxford Essentialn Quotations*, ed. Susan Ratcliffe (Oxford: Oxford University Press, 2018), accessed 3 July 2024, https://www.oxfordreference.com/display/10.1093/acref/9780191866692.001.0001/q-oro-ed6-00005253.
188. "The Ocean Economy in 2030" (Organisation for Economic Co-operation and Development, 2016), accessed 3 July 2024, https://www.oecd.org/environment/the-ocean-economy-in-2030-9789264251724-en.htm.
189. "Three Decades of Ocean Warming Impacts on Marine Ecosystems: A Review and Perspective," Science Direct, December 2023, https://www.sciencedirect.com/science/article/pii/S0967064523000681#:~:text=Over%20the%20past%2050%20years%2C%20the%20ocean%20has%20absorbed%20%E2%88%BC,over%20the%20last%2050%20years.

190. "How is Climate Change Impacting the World's Oceans?" United Nations, https://www.un.org/en/climatechange/science/climate-issues/ocean-impacts#:~:text=These%20changes%20ultimately%20cause%20a,nearly%20half%20of%20the%20world's
191. "Sea Level 101, Part Two: All Sea Level is 'Local'" (NASA), last modified 14 July 2020, https://climate.nasa.gov/explore/ask-nasa-climate/3002/sea-level-101-part-two-all-sea-level-is-local.
192. "How is Climate Change Impacting the World's Oceans?" United Nations, https://www.un.org/en/climatechange/science/climate-issues/ocean-impacts#:~:text=These%20changes%20ultimately%20cause%20a,nearly%20half%20of%20the%20world's
193. "Consequences of Climate Change, Marine Heatwaves Pose Enduring Threats Both at Sea and on Land," Ocean & Climate Platform, August 2023, https://ocean-climate.org/en/consequences-of-climate-change-marine-heatwaves-pose-enduring-threats-both-at-sea-and-on-land/#:~:text=By%202021%2C%20nearly%2060%25%20of,particularly%20exposed%20to%20these%20episodes.
194. "Projections of Future Coral Bleaching Conditions Using IPCC CMIP6 Models: Climate Policy Implications, Management Applications, and Regional Seas Summaries" (UN Environment Programme, 2020), accessed 3 July 2024, https://www.unep.org/resources/report/projections-future-coral-bleaching-conditions-using-ipcc-cmip6-models-climate.
195. "An Inside Look at the Beauty and Benefits of Mangroves," United Nations Environment Programme, July 2023, https://www.unep.org/news-and-stories/story/inside-look-beauty-and-benefits-mangroves
196. "Facing Extinction, Tuvalu Considers the Digital Clone of a Country," *The Guardian*, June 2023, https://www.theguardian.com/world/2023/jun/27/tuvalu-climate-crisis-rising-sea-levels-pacific-island-nation-country-digital-clone
197. "Building Higher Islands Could Save the Maldives From Sea-level Rise, Says Study," The Tyndall Centre for Climate Change, February 2023, https://tyndall.ac.uk/news/building-higher-islands-could-save-the-maldives-from-sea-level-rise-says-study/
198. "Prime Minister's Address at the Launch of 'Infrastructure for Resilient Island States' Initiative at COP26 Summit in Glasgow" (Narendra Modi), last modified 2 November 2021, https://www.narendramodi.in/asm/prime-minister-narendra-modi-s-address-at-the-launch-of-infrastructure-for-resilient-island-states-initiative-at-cop26-summit-in-glasgow-558226.
199. El Niño occurs every few years when sea surface temperature increases in the central-east equatorial Pacific.
200. "Will There Be More Plastic Than Fish In The Sea?" WWF, https://www.wwf.org.uk/myfootprint/challenges/will-there-be-more-plastic-fish-sea
201. "Fish and Overfishing - How are Fish Stocks Changing Across the World? How Much is Overfished?" Our World In Data, first published in October 2021 and updated in March 2024, https://ourworldindata.org/fish-and-overfishing#:~:text=One%2Dthird%20(34%25)%20of,can%20be%20very%20different%20sizes.
202. "Biodiversity and Fishing", Marine Stewardship Council, https://www.msc.org/what-we-are-doing/oceans-at-risk/biodiversity-and-fishing#:~:text=Overfishing%20impacts%20not%20only%20the,the%20primary%20cause%20of%20decline.
203. "When will Fish go Extinct?", The World Counts, https://www.theworldcounts.com/challenges/planet-earth/oceans/overfishing-statistics
204. Seaweb, "Only 10% of All Large Fish Are Left in Global Ocean" (*Nature*), last modified 14 May 2003, https://www.eurekalert.org/news-releases/805075.
205. "Life below Water" (World Bank), accessed 3 July 2024, https://datatopics.worldbank.org/sdgatlas/archive/2017/SDG-14-life-below-water.html.
206. Enric Sala et al., "Protecting the Global Ocean for Biodiversity, Food and Climate," *Nature* 592 (2021): 397–402, accessed 3 July 2024, https://www.nature.com/articles/s41586-021-03371-z.epdf?sharing_token=yZ7jFulhml-CGASVyclludRgN0jAjWel9jnR3ZoTv0MwjSp_dqdYRo11ccDn9dqPW5D1xJuK8fpT__q4KFNUwgKdmwi3JyJVwmHRf-bxESQBSr9MbBwkap3XEr49FKSZrw7W6j8yaEyrl67o_vW36vuzGgf5WiXfPupj3TCNKWGPhX2RS00vTHE-B
207. "Industrial Overfishing & Biodiversity Loss", Parley TV, https://parley.tv/threats/biodeiversity-loss#:~:text=an%20average%20of%201.47%20gigatons,ocean%20acidification%20and%20affecting%20biodiversity.
208. "The Ocean – The World's Greatest Ally against Climate Change," United Nations, https://www.un.org/en/climatechange/science/climate-issues/ocean
209. "3 Billion," WWF, https://www.worldwildlife.org/industries/sustainable-seafood#:~:text=of%20people%20worldwide.-,More%20than%203%20billion%20people%20in%20the%20world%20rely%20on,has%20significantly%20impacted%20the%20environment.
210. Sustainable Development Goal.
211. The idea that we are all connected to everyone else by a maximum of six steps in a chain of social connections (e.g., friends of friends).

212. Amitav Ghosh, *The Nutmeg's Curse* (Chicago: University of Chicago Press, 2021).
213. Robyn Vinter and Josh Halliday, "Boy, 16, Arrested after Felling of Famous Sycamore Gap Tree at Hadrian's Wall" (*The Guardian*), last modified 29 September 2023, https://www.theguardian.com/uk-news/2023/sep/28/boy-16-arrested-in-connection-with-felling-of-famous-sycamore-gap-tree-hadrians-wall-england.
214. "Is It Time to Break the Law?" (Channel 4), last modified 20 September 2023, https://www.channel4.com/programmes/chris-packham-is-it-time-to-break-the-law.
215. Swami Vivekananda was an Indian monk and philosopher who lived toward the end of the 19th century.
216. See https://www.caringforcalves.org.
217. Michael Slezak, "'The Blob': How Marine Heatwaves Are Causing Unprecedented Climate Chaos" (*The Guardian*), last modified 14 August 2016, https://www.theguardian.com/science/2016/aug/15/the-blob-how-marine-heatwaves-are-causing-unprecedented-climate-chaos.
218. A process where colder deep ocean water rises to the surface.
219. Ralph Chami, Thomas Cosimano, Connel Fullenkamp and Sena Oztosun, "Nature's Solution to Climate Change" (International Monetary Fund), last modified December 2019, https://www.imf.org/en/Publications/fandd/issues/2019/12/natures-solution-to-climate-change-chami.
220. *Review of the State of World Marine Fishery Resources: Marine Fisheries* (Food and Agriculture Organization of the United Nations, 1997), accessed 3 July 2024, https://www.fao.org/4/w4248e/w4248e00.htm.
221. "Five Things you Need to Know About the State of the World's Fisheries - 2022," Marine Stewardship Council, July 2022, https://www.msc.org/media-centre/news-opinion/news/2022/07/04/five-things-need-to-know-about-the-state-of-the-world's-fisheries-2022
222. Fisheries that use long lines with baited hooks.
223. "Sacred River, Sacred Land: A Community Goes 'Back to Roots' In Kenya," The Gaia Foundation, https://gaiafoundation.org/tharaka-a-community-goes-back-to-roots/#:~:text=In%20Tharaka's%20Story%20of%20Origin,comforting%20humming%20sound%20each%20day.
224. Joseph Millard et al., "Global Effects of Land Use Intensity on Local Pollinator Biodiversity," *Nature Communications* 12 (2021): 2902, accessed 3 July 2024, https://www.nature.com/articles/s41467-021-23228-3.
225. *Storm Henk* (Met Office, 2024), accessed 3 July 2024, https://www.metoffice.gov.uk/binaries/content/assets/metofficegovuk/pdf/weather/learn-about/uk-past-events/interesting/2024/2024_01_storm_henk_v1.pdf.
226. James Gregory and Jeremy Culley, "Storm Isha: Two Dead and Thousands Left without Power" (BBC News), last modified 22 January 2024, https://www.bbc.co.uk/news/uk-68055640.
227. Oliver Slow and Simon King, "Storm Jocelyn: 97mph Gusts Recorded after Heavy Winds Hit UK" (BBC News), last modified 24 January 2024, https://www.bbc.co.uk/news/uk-68062166.
228. "Guardians of the Earth: How Indigenous Peoples can teach the world to safeguard and conserve biodiversity," ICMM, https://nature.icmm.com/working-for-nature/articles/guardians-of-the-earth
229. *From the Heart of the World* (BBC, 1990).
230. *Aluna* (Sunstone Films, 2012).
231. "Variability in Cultural Understandings of Consciousness: A Call for Dialogue with Native Psychologies," (Authors: Lorencova, Radmila; Trnka, Radek), Source: Journal of Consciousness Studies, Volume 30, Numbers 5-6, June 2023.
232. "Science Must Embrace Traditional and Indigenous Knowledge to Solve Our Biodiversity Crisis," (Edwin Ogar, Gretta Pecl and Tero Mustonen), Science Direct, August 2020, https://www.sciencedirect.com/science/article/pii/S259033222030350X
233. Leonardo DiCaprio, "Nemonte Nenquimo" (*Time*), last modified 22 September 2020, https://time.com/collection/100-most-influential-people-2020/5888337/nemonte-nenquimo.
234. "'I Want People to Wake Up:' Nemonte Nenquimo on Growing up in the Rainforest and her Fight to Save it," (*The Guardian*), May 2024, https://www.theguardian.com/books/article/2024/may/25/i-want-people-to-wake-up-nemonte-nenquimo-on-growing-up-in-the-rainforest-and-her-fight-to-save-it
235. Julian Lennon Productions, 2006.
236. 2020.
237. Chlorofluorocarbons.

AUTHOR BIO

Photographer Katrina Campbell

Sangeeta Waldron is a multi-award-winning communications professional who writes for various news platforms specializing in climate change, sustainability and corporate social responsibility. In 2024, she attended Al Gore's Climate Reality Leadership Corps training in Rome, which further reinforced her reasons for writing this book, and she is now a Climate Reality Leader.

Today, Sangeeta also runs her own full-service communications agency, Serendipity PR & Media. She sits on various boards and is currently on the advisory board for Bridge India, an award-winning progressive nonprofit think tank dedicated to discourse on public policy.

In 2021, she published her second book, *Corporate Social Responsibility Is Not Public Relations* (with LID Publishing), which was shortlisted for the 2022 UK Business Book Awards as a Change & Sustainability finalist. This book – her third – is a continuation of her work and legacy.

Sangeeta is a regular international speaker and moderator.

JAICO PUBLISHING HOUSE
Elevate Your Life. Transform Your World.

ESTABLISHED IN 1946, Jaico Publishing House is home to world-transforming authors such as Robin Sharma, Sadhguru, Osho, the Dalai Lama, Deepak Chopra, Eknath Easwaran, Paramhansa Yogananda, Devdutt Pattanaik, Radhakrishnan Pillai, Morgan Housel, Napoleon Hill, John Maxwell, Brian Tracy, and Stephen Hawking.

Our late founder Mr. Jaman Shah first established Jaico as a book distribution company. Sensing that independence was around the corner, he aptly named his company Jaico ('Jai' means victory in Hindi). In order to service the significant demand for affordable books in a developing nation, Mr. Shah initiated Jaico's own publications. Jaico was India's first publisher of paperback books in the English language.

While self-help; religion and philosophy; mind, body and spirit; and business titles form the cornerstone of our non-fiction list, we publish an exciting range of current affairs, history, biography, art and architecture, travel, and popular science books as well. Our renewed focus on popular fiction is evident in our new titles by a host of fresh young talent from India and abroad.

Jaico's translations division publishes select bestselling titles in over 10 regional languages including Gujarati, Hindi, Kannada, Malayalam, Marathi, Tamil, and Telugu. These include titles from renowned national and international authors like Sudha Murthy, Gaur Gopal Das, Swami Mukundananda, Jay Shetty, Simon Sinek, Ankur Warikoo and Jeff Keller.

Visit our Website

Boasting one of India's largest book distribution networks, Jaico has its headquarters in Mumbai, with branches in Ahmedabad, Bangalore, Chennai, Delhi, Hyderabad, and Kolkata. This network ensures that our books reach all parts of the country, both urban and rural.

Jaico
287.9
11/8/25